Elegant Glassware
of the
Depression Era

SEVENTH EDITION

AN IDENTIFICATION
AND VALUE GUIDE

Gene Florence

COLLECTOR BOOKS
A Division of Schroeder Publishing Co., Inc.

The current values in this book should be used only as a guide. They are not intended to set prices, which vary from one section of the country to another. Auction prices as well as dealer prices vary greatly and are affected by condition as well as demand. Neither the Author nor the Publisher assumes responsibility for any losses that might be incurred as a result of consulting this guide.

Searching For A Publisher?

We are always looking for knowledgeable people considered to be experts within their fields. If you feel that there is a real need for a book on your collectible subject and have a large, comprehensive collection, contact Collector Books.

On the Cover:
Top left: Trojan oil bottle, $235.00.
Middle: June Night wine, $27.50.
Top right: Cleo vase, $150.00.
Bottom left: Black Forest pitcher, $1,500.00.
Bottom right: Cadena creamer, $25.00.
Back: Diane bowl, $100.00 – 125.00.

Cover design by Beth Summers

ABOUT THE AUTHOR

Gene M. Florence, Jr., a native Kentuckian, graduated from the University of Kentucky in 1967. He held a double major in mathematics and English which he immediately put to use in industry and subsequently, in teaching junior and senior high school. He taught one year at the Lincoln Institute for gifted, but disadvantaged, students.

A collector since childhood, he progressed from baseball cards, comic books, coins, and bottles to glassware. His buying and selling glassware "hobby" began to usurp his nine-year teaching career. During a teaching hiatus in the summer of 1972, he wrote a book on Depression glassware that was well received by collectors in the field, ultimately persuading him to leave teaching and pursue the glass business full time. This freed him to travel to glass shows throughout the country, where he diligently studied both the glass being marketed and the prices the ware commanded. He was also able to devote more time to research on glass.

Subsequent books written by Mr. Florence include the following titles: *The Collector's Encyclopedia of Depression Glass, The Collector's Encyclopedia of Akro Agate, The Pocket Guide to Depression Glass, Kitchen Glassware of the Depression Years, Collectible Glassware from the 40's, 50's, 60's..., Standard Baseball Card Price Guide,* and five editions of *Very Rare Glassware of the Depression Years.* He has also written five volumes of *The Collector's Encyclopedia of Occupied Japan* and a book on Degenhart Glassware for a museum. His most recent book is *Stemware Identification.* Mr. Florence has now authored 59 books on collectibles.

FOREWORD

"Elegant" glassware, as defined in this book (on glass made from the Depression era through the 1950's) refers to the handmade and acid etched glassware that was sold in the department and jewelry stores as opposed to the dime store and give-away glass that has become known, today, as Depression glass. The word "Elegant" is standard terminology among today's dealers for describing handmade glassware.

The rapid growth of collecting "Elegant" glassware has been exceptional and many dealers who wouldn't gamble on buying that crystal nonsense a few years ago are now acquiring more "Elegant" than basic Depression glass! Depression glass shows used to be stocked with only 15% to 20% "Elegant" glass; now, there is more than 60% at many shows, due mostly to collector focus.

The tremendous reception of the first six books has made this seventh possible. New patterns, more catalog reprints and many new listings await you.

I hope you enjoy this book; and I hope you will feel the years undertaken to give you the finest books on "Elegant" glassware have been well spent.

PRICING

All prices in this book are retail prices for mint condition glassware. This book is only intended as *a guide to prices.* There remain regional price differences that cannot be reasonably dealt with herein.

You may expect dealers to pay approximately thirty to sixty percent less than the prices listed. My knowledge of prices comes from experience of traveling to and selling at shows in various parts of the United States for almost thirty years. I readily admit to soliciting price information from persons known to be experts in these various glass fields in order to provide you with the latest, most accurate pricing information possible. However, final pricing judgments are mine!

MEASUREMENTS AND TERMS

All measurements and terms in this book are from factory catalogs or actual measurements from the piece. It has been my experience that actual measurements vary slightly from those listed in catalogs; so don't get unduly concerned over slight variations. For example, Fostoria always measured plates to the nearest inch, but I have found that most Fostoria plates are never exact inches in measurement.

ACKNOWLEDGMENTS

Photography sessions for this book were spread over a two year period with one session lasting seven days. I took a lot of heat for telling my help not to set their clocks back on that last Sunday in October. We worked on daylight time and were able to finish by 4 pm!

A special accolade is due Dick and Pat Spencer for lending their glass, gathering glassware from other collectors and transporting it to Paducah, working at the photography sessions, and supplying prices and information on Heisey in this book. Friends such as these are incomparable!

There are many people behind the scenes in the production of this book! Collectors have lent glass, others, their time; some lent talents and expertise. Many of these people remain friends even after wearying hours of packing, unpacking, arranging, sorting, and repacking glass! Some traveled hundreds of miles to bring their valuable glass to share with you. Others spent hours discussing and recording prices, often after already long show hours. Without the following extraordinary people, this book would not exist: Earl and Beverly Hines, Dan Tucker and Lorrie Kitchen, Charles Larson, Paul and Margaret Arras, Gary and Sue Clark, John and Judy Bine, Bill and Lottie Porter, Quinten Keech, Charlie and Ruth Collins, Yvonne Heil, Ralph and Fran Leslie, John and Raymond Day, Dale Mitchell, John and Linda Neary, Chuck Bails, Tom Schmidt, Kevin Kiley, Leroy and Susan Allen, Joe and Florence Solito, Jane White, Bill and Billy Schroeder, Terri Stalions, Lisa Stroup, the guys from Collector Books shipping department, and numerous unnamed readers throughout the U.S., England, and Canada who shared pictures and information about their previously unlisted pieces. Richard Walker, Zibby Walker, and Charley Lynch did all the new photography for this book. Zibby did double duty with set-ups and conscientiously recorded my "work" shots.

Family is the single most important aid in my work. Charles helped cart boxes from storage and built shelves while Sybil spent several days helping Cathy sort glass into various patterns and boxes. Chad, Marc, and their friends, Gary and Blake, helped load and unload van loads of glass for each photography session, not to mention seeing to home fires while I traveled.

Cathy, with her "sharp" pencil, endeavored to make sense out of the reams of material that I wrote. I tend to deal with broader concepts; she tries to organize subjects and verbs into what I meant to say! This year we worked on this book together in Florida; thus things have gone much smoother than last time when we were dealing with overnight packages of writing and long-distance phone editing. She's had twenty-five years of this glass and book business (researching, note taking, typing, editing, proofing, traveling, packing, and unpacking, both the glassware and me). Twenty-five of the thirty-two years we've been married have been wrapped up in deadlines for books! We both worked as teachers, parents, and authors. I hope we have been successful at educating in fashions we never dreamed of in our youth!

You give us the encouragement to continue this genuinely arduous work year after year. As long as you keep sending applicable information, further listings, lending glassware, calling attention to new finds, exclusions, or oversights, I'll continue to pass the information along to the public. Your support keeps me going, personally, and is a great help to the body of knowledge emerging about older glassware in general! Enjoy the glassware! This is the ultimate satisfaction in collecting!

CONTENTS

CONTENTS BY COMPANY

AMERICAN, Line #2056, Fostoria Glass Company, 1915 – 1986

Colors: crystal; some amber, blue, green, yellow, pink tinting to purple in late 1920's; white, red in 1980's, and currently being made in red and crystal for Lancaster Colony by Dalzell Viking

Lancaster Colony continues to manufacture Fostoria's American pattern. This newly made American can be found in all the Fostoria outlet stores throughout the Midwest. Those pieces currently being remade or pieces that have been made in recent years are marked with an asterisk (*) in the price listing. Even before the closing of the original Fostoria factory in 1986, Lancaster Colony marketed its "Whitehall" glassware line that is similar to American, and made by Indiana Glass at Dunkirk, Indiana. You will find an abundance of "Whitehall" in colors of pink, an avocado green, and several shades of blue. Check the glassware section of your local discount store for new colors and items being made. Many of the specialty catalogs have this colored glassware alluded to as "Depression Glass" in their pages. Whitehall's pink colored ware is frequently confused by novice collectors with Jeannette's Depression era Cube pattern.

None of the American or "look-alike" American pieces are marked in any way. Red is still being sold at the Fostoria outlet stores in an abundance of pieces. American was never made in red until the 1980's and then it was made by Viking Glass for Fostoria. Dalzell Viking has now taken over the manufacturing of red for Lancaster Colony. Colored pieces of older American are still in demand.

You can see the original green on the top of page 9. The green sugar shown in that picture is often confused with Jeannette's Cube. Learn to differentiate patterns. For instance, the edge of Jeannette's sugar bowl is smooth.

There are some major price adjustments of American pieces that are being found in England. So many British antique dealers have become aware of our collecting habits, that the hard-to-find Fostoria American there is no longer so hard to find — here! Prices on some pieces have **plummeted.** Many dealers had been asking large prices for these items, especially the wash bowl and pitcher sets. One dealer now owns five of these and is struggling to find that higher priced market. My feeling is that collectors willing to spend thousands of dollars to get these sets already own them. Once glass items reach prices in the four digit area, many collectors of the pattern are willing to do without!

Reissued cookie jars pose a problem for collectors! Most of the new issues I have seen have wavy lines in the pattern itself and crooked knobs on the top. Old cookie jars do not. (A telling point that works 80% of the time is to try to turn the lid around while it rests inside the cookie jar. The new lids seem to hang-up and stop somewhere along the inside making the whole cookie jar turn. The old jars will allow you to turn the lid completely around without catching on the sides!)

Both styles of ice cream saucers shown only in the 1941 Fostoria catalog are in the top photo on page 9.

	*Crystal
Appetizer, tray, 10½", w/6 inserts	240.00
Appetizer, insert, 3¼"	27.50
Ash tray, 2⅞", sq.	7.50
Ash tray, 3⅞", oval	9.00
Ash tray, 5", sq.	40.00
Ash tray, 5½", oval	18.00
Basket, w/reed handle, 7" x 9"	90.00
Basket, 10", new in 1988	30.00
Bell	365.00
Bottle, bitters, w/tube, 5¾", 4½ oz.	70.00
Bottle, condiment/ketchup w/stopper	125.00
Bottle, cologne, w/stopper, 6 oz., 5¾"	70.00
Bottle, cologne, w/stopper, 7¼", 8 oz.	80.00
Bottle, cordial, w/stopper, 7¼", 9 oz.	90.00
Bottle, water, 44 oz., 9¼"	550.00
Bowl, banana split, 9" x 3½"	350.00
Bowl, finger, 4½" diam., smooth edge	40.00
Bowl, 3½", rose	20.00
Bowl, 3¾", almond, oval	18.00
Bowl, 4¼", jelly, 4¼" h.	15.00
* Bowl, 4½", 1 hdld.	10.00
Bowl, 4½", 1 hdld., sq.	11.00
Bowl, 4½", jelly, w/cover, 6¾" h.	22.00
* Bowl, 4½", nappy	12.00
Bowl, 4½", oval	15.00

	*Crystal
Bowl, 4¾", fruit, flared	15.00
Bowl, 5", cream soup, 2 hdld.	45.00
Bowl, 5", 1 hdld., tri-corner	12.00
* Bowl, 5", nappy	10.00
Bowl, 5", nappy, w/cover	27.50
Bowl, 5", rose	25.00
Bowl, 5½", lemon, w/cover	42.50
Bowl, 5½", preserve, 2 hdld., w/cover.	85.00
Bowl, 6", bonbon, 3 ftd.	15.00
* Bowl, 6", nappy	15.00
Bowl, 6", olive, oblong	12.00
Bowl, 6½", wedding, w/cover, sq., ped.ft., 8" h.	90.00
Bowl, 6½", wedding, sq., ped. ft., 5¼" h.	55.00
Bowl, 7", bonbon, 3 ftd.	12.50
Bowl, 7", cupped, 4½" h.	50.00
* Bowl, 7", nappy	25.00
Bowl, 8", bonbon, 3 ftd.	17.50
Bowl, 8", deep	60.00
Bowl, 8", ftd.	60.00
Bowl, 8", ftd., 2 hdld., "trophy" cup	110.00
* Bowl, 8", nappy	22.00
* Bowl, 8", pickle, oblong	13.00
Bowl, 8½", 2 hdld.	45.00
* Bowl, 8½", boat	15.00

AMERICAN

	*Crystal
Bowl, 9", boat, 2 pt.	11.00
* Bowl, 9", oval veg.	25.00
Bowl, 9½", centerpiece	42.50
Bowl, 9½", 3 pt., 6" w.	37.50
Bowl, 10", celery, oblong	20.00
* Bowl, 10", deep	35.00
Bowl, 10", float	45.00
Bowl, 10", oval, float	32.50
Bowl, 10", oval, veg., 2 pt.	35.00
Bowl, 10½", fruit, 3 ftd.	35.00
Bowl, 11", centerpiece	40.00
Bowl, 11", centerpiece, tri-corner	42.50
Bowl, 11", relish/celery, 3 pt.	30.00
Bowl, 11½", float	55.00
Bowl, 11½", fruit, rolled edge, 2¾" h.	42.50
Bowl, 11½", oval, float	45.00
Bowl, 11½", rolled edge	45.00
Bowl, 11¾", oval, deep	42.50
Bowl, 12", boat	17.50
Bowl, 12", fruit/sm. punch, ped. ft., (Tom & Jerry)	170.00
Bowl, 12", lily pond	65.00
Bowl, 12", relish "boat," 2 pt.	20.00
Bowl, 13", fruit, shallow	65.00
Bowl, 14", punch, w/high ft. base (2 gal.)	250.00
Bowl, 14", punch, w/low ft. base	225.00
Bowl, 15", centerpiece, "hat" shape	165.00
Bowl, 16", flat, fruit, ped. ft.	175.00
Bowl, 18", punch, w/low ft. base (3¾ gal.)	335.00
Box, pomade, 2" square	250.00
* Box, w/cover, puff, 3⅛" x 2¾"	175.00
Box, w/cover, 4½" x 4½"	175.00
Box, w/cover, handkerchief, 5⅝" x 4⅝"	250.00
Box, w/cover, hairpin, 3½" x 1¾"	275.00
Box, w/cover, jewel, 5¼" x 2¼"	275.00
Box, w/cover, jewel, 2 drawer, 4¼" x 3¼"	2,000.00
* Box, w/cover, glove, 9½" x 3½"	250.00
* Butter, w/cover, rnd. plate, 7¼"	115.00
* Butter, w/cover, ¼ lb.	25.00
Cake stand, (see salver)	
Candelabrum, 6½", 2-lite, bell base w/bobeche & prisms	110.00
Candle lamp, 8½", w/chimney, candle part, 3½"	125.00
Candlestick, twin, 4⅛" h., 8½" spread	55.00
Candlestick, 2", chamber with fingerhold	42.50
Candlestick, 3", rnd. ft.	15.00
Candlestick, 4⅜", 2-lite, rnd. ft.	35.00
Candlestick, 6", octagon ft.	25.00
Candlestick, 6½", 2-lite, bell base	95.00
Candlestick, 6¼", round ft.	175.00
* Candlestick, 7", sq. column	95.00
Candlestick, 7¼", "Eiffel" tower	125.00
Candy box, w/cover, 3 pt., triangular	75.00
Candy, w/cover, ped. ft.	37.50

	*Crystal
Cheese (5¾" compote) & cracker (11½" plate)	55.00
Cigarette box, w/cover, 4¾"	37.50
Coaster, 3¾"	9.00
Comport, 4½", jelly	15.00
* Comport, 5", jelly, flared	15.00
* Comport, 6¾", jelly, w/cover	35.00
Comport, 8½", 4" high	40.00
Comport, 9½", 5¼" high	50.00
Comport, w/cover, 5"	25.00
* Cookie jar, w/cover, 8⅞" h.	275.00
Creamer, tea, 3 oz., 2⅜" (#2056½)	9.00
Creamer, individual, 4¾ oz.	9.00
Creamer, 9½ oz.	12.50
Crushed fruit, w/cover & spoon, 10"	1,350.00
Cup, flat	7.50
Cup, ftd., 7 oz.	8.00
Cup, punch, flared rim	11.00
Cup, punch, straight edge	10.00
Decanter, w/stopper, 24 oz., 9¼" h.	100.00
Dresser set: powder boxes w/covers & tray	400.00
Flower pot, w/perforated cover, 9½" diam.; 5½" h.	1,350.00
Goblet, #2056, 2½ oz., wine, hex ft., 4⅜" h.	12.00
Goblet, #2056, 4½ oz., oyster cocktail, 3½" h.	17.50
Goblet, #2056, 4½ oz., sherbet, flared, 4⅜" h.	9.00
Goblet, #2056, 4½ oz., fruit, hex ft., 4¾" h.	9.00
Goblet, #2056, 5 oz., low ft., sherbet, flared, 3¼" h.	9.00
Goblet, #2056, 6 oz., low ft., sundae, 3⅛" h.	9.00
Goblet, #2056, 7 oz., claret, 4⅞" h.	50.00
* Goblet, #2056, 9 oz., low ft., 4⅜" h.	11.00
Goblet, #2056, 10 oz., hex ft., water, 6⅞" h.	13.00
Goblet, #2056, 12 oz., low ft., tea, 5¾" h.	14.00
Goblet, #2056½, 4½ oz., sherbet, 4½" h.	10.00
Goblet, #2056½, 5 oz., low sherbet, 3½" h.	10.00
Goblet, #5056, 1 oz., cordial, 3⅛", w/plain bowl	25.00
Goblet, #5056, 3½ oz., claret, 4⅝", w/plain bowl	13.50
Goblet, #5056, 3½ oz., cocktail, 4", w/plain bowl	11.00
Goblet, #5056, 4 oz., oyster cocktail, 3½", w/plain bowl	10.00
Goblet, #5056, 5½ oz., sherbet, 4⅛", w/plain bowl	10.00
Goblet, #5056, 10 oz., water, 6⅛", w/plain bowl	12.00

AMERICAN

	*Crystal		*Crystal
Hair receiver, 3" x 3"	275.00	* Platter, 10½", oval	40.00
Hat, 2⅛", (sm. ash tray)	15.00	Platter, 12", oval	55.00
Hat, 3" tall	25.00	Ring holder	200.00
Hat, 4" tall	45.00	Salad set: 10" bowl, 14" torte, wood	
Hat, western style	250.00	fork & spoon	67.50
Hotel washbowl and pitcher	3,500.00	Salt, individual	9.00
Hurricane lamp, 12" complete	165.00	Salver, 10", sq., ped. ft. (cake stand)	85.00
Hurricane lamp base	55.00	Salver, 10", rnd., ped. ft. (cake stand)	60.00
Ice bucket, w/tongs	60.00	* Salver, 11", rnd., ped. ft. (cake stand)	30.00
Ice cream saucer (2 styles)	55.00	Sauce boat & liner	47.50
Ice dish for 4 oz. crab or 5 oz. tomato		Saucer	3.00
liner	32.50	Set: 2 jam pots w/tray	145.00
Ice dish insert	10.00	Set: decanter, 6 - 2 oz. whiskeys on	
Ice tub, w/liner, 5⅝"	85.00	10½" tray	215.00
Ice tub, w/liner, 6½"	90.00	Set: toddler, w/baby tumbler & bowl	90.00
Jam pot, w/cover	60.00	Set: youth, w/bowl, hdld. mug, 6" plate	90.00
Jar, pickle, w/pointed cover, 6" h.	310.00	Set: condiment, 2 oils, 2 shakers,	
Marmalade, w/cover & chrome spoon	50.00	mustard w/cover & spoon w/tray	275.00
* Mayonnaise, div.	15.00	Shaker, 3", ea.	10.00
Mayonnaise, w/ladle, ped. ft.	45.00	* Shaker, 3½", ea.	7.00
Mayonnaise, w/liner & ladle	32.50	Shaker, 3¼", ea.	10.00
Molasses can, 11 oz., 6¾" h., 1 hdld.	335.00	Shakers w/tray, individual, 2"	22.00
* Mug, 5½ oz., "Tom & Jerry," 3¼" h.	40.00	Sherbet, handled, 3½" high, 4½ oz.	85.00
* Mug, 12 oz., beer, 4½" h.	65.00	Shrimp bowl, 12¼"	345.00
Mustard, w/cover	30.00	Spooner, 3¾"	35.00
Napkin ring	11.00	** Strawholder, 10", w/cover	225.00
Oil, 5 oz.	35.00	Sugar, tea, 2¼" (#2056½)	13.00
Oil, 7 oz.	35.00	Sugar, hdld., 3¼" h.	12.00
Picture frame	15.00	Sugar shaker	50.00
Pitcher, ½ gal. w/ice lip, 8¼", flat bottom	85.00	Sugar, w/o cover	10.00
Pitcher, ½ gal., w/o ice lip	260.00	Sugar, w/cover, no hdl., 6¼" (cover	
Pitcher, ½ gal., 8", ftd.	70.00	fits strawholder)	60.00
Pitcher, 1 pt., 5⅜", flat	27.50	Sugar, w/cover, 2 hdld.	20.00
Pitcher, 2 pt., 7¼", ftd.	65.00	Syrup, 6½ oz., #2056½, Sani-cut server	75.00
Pitcher, 3 pt., 8", ftd.	70.00	Syrup, 6 oz., non pour screw top, 5¼" h.	215.00
Pitcher, 3 pt., w/ice lip, 6½", ftd., "fat"	50.00	Syrup, 10 oz., w/glass cover &	
* Pitcher, 1 qt., flat	30.00	6" liner plate	145.00
Plate, cream soup liner	12.00	Syrup, w/drip proof top	35.00
Plate, 6", bread & butter	12.00	Toothpick	25.00
Plate, 7", salad	10.00	Tray, cloverleaf for condiment set	165.00
Plate, 7½" x 4⅜", crescent salad	47.50	Tray, tid bit, w/question mark metal	
Plate, 8", sauce liner, oval	25.00	handle	35.00
Plate, 8½", salad	12.00	Tray, 5" x 2½", rect.	80.00
Plate, 9", sandwich (sm. center)	14.00	Tray, 6" oval, hdld.	35.00
Plate, 9½", dinner	22.50	Tray, pin, oval, 5½" x 4½"	125.00
Plate, 10", cake, 2 hdld.	25.00	Tray, 6½" x 9" relish, 4 part	45.00
Plate, 10½" sandwich (sm. center)	20.00	Tray, 9½", service, 2 hdld.	35.00
Plate, 11½", sandwich (sm. center)	20.00	Tray, 10", muffin (2 upturned sides)	30.00
Plate, 12", cake, 3 ftd.	22.50	Tray, 10", square, 4 part	80.00
Plate, 13½", oval torte	45.00	Tray, 10", square	110.00
Plate, 14", torte	50.00	Tray, 10½", cake, w/question mark	
Plate, 18", torte	125.00	metal hdl.	30.00
Plate, 20", torte	150.00	Tray, 10½" x 7½", rect.	70.00
Plate 24", torte	225.00	Tray, 10½" x 5", oval hdld.	45.00

** Bottom only

10

	*Crystal
Tray, 10¾", square, 4 part	125.00
Tray, 12", sand. w/ctr. handle	35.00
Tray, 12", round	135.00
Tray, 13½", oval, ice cream	160.00
Tray for sugar & creamer, tab. hdld., 6¾"	12.00
Tumbler, hdld. iced tea	225.00
Tumbler, #2056, 2 oz., whiskey, 2½" h.	11.00
Tumbler, #2056, 3 oz., ftd. cone, cocktail, 2⅞" h.	14.00
Tumbler, #2056, 5 oz., ftd., juice, 4¾"	12.00
Tumbler, #2056, 6 oz., flat, old-fashioned, 3⅜" h.	14.00
Tumbler, #2056, 8 oz. flat, water, flared, 4⅛" h.	14.00
* Tumbler, #2056, 9 oz. ftd., water, 4⅞" h.	14.00
Tumbler, #2056, 12 oz., flat, tea, flared, 5¼" h.	16.00
Tumbler, #2056½, 5 oz., straight side, juice	12.00
Tumbler, #2056½, 8 oz., straight side, water, 3⅞" h.	12.00
Tumbler, #2056½, 12 oz., straight side, tea, 5" h.	17.50
Tumbler, #5056, 5 oz., ftd., juice, 4⅛" w/plain bowl	12.00

	*Crystal
Tumbler, #5056, 12 oz., ftd., tea, 5½" w/plain bowl	12.00
Urn, 6", sq., ped. ft	30.00
Urn, 7½", sq. ped. ft	35.00
Vase, 4½", sweet pea	65.00
Vase, 6", bud, ftd.	18.00
* Vase, 6", bud, flared	18.00
Vase, 6", straight side	35.00
Vase, 6½", flared rim	15.00
Vase, 7", flared	75.00
* Vase, 8", straight side	40.00
* Vase, 8", flared	80.00
Vase, 8", porch, 5" diam.	350.00
Vase, 8½", bud, flared	25.00
Vase, 8½", bud, cupped	25.00
Vase, 9", w/sq. ped. ft.	45.00
Vase, 9½", flared	115.00
Vase, 10", cupped in top	175.00
Vase, 10", porch, 8" diam.	350.00
* Vase, 10", straight side	90.00
Vase, 10", swung	195.00
Vase, 10", flared	90.00
Vase, 12", straight side	135.00
Vase, 12", swung	195.00
Vase, 14", swung	225.00
Vase, 20", swung	350.00

APPLE BLOSSOM, Line #3400, Cambridge Glass Company, 1930's

Colors: blue, pink, light and dark green, yellow, crystal, amber

Yellow Apple Blossom can be collected in sets more easily than any other color; still some diehards are working on putting green sets together. Few pitchers and even fewer butter dishes are seen in the light emerald green. Although several yellow sets entered the market a few years ago, those sets have now been absorbed by eager collectors. A few hardy souls search for pink, blue, and crystal. Putting any of these colored sets together a piece at a time will probably take years; but, if you are up to a challenge, go for it! Recently, monetary gains have caused gathered Elegant glass sets to return to the collecting arena. Financial considerations are a powerful force!

Apple Blossom pitchers, displayed on page 15, are not as plentiful as that picture would lead you to believe. You will search long and hard to round up any of these. The #3130 stemware line shown best at the top of page 15 is the most often seen; keep that in mind when you select a stem line to collect. Serving pieces, dinner plates, and unusual items are elusive. Buy when you have the chance or regret it later. Patience is prudent when searching for this pattern!

	Crystal	Yellow Amber	Pink *Green
Ash tray, 6", heavy	50.00	150.00	
Bowl, #3025, ftd., finger, w/plate	25.00	40.00	45.00
Bowl, #3130, finger, w/plate	30.00	40.00	45.00
Bowl, 3", indiv. nut, 4 ftd	50.00	65.00	65.00
Bowl, 5¼", 2 hdld., bonbon	12.50	25.00	25.00
Bowl, 5½", 2 hdld., bonbon	12.50	25.00	25.00
Bowl, 5½", fruit "saucer"	10.00	18.00	20.00
Bowl, 6", 2 hdld., "basket" (sides up)	20.00	30.00	35.00
Bowl, 6", cereal	18.00	28.00	32.00
Bowl, 9", pickle	17.00	35.00	40.00
Bowl, 10", 2 hdld.	35.00	70.00	85.00
Bowl, 10", baker	35.00	70.00	85.00
Bowl, 11", fruit, tab hdld.	35.00	75.00	80.00
Bowl, 11", low ftd.	30.00	75.00	90.00
Bowl, 12", relish, 4 pt.	30.00	50.00	65.00
Bowl, 12", 4 ftd.	40.00	70.00	85.00
Bowl, 12", flat	35.00	60.00	65.00
Bowl, 12", oval, 4 ftd.	40.00	60.00	85.00
Bowl, 12½", console	35.00	50.00	55.00
Bowl, 13"	35.00	60.00	65.00
Bowl, cream soup, w/liner plate	20.00	32.00	40.00
Butter w/cover, 5½"	125.00	250.00	375.00
Candelabrum, 3-lite, keyhole	27.50	45.00	55.00
Candlestick, 1-lite, keyhole	17.50	25.00	27.50
Candlestick, 2-lite, keyhole	22.50	30.00	35.00
Candy box w/cover, 4 ftd. "bowl"	70.00	90.00	125.00
Cheese (compote) & cracker (11½" plate)	40.00	60.00	80.00
Comport, 4", fruit cocktail	12.50	20.00	25.00
Comport, 7", tall	35.00	50.00	65.00
Creamer, ftd.	12.50	17.50	22.50
Creamer, tall ftd.	12.50	20.00	25.00
Cup	15.00	22.00	26.00
Cup, A.D.	40.00	50.00	80.00
Fruit/oyster cocktail, #3025, 4½ oz.	12.50	17.50	20.00
Mayonnaise, w/liner & ladle, (4 ftd. bowl)	35.00	55.00	70.00
Pitcher, 50 oz., ftd., flattened sides	125.00	210.00	275.00
Pitcher, 64 oz., #3130	135.00	250.00	300.00
Pitcher, 64 oz., #3025	135.00	250.00	300.00
Pitcher, 67 oz., squeezed middle, loop hdld.	135.00	275.00	325.00
Pitcher, 76 oz.	145.00	250.00	325.00
Pitcher, 80 oz., ball	125.00	165.00	300.00
Pitcher w/cover, 76 oz., ftd., #3135	195.00	375.00	495.00
Plate, 6", bread/butter	6.00	7.00	8.00
Plate, 6", sq., 2 hdld.	8.00	9.00	10.00
Plate, 7½", tea	9.00	12.00	13.00

* Blue prices 25% to 30% more.

APPLE BLOSSOM

	Crystal	Yellow Amber	Pink *Green
Plate, 8½"	14.00	20.00	22.00
Plate, 9½", dinner	45.00	65.00	75.00
Plate, 10", grill	25.00	45.00	55.00
Plate, sandwich, 11½", tab hdld.	22.00	32.50	35.00
Plate, sandwich, 12½", 2 hdld.	25.00	37.50	40.00
Plate, sq., bread/butter	5.00	7.00	8.00
Plate, sq., dinner	45.00	65.00	75.00
Plate, sq., salad	10.00	12.00	13.00
Plate, sq., service	17.50	20.00	22.00
Platter, 11½	37.50	65.00	75.00
Platter, 13½" rect., w/tab handle	40.00	90.00	110.00
Salt & pepper, pr.	37.50	75.00	90.00
Saucer	4.00	5.00	5.00
Saucer, A.D.	12.00	15.00	17.50
Stem, #1066, parfait	65.00	100.00	150.00
Stem, #3025, 7 oz., low fancy ft., sherbet	11.00	15.00	16.00
Stem, #3025, 7 oz., high sherbet	12.00	18.00	20.00
Stem, #3025, 10 oz.	18.00	22.00	25.00
Stem, #3130, 1 oz., cordial	55.00	95.00	145.00
Stem, #3130, 3 oz., cocktail	15.00	24.00	27.50
Stem, #3130, 6 oz., low sherbet	10.00	15.00	16.00
Stem, #3130, 6 oz., tall sherbet	10.00	18.00	20.00
Stem, #3130, 8 oz., water	15.00	25.00	32.50
Stem, #3135, 3 oz., cocktail	13.00	24.00	27.50
Stem, #3135, 6 oz., low sherbet	10.00	15.00	16.00
Stem, #3135, 6 oz., tall sherbet	10.00	18.00	20.00
Stem, #3135, 8 oz., water	14.00	22.00	30.00
Stem, #3400, 6 oz., ftd., sherbet	9.00	15.00	16.00
Stem, #3400, 9 oz., water	12.50	22.00	30.00
Sugar, ftd.	12.00	16.00	20.00
Sugar, tall ftd.	12.00	18.00	22.50
Tray, 7" hdld. relish	15.00	25.00	30.00
Tray, 11" ctr. hdld. sand.	25.00	37.50	45.00
Tumbler, #3025, 4 oz.	12.00	18.00	20.00
Tumbler, #3025, 10 oz.	15.00	22.00	24.00
Tumbler, #3025, 12 oz.	18.00	32.50	40.00
Tumbler, #3130, 5 oz., ftd.	11.00	22.00	28.00
Tumbler, #3130, 8 oz., ftd.	12.00	25.00	27.50
Tumbler, #3130, 10 oz., ftd.	13.00	25.00	27.50
Tumbler, #3130, 12 oz., ftd.	17.50	35.00	42.50
Tumbler, #3135, 5 oz., ftd.	10.00	22.00	28.00
Tumbler, #3135, 8 oz., ftd.	12.00	25.00	27.50
Tumbler, #3135, 10 oz., ftd.	13.00	25.00	27.50
Tumbler, #3135, 12 oz., ftd.	17.50	35.00	42.50
Tumbler, #3400, 2½ oz., ftd.	20.00	50.00	65.00
Tumbler, #3400, 9 oz., ftd.	12.00	25.00	27.50
Tumbler, #3400, 12 oz., ftd.	17.50	35.00	42.50
Tumbler, 12 oz., flat (2 styles) - 1 mid indent to match 67 oz. pitcher	20.00	35.00	40.00
Tumbler, 6"	15.00	30.00	35.00
Vase, 5"	25.00	45.00	50.00
Vase, 6", rippled sides	30.00	55.00	75.00
Vase, 8", 2 styles	40.00	90.00	125.00
Vase, 12", keyhole base w/neck indent	45.00	150.00	225.00

* Blue prices 25% to 30% more.

Note: See Pages 228-229 for stem identification.   14

BAROQUE, Line #2496, Fostoria Glass Company, 1936 – 1966

Colors: crystal, "Azure" blue, "Topaz" yellow, green, pink, red, cobalt blue, black amethyst

A green Baroque console bowl (to match the green candlestick pictured on page 19) has been found in California. Those two items are all that have been reported in green. Now, someone needs to locate a red or amethyst bowl to match those unusual colored candles that have surfaced.

Several pieces of Baroque are beginning to be elusive. Cream soups and individual shakers are the most troublesome, although pitchers and punch bowls have never been plentiful. They, at least, have always been pricey; whereas the other items were merely expensive, but affordable, if they could be found!

The sweetmeat is the 9" tall covered dish at the rear of the lower photograph on page 17. This is to distinguish it from the jelly that is only 7½" tall. Note the tops on the shakers. They came with both metal and glass tops, although most collectors prefer glass lids.

New collectors, notice that the yellow pitcher on the top of page 17 has no ice lip while the blue one on the top of page 19 has an ice lip. The pitcher with ice lip seems to be more desirable. That covered jar with spoon (top right of page 17) is a mustard and the little rounded ball-shaped vase at the bottom of the same page is the rose or ivy bowl.

Candlesticks are available in a variety of styles! Pictured in blue (top of page 19) is a 5½" single lite and a pair of 4" candles. The 6", 3-lite versions are shown in red and green at the bottom of that page.

Color variations in blue are depicted in the lower photo. This is a concern to many collectors. Most tend to shy away from the green tint. If color deviations do not bother you, then you will have more selections as you search for Baroque!

Straight tumblers are more difficult to find than footed ones, but many seem to prefer them to those cone-shaped, footed pieces. Price concerns may enter into that decision! If everyone were to like the same style though, demand would quickly exceed the supply!

Baroque blank (#2496) was used for many of Fostoria's etched lines including Navarre, Chintz, and Meadow Rose.

	Crystal	Blue	Yellow
Ash tray	7.50	15.00	13.00
Bowl, cream soup	35.00	75.00	75.00
Bowl, ftd., punch	400.00	1,250.00	
Bowl, 3¾", rose	25.00	55.00	45.00
Bowl, 4", hdld. (4 styles)	11.00	22.50	20.00
Bowl, 5", fruit	15.00	30.00	25.00
Bowl, 6", cereal	20.00	40.00	32.00
Bowl, 6", sq.	8.00	20.00	22.00
Bowl, 6½", 2 pt.	9.00	25.00	20.00
Bowl, 7", 3 ftd.	12.50	25.00	25.00
Bowl, 7½", jelly, w/cover	30.00	90.00	55.00
Bowl, 8", pickle	8.50	27.50	22.50
Bowl, 8½", hdld.	14.00	35.00	30.00
Bowl, 9½", veg., oval	25.00	65.00	50.00
Bowl, 10", hdld.	15.00	60.00	40.00
Bowl, 10½", hdld., 4 ftd.	17.50	47.50	37.50
Bowl, 10" x 7½"	25.00		
Bowl, 10", relish, 3 pt.	20.00	30.00	22.50
Bowl, 11", celery	12.00	45.00	25.00
Bowl, 11", rolled edge	20.00	50.00	37.50
* Bowl, 12", flared	21.50	40.00	32.50
Candelabrum, 8¼", 2-lite, 16 lustre	85.00	120.00	95.00
Candelabrum, 9½", 3-lite, 24 lustre	110.00	175.00	150.00
Candle, 7¾", 8 lustre	50.00	90.00	80.00
Candlestick, 4"	12.50	35.00	30.00
Candlestick, 4½", 2-lite	15.00	55.00	50.00

*Pink just discovered.

BAROQUE

	Crystal	Blue	Yellow
Candlestick, 5½"	9.00	40.00	35.00
* Candlestick, 6", 3-lite	17.50	75.00	60.00
Candy, 3 part w/cover	30.00	125.00	85.00
Comport, 4¾"	15.00	30.00	25.00
Comport, 6½"	17.50	35.00	30.00
Creamer, 3¼", indiv.	9.00	30.00	25.00
Creamer, 3¾", ftd.	8.00	14.00	14.00
Cup	9.00	30.00	20.00
Cup, 6 oz., punch	12.00	30.00	
Ice bucket	35.00	125.00	80.00
Mayonnaise, 5½", w/liner	15.00	55.00	40.00
Mustard, w/cover	22.00	60.00	45.00
Oil, w/stopper, 5½"	85.00	400.00	210.00
Pitcher, 6½"	110.00	750.00	450.00
Pitcher, 7", ice lip	110.00	700.00	400.00
Plate, 6"	3.00	10.00	8.00
Plate, 7½"	4.00	12.50	10.00
Plate, 8½"	6.00	20.00	17.50
Plate, 9½"	15.00	60.00	47.50
Plate, 10", cake	20.00	35.00	30.00
Plate, 11", ctr. hdld., sand	25.00		
Plate, 14", torte	13.00	40.00	25.00
Platter, 12", oval	22.00	65.00	45.00
Salt & pepper, pr.	45.00	120.00	100.00
Salt & pepper, indiv., pr.	50.00	225.00	130.00
Saucer	2.00	5.00	4.00
Sherbet, 3¾", 5 oz.	10.00	27.50	17.50
Stem, 6¾", 9 oz., water	12.00	27.50	22.50
Sugar, 3", indiv.	5.00	27.50	22.50
Sugar, 3½", ftd.	6.00	15.00	11.00
Sweetmeat, covered, 9"	75.00	195.00	145.00
Tray, 11", oval	15.00	47.50	37.50
Tray, 6¼" for indiv. cream/sugar	15.00	25.00	20.00
Tumbler, 3½", 6½ oz., old-fashioned	22.50	90.00	60.00
Tumbler, 3", 3½ oz., ftd., cocktail	10.00	20.00	15.00
Tumbler, 6", 12 oz., ftd., tea	20.00	40.00	30.00
Tumbler, 3¾", 5 oz., juice	12.00	40.00	25.00
Tumbler, 5½", 9 oz., ftd., water	12.00	30.00	25.00
Tumbler, 4¼", 9 oz., water	25.00	50.00	25.00
Tumbler, 5¾", 14 oz., tea	27.50	75.00	50.00
Vase, 6½"	45.00	125.00	100.00
Vase, 7"	40.00	125.00	85.00

* Red $150.00
Green $120.00
Black Amethyst $140.00
Cobalt Blue $140.00

BLACK FOREST, Possibly Paden City for Van Deman & Son, Late 1920's – Early 1930's

Colors: amber, black, ice blue, crystal, green, pink, red, cobalt

Black Forest is often confused with U.S. Glass Deerwood pattern. A reader mentioned that some pieces of Deerwood are found on Paden City blanks which adds to the confusion. In fact, you can see a pink Deerwood candy on page 79 which is a typical flat divided blank of Paden City. Study the pattern shots of each. Black Forest portrays moose and trees, while deer and trees are dominant on Deerwood. Now, all you have to know is a deer from a moose and have some luck in spotting either!

The night set (pitcher and tumbler) in Black Forest is missing from most collections. These have only been found in pink and green to date. The tumbler has an extended band that will only allow it to drop down as far as the neck of the pitcher when inverted.

The question I am most asked about Black Forest concerns goblets that were made in the 1970's. An amber one is pictured on the right. These were made in amber, dark green, blue, crystal, and red. Since these are newer than the original Black Forest, they are easier to find and are selling in the $20.00 to $30.00 range, although you may see them offered for much more by unknowing dealers. Red and blue are on the upper side of that price. All these reproduced items have that heavy, predominant "Daisy and Button" stem shown here.

Even though there are some expensive pieces in Black Forest, it will not rapidly drain your bank account since so little of it is being offered for sale. You will only find a piece or two at a time — even at Depression glass shows. However, don't let difficulty deter you from collecting! I receive hundreds of letters yearly advising me how much joy collectors obtain from possessing even a piece or two of their favorite patterns!

	Amber	*Black	Crystal	Green	Pink	Red
Batter jug			135.00			
Bowl, 4½", finger				15.00		
Bowl, 9¼", center hdld.				75.00	75.00	
Bowl, 11", console	50.00	50.00	35.00	30.00	30.00	
Bowl, 11", fruit		30.00		25.00	25.00	
Bowl, 13", console		75.00				
Bowl, 3 ftd.			60.00			
Cake plate, 2" pedestal	40.00	50.00		40.00	35.00	
Candlestick, mushroom style	30.00	35.00	15.00	30.00	30.00	
Candlestick double			35.00			
Candy dish, w/cover, several styles	85.00	125.00		110.00	110.00	
Creamer, 2 styles		35.00	20.00	35.00	35.00	65.00
Comport, 4", low ftd.				25.00	25.00	
Comport, 5½", high ftd.		30.00		28.00	25.00	
Cup and saucer, 3 styles		90.00		85.00	85.00	110.00
Decanter, w/stopper, 8½", 28 oz., bulbous					165.00	
Decanter w/stopper, 8¾", 24 oz., straight			75.00	145.00	145.00	
Ice bucket	90.00			75.00	75.00	
Ice pail, 6", 3" high	75.00					
Ice tub, 2 styles (Ice blue $195.00)	80.00	85.00		85.00	75.00	
Mayonnaise, with liner		60.00		60.00	60.00	
Night Set: pitcher, 6½", 42 oz. & tumbler				400.00	400.00	
Pitcher, 8", 40 oz., (Cobalt $750.00)						
Pitcher, 8", 62 oz.			175.00			
Pitcher, 9", 80 oz.					400.00	
Pitcher, 10½", 72 oz.				425.00	425.00	
Plate, 6½", bread/butter		22.00		22.00		30.00
Plate, 8", luncheon		25.00			25.00	30.00
Plate, 11", 2 hdld.		45.00		25.00	25.00	
Plate, 13¾", 2 hdld.				75.00	75.00	
Relish, 10½", 5 pt. covered				175.00	175.00	
Salt and pepper, pr.			125.00		175.00	
Server, center hdld.	50.00	40.00	35.00	35.00	35.00	
Shot Glass, 2 oz., 2½"	40.00					
Stem, 2 oz., wine, 4¼"			17.50	50.00		
Stem, 6 oz., champagne, 4¾"			17.50		30.00	
Stem, 9 oz., water, 6"			22.50			
Sugar, 2 styles		35.00	20.00	35.00	35.00	65.00
Tumbler, 3 oz., juice, flat or footed, 3½"			25.00	35.00	35.00	
Tumbler, 8 oz., old fashioned, 3⅞"					35.00	
Tumbler, 9 oz., ftd., 5½"	30.00					
Tumbler, 12 oz., tea, 5½"				45.00	45.00	
Vase, 6½" (Cobalt $125.00)		55.00	45.00	50.00	50.00	
Vase, 10", 2 styles in black		85.00		75.00	75.00	
Whipped cream pail	75.00					

*Add 20% for gold decorated.

CADENA, Tiffin Glass Company, Early 1930's

Colors: crystal, yellow; some pink

Tiffin patterns have always driven collectors to distraction trying to find serving pieces; and Cadena is no exception. Note the lack of those items in my photograph! Stemware can be found with some searching; but even if you are willing to pay the price for other items, they are rarely available. Pitchers were sold both with and without a lid. If you try to put a lid on one of the pitchers originally sold without one, you may find that the lid will not fit. Pitchers sold without lids were often curved in so much that a lid will not fit inside the top rim. Bear in mind also that the pitcher cover is plain; no pattern is etched on it.

Very few pieces of pink are being found. Cadena is rarely seen at Depression shows and that makes for fewer collectors. The days of finding a large set at one time have mostly disappeared into the past. Occasionally, you will find a piece or two. Seemingly, Tiffin did not market this pattern as extensively as they did their Cherokee Rose, Fuchsia, and Flanders patterns, all of which are popular with today's collectors!

One question I am asked frequently is why I can't show individual items in specific patterns and identify them piece by piece. A major reason is cost and another is availability! I couldn't afford to buy every piece in every pattern if I could find them, and you couldn't lift the book (or would have to read it with a magnifying glass) if I did.

I have always tried to show you as much glass as possible to whet your collecting appetite. Where feasible, a close-up shot has been included to enhance pattern identification. Colors and items are changed in every other edition, and major patterns are changed with every edition as new items are discovered. Believe me, we keep trying to improve with each edition!

	Crystal	Pink/ Yellow
Bowl, cream soup	20.00	30.00
Bowl, finger, ftd.	15.00	25.00
Bowl, grapefruit, ftd.	22.00	50.00
Bowl, 6", hdld.	10.00	22.00
Bowl, 10", pickle	15.00	27.50
Bowl, 12", console	25.00	47.50
Candlestick	20.00	35.00
Creamer	15.00	25.00
Cup	25.00	65.00
Mayonnaise, ftd., w/liner	30.00	50.00
Oyster cocktail	15.00	25.00
Pitcher, ftd.	175.00	250.00
Pitcher, ftd., w/cover	235.00	350.00
Plate, 6"	5.00	8.00
Plate, 7¾"	7.00	12.00
Plate, 9¼"	30.00	40.00
Saucer	10.00	12.50
Stem, 4¾", sherbet	15.00	22.00
Stem, 5¼", cocktail	17.50	25.00
Stem, 5¼", ¾ oz., cordial	60.00	90.00
Stem, 6", wine	25.00	40.00
Stem, 6⁵⁄₁₆", 8 oz., parfait	25.00	35.00
Stem, 6½", champagne	17.00	30.00
Stem, 7½", water	20.00	35.00
Sugar	15.00	23.00
Tumbler, 4¼", ftd., juice	17.50	27.50
Tumbler, 5¼", ftd., water	20.00	30.00
Vase, 9"	40.00	75.00

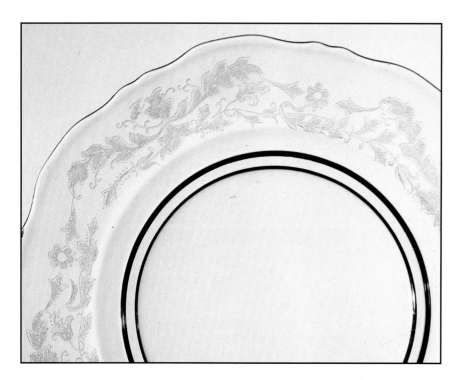

CANDLELIGHT, Cambridge Glass Company, 1940's – Early 1950's

Colors: crystal, Crown Tuscan with gold decoration

I received a letter from a lady in California who was searching for pieces of a glassware pattern she had inherited. After five years of looking, she saw the pattern in my book and wrote to ask for help. Unfortunately for her search, her Candlelight pattern was the cut version and not the etched. Cut Candlelight is even more rarely found than its etched counterpart. At least she now knows her pattern's name and scarcity.

Prices for Candlelight have escalated over the past two years. Stemware pieces are easiest found, but cordials and wines are quite difficult to obtain. You will look long and hard for shakers, basic serving pieces, and lamps. I have been unable to find a cup and saucer, but I finally located a pair of shakers. There are two icers and liners in the photograph. One represents the etched and the other cut Candlelight. Note the difference! The pattern is harder to see on the cut!

Of course, Candlelight is not as collected as other Cambridge patterns, even though almost everyone recognizes the pattern! That bowl used as a pattern shot also has a cut Candlelight pattern instead of acid etched. Admittedly, Candlelight pieces are not commonly found; but even one or two pieces can improve the looks of a table or mantle.

Bill Schroeder of Collector Books just found a 1951 Candlelight brochure which added an additional 20 items to my listings!

	Crystal		Crystal
Bonbon, 7", ftd., 2 hdld., #3900/130	35.00	Plate, 13½", cake, 2 hdld., #3900/35	75.00
Bowl, 10", 4 toed, flared, #3900/54	60.00	Plate, 13½", cracker, #3900/135	65.00
Bowl, 11", 2 hdld., #3900/34	70.00	Plate, 14", rolled edge, #3900/166	70.00
Bowl, 11", 4 ftd., fancy edge, #3400/48	65.00	Relish, 7", 2 hdld., #3900/123	35.00
Bowl, 11½", ftd., 2 hdld., #3900/28	75.00	Relish, 7", div., 2 hdld., #3900/124	40.00
Bowl, 12", 4 ftd., flared, #3400/4	70.00	Relish, 8", 3-part, #3400/91	45.00
Bowl, 12", 4 ftd., oblong, #3400/160	75.00	Relish, 9", 3 pt., #3900/125	47.50
Bowl, 12", 4 toed, flared, #3900/62	75.00	Relish, 12", 3 pt., #3900/126	55.00
Bowl, 12", 4 toed, oval, hdld., #3900/65	95.00	Relish, 12", 5 pt., #3900/120	65.00
Butter dish, 5", #3400/52	150.00	Salt & pepper, pr., #3900/1177	95.00
Candle, 5", #3900/67	40.00	Saucer, #3900/17	5.00
Candle, 6", 2-lite, #3900/72	45.00	Stem, 1 oz., cordial, #3776	75.00
Candle, 6", 3-lite, #3900/74	55.00	Stem, 2 oz., sherry, #7966	65.00
Candlestick, 5", #646	40.00	Stem, 2½ oz., wine, #3111	60.00
Candlestick, 6", 2-lite, #647	45.00	Stem, 3 oz., cocktail, #3111	35.00
Candlestick, 6", 3-lite, #1338	55.00	Stem, 3 oz., cocktail, #3776	30.00
Candy box and cover, 3-part, #3500/57	100.00	Stem, 3½ oz., wine, #3776	55.00
Candy w/lid, rnd. #3900/165	110.00	Stem, 4 oz., cocktail, #7801	30.00
Cocktail shaker, 36 oz., #P101	150.00	Stem, 4½ oz., claret, #3776	60.00
Comport, 5", cheese, #3900/135	35.00	Stem, 4½ oz., oyster cocktail, #3111	30.00
Comport, 5⅜", blown, #3121	60.00	Stem, 4½ oz., oyster cocktail, #3776	25.00
Comport, 5½", #3900/136	52.50	Stem, 7 oz., low sherbet, #3111	17.50
Creamer, #3900/41	20.00	Stem, 7 oz., low sherbet, #3776	16.50
Creamer, indiv., #3900/40	22.50	Stem, 7 oz., tall sherbet, #3111	22.50
Cruet, 6 oz., w/stopper, #3900/100	110.00	Stem, 7 oz., tall sherbet, #3776	20.00
Cup, #3900/17	30.00	Stem, 9 oz., water, #3776	35.00
Decanter, 28 oz., ftd., #1321	175.00	Stem, 10 oz., water, #3111	35.00
Ice bucket, #3900/671	125.00	Sugar, #3900/41	20.00
Icer, 2 pc., cocktail, #968	85.00	Sugar, indiv., #3900/40	20.00
Lamp, hurricane, #1617	150.00	Tumbler, 5 oz., ftd., juice, #3111	22.00
Lamp, hurricane, keyhole, w/bobeche,#1603	190.00	Tumbler, 5 oz., juice, #3776	20.00
Lamp, hurricane, w/bobeche, #1613	275.00	Tumbler, 12 oz., ftd., iced tea., #3111	30.00
Mayonnaise, 3 pc., #3900/129	57.50	Tumbler, 12 oz., iced tea, #3776	27.50
Mayonnaise, div., 4 pc., #3900/111	65.00	Tumbler, 13 oz., #3900/115	40.00
Mayonnaise, ftd., 2 pc., #3900/19	47.50	Vase, 5", ftd., bud, #6004	40.00
Nut cup, 3", 4 ftd., #3400/71	60.00	Vase, 5", globe, #1309	55.00
Oil, 6 oz., #3900/100	75.00	Vase, 6", ftd., #6004	45.00
Pitcher, Doulton, #3400/141	325.00	Vase, 8", ftd., #6004	55.00
Plate, 6½", #3900/20	12.50	Vase, 9", ftd., keyhole, #1237	65.00
Plate, 8", 2 hdld., #3900/131	25.00	Vase, 10", bud, #274	50.00
Plate, 8", salad, #3900/22	17.00	Vase, 11", ftd. pedestal, #1299	120.00
Plate, 10½", dinner, #3900/24	70.00	Vase, 11", ftd., #278	75.00
Plate, 12", 4 toed, #3900/26	60.00	Vase, 12", ftd., keyhole, #1238	95.00
Plate, 13", torte, 4 toed, #3900/33	60.00	Vase, 13", ftd, #279	125.00

CANDLEWICK, Line #400, Imperial Glass Company, 1936 – 1984

Colors: crystal, blue, pink, yellow, black, red, cobalt blue, green, carmel slag

Candlewick stemware and tumbler identification usually gives collectors fits until they learn all the different lines. In the bottom photo on page 29 are two different stem lines on which ruby and cobalt Candlewick is found. The round stems and tumblers are 3800 while the flared style is 3400 line. If your red or cobalt stemware has some other shape, then it is not Candlewick. Another stemware line is 400/190 and is found with a hollow stem. These can easily be seen in the ad on page 35 or in the picture at the bottom of page 27. The tumblers shown on the bottom left of page 33 have the designation 400/19. The bases on these tumblers are flat as opposed to 400/18 which has a domed foot (not pictured in this edition). The 400/... was Imperial's factory listing for each piece.

Viennese blue pieces of Candlewick (light colored blue shown below) are selling well, but sales of higher priced red and black items have slowed. In the recent past, prices on colored Candlewick escalated very rapidly; now, those prices have moderated, a characteristic of a too rapid price rise. Ruby red and black fancy bowls have steadied in the ball park of $210.00 – 225.00 with the Viennese blue pieces bringing fifty to sixty percent of that. Ruby red stems continue to be found in the 3400 and 3800 lines with most of these selling in the $40.00 to $65.00 range. However, cordials are selling in ruby red and Ritz blue (cobalt) from $100.00 to $140.00. Other Ritz blue stems are fetching $70.00 to $100.00. All of these colored pieces of Candlewick were made before 1940.

The family punch bowl (400/139/2) is shown at the top of page 27. Note the notched lid for the ladle. That bottom without a notched lid is the snack jar (400/139/1) pictured on the top of page 31. Everyone seeks the 14" birthday cake plate (400/160) shown top of page 27 with fewer candles than its seventy-two candles capacity. "After seventy-two, you ought to stop blowing out candles," explained one elderly Candlewick collector at a recent show. Scratches from years of use devalue these cake plates; so be aware of that on all Candlewick plates.

One of the rarely seen gold decorated punch sets is shown on page 31. Enjoy that along with ads from a couple of 1940's magazines on pages 34 and 35.

There are several unusual and rare Candlewick items shown in the four and soon to be five volumes of *Very Rare Glassware of the Depression Years.*

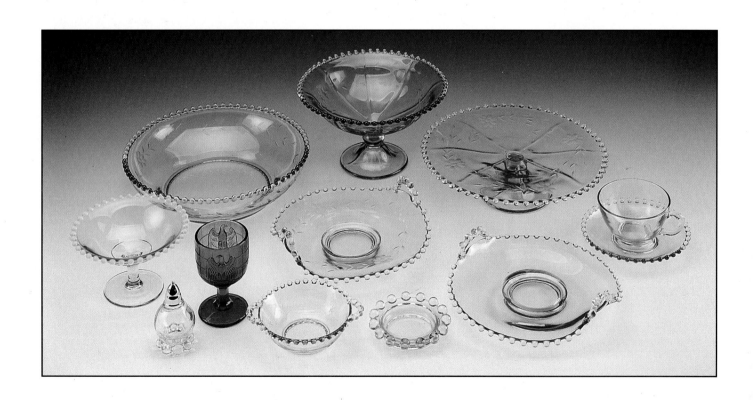

CANDLEWICK

	Crystal
Ash tray, eagle, 6½", 1776/1	55.00
Ash tray, heart, 4½", 400/172	10.00
Ash tray, heart, 5½", 400/173	12.00
Ash tray, heart, 6½", 400/174	15.00
Ash tray, indiv 400/64.	8.00
Ash tray, oblong, 4½", 400/134/1	6.00
Ash tray, round, 2¾", 400/19	9.00
Ash tray, round, 4", 400/33	11.00
Ash tray, round, 5", 400/133	8.00
Ash tray, square, 3¼", 400/651	35.00
Ash tray, square, 4½", 400/652	35.00
Ash tray, square, 5¾", 400/653	40.00
Ash tray, 6", matchbook holder center, 400/60	100.00
Ash tray set, 3 pc. rnd. nest. (crys. or colors), 400/550	30.00
Ash tray set, 3 pc. sq. nesting, 400/650	110.00
Ash tray set, 4 pc. bridge (cig. hold at side), 400/118	37.50
Basket, 5", beaded hdld., 400/273	200.00
Basket, 6½", hdld., 400/40/0	30.00
Basket, 11", hdld., 400/73/0	210.00
Bell, 4", 400/179	65.00
Bell, 5", 400/108	75.00
Bottle, bitters, w/tube, 4 oz. 400/117	60.00
Bowl, bouillon, 2 hdld., 400/126	42.50
Bowl, #3400, finger, ftd.	30.00
Bowl, #3800, finger	30.00
Bowl, 4½", nappy, 3 ftd., 400/206	67.50
Bowl, 4¾", round, 2 hdld., 400/42B	12.00
Bowl, 5", cream soup, 400/50	42.50
Bowl, 5", fruit, 400/1F	12.00
Bowl, 5", heart w/hand., 400/49H	20.00
Bowl, 5", square, 400/231	85.00
Bowl, 5½", heart, 400/53H	20.00
Bowl, 5½", jelly, w/cover, 400/59	60.00
Bowl, 5½", sauce, deep, 400/243	37.50
Bowl, 6", baked apple, rolled edge, 400/53X	27.50
Bowl, 6", cottage cheese, 400/85	25.00
Bowl, 6", fruit, 400/3F	12.00
Bowl, 6", heart w/hand., 400/51H	25.00
Bowl, 6", mint w/hand., 400/51F	20.00
Bowl, 6", round, div., 2 hdld., 400/52	25.00
Bowl, 6", 2 hdld., 400/52B	15.00
Bowl, 6", 3 ftd., 400/183	60.00
Bowl, 6", sq., 400/232	115.00
Bowl, 6½", relish, 2 pt., 400/84	25.00
Bowl, 6½", 2 hdld., 400/181	30.00
Bowl, 7", round, 400/5F	25.00
Bowl, 7", round, 2 hdld., 400/62B	17.50
Bowl, 7", relish, sq., div., 400/234	125.00
Bowl, 7", ivy, high, bead ft., 400/188	175.00
Bowl, 7", lily, 4 ft., 400/74J	65.00
Bowl, 7", relish, 400/60	25.00
Bowl, 7", sq., 400/233	135.00
Bowl, 7¼", rose, ftd. w/crimp edge, 400/132C	395.00
Bowl, 7½", pickle/celery 400/57	27.50
Bowl, 7½", lily, bead rim, ftd., 400/75N	295.00
Bowl, 7½", belled, (console base), 400/127B	85.00

	Crystal
Bowl, 8", round, 400/7F	37.50
Bowl, 8", relish, 2 pt., 400/268	20.00
Bowl, 8", cov. veg., 400/65/1	265.00
Bowl, 8½", rnd., 400/69B	35.00
Bowl, 8½", nappy, 4 ftd., 400/74B	65.00
Bowl, 8½", 3 ftd., 400/182	110.00
Bowl, 8½", 2 hdld., 400/72B	22.00
Bowl, 8½", pickle/celery, 400/58	20.00
Bowl, 8½", relish, 4 pt., 400/55	22.00
Bowl, 9", round, 400/10F	42.50
Bowl, 9", crimp, ftd., 400/67C	135.00
Bowl, 9", sq., fancy crimp edge, 4 ft., 400/74SC	70.00
Bowl, 9", heart, 400/49H	110.00
Bowl, 9", heart w/hand., 400/73H	115.00
Bowl, 10", 400/13F	45.00
Bowl, 10", banana, 400/103E	1,250.00
Bowl, 10", 3 toed, 400/205	140.00
Bowl, 10", belled, (punch base), 400/128B	70.00
Bowl, 10", cupped edge, 400/75F	45.00
Bowl, 10", deep, 2 hdld., 400/113A	115.00
Bowl, 10", divided, deep, 2 hdld., 400/114A	135.00
Bowl, 10", fruit, bead stem (like compote), 400/103F	175.00
Bowl, 10", relish, oval, 2 hdld., 400/217	40.00
Bowl, 10", relish, 3 pt., 3 ft., 400/208	90.00
Bowl, 10", 3 pt., w/cover, 400/216	300.00
Bowl, 10½", belled, 400/63B	60.00
Bowl, 10½", butter/jam, 3 pt., 400/262	135.00
Bowl, 10½", salad, 400/75B	40.00
Bowl, 10½", relish, 3 section, 400/256	30.00
Bowl, 11", celery boat, oval, 400/46	60.00
Bowl, 11", centerpiece, flared, 400/13B	55.00
Bowl, 11", float, inward rim, ftd., 400/75F	40.00
Bowl, 11", oval, 400/124A	240.00
Bowl, 11", oval w/partition, 400/125A	265.00
Bowl, 12", round, 400/92B	40.00
Bowl, 12", belled, 400/106B	90.00
Bowl, 12", float, 400/92F	40.00
Bowl, 12", hdld., 400/113B	165.00
Bowl, 12", shallow, 400/17F	47.50
Bowl, 12", relish, oblong, 4 sect., 400/215	115.00
Bowl, 13", centerpiece, mushroom, 400/92L	50.00
Bowl, 13", float, 1½" deep, 400/101	65.00
Bowl, 13½", relish, 5 pt., 400/209	77.50
Bowl, 14", belled, 400/104B	90.00
Bowl, 14", oval, flared, 400/131B	225.00
Butter and jam set, 5 piece, 400/204	295.00
Butter, w/ cover, rnd., 5½", 400/144	32.50
Butter, w/ cover, no beads, California, 400/276	125.00
Butter, w/ bead top, ¼ lb., 400/161	30.00
Cake stand, 10", low foot, 400/67D	52.50
Cake stand, 11", high foot, 400/103D	70.00
Calendar, 1947, desk	175.00
Candleholder, 3 way, beaded base, 400/115	110.00
Candleholder, 2-lite, 400/100	20.00
Candleholder, flat, 3½", 400/280	50.00
Candleholder, 3½", rolled edge, 400/79R	12.00
Candleholder, 3½", w/fingerhold, 400/81	48.00
Candleholder, flower, 4", 2 bead stem, 400/66F	50.00
Candleholder, flower, 4½", 2 bead stem, 400/66C	60.00

CANDLEWICK

	Crystal
Candleholder, 4½", 3 toed, 400/207	60.00
Candleholder, 3-lite on cir. bead. ctr., 400/147	25.00
Candleholder, 5", hdld./bowled up base, 400/90	45.00
Candleholder, 5" heart shape, 400/40HC	75.00
Candleholder, 5½", 3 bead stems, 400/224	90.00
Candleholder, flower, 5", (epergne inset), 400/40CV	95.00
Candleholder, 5", flower, 400/40C	35.00
Candleholder, 6½", tall, 3 bead stems, 400/175	95.00
Candleholder, flower, 6", round, 400/40F	25.00
Candleholder, urn, 6", holders on cir. ctr. bead, 400/129R	125.00
Candleholder, flower, 6½", square, 400/40S	40.00
Candleholder, mushroom, 400/86	35.00
Candleholder, flower 9" centerpiece, 400/196FC	165.00
Candy box, round, 5½", 400/59	45.00
Candy box, sq., 6½", rnd. lid, 400/245	195.00
Candy box, w/ cover, 7", 400/259	135.00
Candy box, w/ cover, 7" partitioned, 400/110	70.00
Candy box, w/ cover, round, 7", 3 sect., 400/158	165.00
Candy box, w/ cover, beaded, ft., 400/140	250.00
Cigarette box w/cover, 400/134	35.00
Cigarette holder, 3", bead ft., 400/44	35.00
Cigarette set: 6 pc., (cigarette box & 4 rect. ash trays), 400/134/6	67.50
Clock, 4", round	265.00
Coaster, 4", 400/78	7.00
Coaster, w/spoon rest, 400/226	16.00
Cocktail, seafood w/bead ft., 400/190	55.00
Cocktail set: 2 pc., plate w/indent; cocktail, 400/97	35.00
Compote, 4½", 400/63B	40.00
Compote, 5", 3 bead stems, 400/220	70.00
Compote, 5½", 4 bead stem, 400/45	25.00
Compote, 5½, low, plain stem, 400/66B	22.00
Compote, 5½", 2 bead stem, 400/66B	22.00
Compote, 8", bead stem, 400/48F	80.00
Compote, 10", ftd. fruit, crimped, 40/103C	150.00
Compote, ft. oval, 400/137	995.00
Condiment set: 4 pc., (2 squat bead ft. shakers, marmalade), 400/1786	67.50
Console sets: 3 pc. (14" oval bowl, two 3-lite candles), 400/1531B	295.00
3 pc. (mushroom bowl, w/mushroom candles), 400/8692L	105.00
Creamer, domed foot, 400/18	115.00
Creamer, 6 oz., bead handle, 400/30	8.00
Creamer, indiv. bridge, 400/122	7.50
Creamer, plain ft., 400/31	9.00
Creamer, flat, bead handle, 400/126	32.50
Cup, after dinner, 400/77	17.50
Cup, coffee, 400/37	7.50
Cup, punch, 400/211	7.50
Cup, tea, 400/35	8.00
Decanter, w/stopper, 15 oz. cordial, 400/82/2	295.00
Decanter w/stopper, 18 oz., 400/18	395.00
Decanter w/stopper, 26 oz., 400/163	295.00
Deviled egg server, 12", ctr. hdld., 400/154	110.00
Egg cup, bead. ft., 400/19	47.50

	Crystal
Fork & spoon, set, 400/75	35.00
Hurricane lamp, 2 pc. candle base, 400/79	120.00
Hurricane lamp, 2 pc., hdld. candle base, 400/76	150.00
Hurricane lamp, 3 pc. flared & crimped edge globe, 400/152	150.00
Ice tub, 5½" deep, 8" diam., 400/63	95.00
Ice tub, 7", 2 hdld., 400/168	195.00
Icer, 2 pc., seafood/fruit cocktail, 400/53/3	95.00
Icer, 2 pc., seafood/fruit cocktail #3800 line, one bead stem	65.00
Jam set, 5 pc., oval tray w/2 marmalade jars w/ladles, 400/1589	115.00
Jar tower, 3 sect., 400/655	325.00
Knife, butter, 4000	295.00
Ladle, marmalade, 3 bead stem, 400/130	12.00
Ladle, mayonnaise, 6¼", 400/135	12.00
Marmalade set, 3 pc., beaded ft. w/cover & spoon, 400/1989	40.00
Marmalade set, 3 pc. tall jar, domed bead ft., lid, spoon, 400/8918	65.00
Marmalade set, 4 pc., liner saucer, jar, lid, spoon, 400/89	42.50
Mayonnaise set, 2 pc. scoop side bowl, spoon, 400/23	37.50
Mayonnaise set, 3 pc. hdld. tray/hdld. bowl/ladle, 400/52/3	45.00
Mayonnaise set, 3 pc. plate, heart bowl, spoon, 400/49	33.00
Mayonnaise set, 3 pc. scoop side bowl, spoon, tray, 400/496	40.00
Mayonnaise 4 pc., plate, divided bowl, 2 ladles, 400/84	40.00
Mirror, 4½", rnd., standing	110.00
Mustard jar, w/spoon, 400/156	30.00
Oil, 4 oz., bead base, 400/164	55.00
Oil, 6 oz., bead base, 400/166	65.00
Oil, 4 oz., bulbous bottom, 400/274	45.00
Oil, 4 oz., hdld., bulbous bottom, 400/278	65.00
Oil, 6 oz., hdld., bulbous bottom, 400/279	80.00
Oil, 6 oz., bulbous bottom, 400/275	55.00
Oil, w/stopper, etched "Oil," 400/121	60.00
Oil, w/stopper, etched "Vinegar," 400/121	60.00
Party set, 2 pc., oval plate w/indent for cup, 400/98	27.50
Pitcher, 14 oz., short rnd., 400/330	175.00
Pitcher, 16 oz., low ft., 400/19	210.00
Pitcher, 16 oz., no ft., 400/16	175.00
Pitcher, 20 oz., plain, 400/416	40.00
Pitcher, 40 oz., juice/cocktail, 400/19	175.00
Pitcher, 40 oz., manhattan, 400/18	225.00
Pitcher, 40 oz., plain, 400/419	40.00
Pitcher, 64 oz., plain, 400/424	50.00
Pitcher, 80 oz., plain, 400/424	55.00
Pitcher, 80 oz., 400/24	130.00
Pitcher, 80 oz., beaded ft., 400/18	225.00
Plate, 4½", 400/34	6.00
Plate, 5½", 2 hdld., 400/42D	10.00
Plate, 6", bread/butter, 400/1D	8.00
Plate, 6", canape w/off ctr. indent, 400/36	14.00
Plate, 6¾", 2 hdld. crimped, 400/52C	25.00
Plate, 7", salad, 400/3D	8.00

CANDLEWICK

	Crystal
Plate, 7½", 2 hdld., 400/52D	10.00
Plate, 7½", triangular, 400/266	85.00
Plate, 8", oval, 400/169	22.50
Plate, 8", salad, 400/5D	9.00
Plate, 8", w/indent, 400/50	11.00
Plate, 8¼", crescent salad, 400/120	45.00
Plate, 8½", 2 hdld., crimped, 400/62C	20.00
Plate, 8½", 2 hdld., 400/62D	12.00
Plate, 8½", salad, 400/5D	10.00
Plate, 8½", 2 hdld. (sides upturned), 400/62E	25.00
Plate, 9", luncheon, 400/7D	13.50
Plate, 9", oval, salad, 400/38	37.50
Plate, 9", w/indent, oval, 400/98	15.00
Plate, 10", 2 hdld., sides upturned, 400/72E	22.50
Plate, 10", 2 hdld. crimped, 400/72C	30.00
Plate, 10", 2 hdld., 400/72D	17.50
Plate, 10½", dinner, 400/10D	37.50
Plate, 12", 2 hdld., 400/145D	27.50
Plate, 12", 2 hdld. crimp., 400/145C	32.50
Plate, 12", service, 400/13D	30.00
Plate, 12½", cupped edge, torte, 400/75V	27.50
Plate, 12½", oval, 400/124	75.00
Plate, 13½", cupped edge, serving, 400/92V	40.00
Plate, 14" birthday cake (holes for 72 candles), 400/160	425.00
Plate, 14", 2 hdld., sides upturned, 400/113E	35.00
Plate, 14", 2 hdld., torte, 400/113D	30.00
Plate, 14", service, 400/92D	30.00
Plate, 14", torte, 400/17D	42.50
Plate, 17", cupped edge, 400/20V	50.00
Plate, 17", torte, 400/20D	50.00
Platter, 13", 400/124D	90.00
Platter, 16", 400/131D	185.00
Punch ladle, 400/91	30.00
Punch set, family, 8 demi cups, ladle, lid, 400/139/77	550.00
Punch set, 15 pc. bowl on base, 12 cups, ladle, 400/20	245.00
Relish & dressing set, 4 pc. (10½" 4 pt. relish w/marmalade), 400/1112	90.00
Salad set, 4 pc., buffet; lg. rnd. tray, div. bowl, 2 spoons, 400/17	120.00
Salad set, 4 pc. (rnd. plate, flared bowl, fork, spoon), 400/75B	85.00
Salt & pepper pr., bead ft., straight side, chrome top, 400/247	16.00
Salt & pepper pr., bead ft., bulbous, chrome top, 400/96	15.00
Salt & pepper pr., bulbous w/bead stem, plastic top, 400/116	65.00
Salt & pepper, pr., indiv., 400/109	11.00
Salt & pepper, pr., ftd. bead base, 400/190	47.50
Salt dip, 2", 400/61	11.00
Salt dip, 2¼", 400/19	11.00
Salt spoon, 3, 400/616	11.00
Salt spoon, w/ribbed bowl, 4000	11.00
Sauce boat, 400/169	105.00
Sauce boat liner, 400/169	40.00
Saucer, after dinner, 400/77AD	5.00
Saucer, tea or coffee, 400/35 or 400/37	2.50

	Crystal
Set: 2 pc. hdld. cracker w/cheese compote, 400/88	37.50
Set: 2 pc. rnd. cracker plate w/indent; cheese compote, 400/145	45.00
Snack jar w/cover, bead ft., 400/139/1	425.00
Stem, 1 oz., cordial, 400/190	70.00
Stem, 4 oz., cocktail, 400/190	18.00
Stem, 5 oz., tall sherbet, 400/190	15.00
Stem, 5 oz., wine, 400/190	21.00
Stem, 6 oz., sherbet, 400/190	14.00
Stem, 10 oz., water 400/190	18.00
Stem, #3400, 1 oz., cordial	37.50
Stem, #3400, 4 oz., cocktail	16.00
Stem, #3400, 4 oz. oyster cocktail	14.00
Stem, #3400, 4 oz., wine	25.00
Stem, #3400, 5 oz., claret	50.00
Stem, #3400, 5 oz., low sherbet	10.00
Stem, #3400, 6 oz., parfait	50.00
Stem, #3400, 6 oz., sherbet/saucer champagne	17.50
Stem, #3400, 9 oz., goblet, water	16.00
Stem, #3800, low sherbet	25.00
Stem, #3800, brandy	27.50
Stem, #3800, 1 oz. cordial	42.50
Stem, #3800, 4 oz., cocktail	25.00
Stem, #3800, 4 oz. wine	27.50
Stem, #3800, 6 oz., champagne/sherbet	25.00
Stem, #3800, 9 oz. water goblet	25.00
Stem, #3800, claret	30.00
Stem, #4000, 1¼ oz., cordial	30.00
Stem, #4000, cocktail	22.00
Stem, #4000, 5 oz., wine	25.00
Stem, #4000, 6 oz., tall sherbet	22.00
Stem, #4000, 11 oz., goblet	30.00
Stem, #4000, 12 oz., tea	25.00
Strawberry set, 2 pc. (7" plate/sugar dip bowl), 400/83	50.00
Sugar, domed foot, 400/18	115.00
Sugar, 6 oz., bead hdld., 400/30	7.00
Sugar, flat, bead handle, 400/126	40.00
Sugar, indiv. bridge, 400/122	6.00
Sugar, plain ft., 400/31	6.50
Tete-a-tete 3 pc. brandy, a.d. cup, 6½" oval tray, 400/111	65.00
Tid bit server, 2 tier, cupped, 400/2701	50.00
Tid bit set, 3 pc., 400/18TB	195.00
Toast, w/cover, set, 7¾", 400/123	275.00
Tray, 5½", hdld., upturned handles, 400/42E	18.00
Tray, 5½", lemon, ctr. hdld., 400/221	30.00
Tray, 5¼" x 9¼", condiment, 400/148	42.50
Tray, 6½", 400/29	15.00
Tray, 6", wafer, handle bent to ctr. of dish, 400/51T	22.00
Tray, 10½", ctr. hdld. fruit, 400/68F	100.00
Tray, 11½", ctr. hdld. party, 400/68D	30.00
Tray, 13½", 2 hdld. celery, oval, 400/105	30.00
Tray, 13", relish, 5 sections, 400/102	70.00
Tray, 14", hdld., 400/113E	40.00
Tumbler, 3½ oz., cocktail, 400/18	40.00
Tumbler, 5 oz., juice, 400/18	37.50
Tumbler, 6 oz., sherbet, 400/18	40.00

	Crystal
Tumbler, 7 oz., old-fashioned 400/18	35.00
Tumbler, 7 oz., parfait, 400/18	45.00
Tumbler, 9 oz., water, 400/18	40.00
Tumbler, 12 oz., tea, 400/18	47.50
Tumbler, 3 oz., ftd., cocktail, 400/19	15.00
Tumbler, 3 oz., ftd., wine, 400/19	20.00
Tumbler, 5 oz., low sherbet, 400/19	15.00
Tumbler, 5 oz., juice, 400/19	10.00
Tumbler, 7 oz., old-fashioned, 400/19	32.50
Tumbler, 10 oz., 400/19	12.00
Tumbler, 12 oz., 400/19	22.00
Tumbler, 14 oz., 400/19, tea	22.00
Tumbler, #3400, 5 oz., ft., juice	17.50
Tumbler, #3400, 9 oz., ftd.	16.00
Tumbler, #3400, 10 oz., ftd.	15.00
Tumbler, #3400, 12 oz., ftd.	17.00
Tumbler, #3800, 5 oz., juice	25.00
Tumbler, #3800, 9 oz.	25.00
Tumbler, #3800, 12 oz.	30.00
Vase, 4", bead ft., sm. neck, ball, 400/25	42.50
Vase, 5¾", bead ft., bud, 400/107	55.00
Vase, 5¾", bead ft., mini bud, 400/107	55.00

	Crystal
Vase, 6", flat, crimped edge, 400/287C	30.00
Vase, 6", ftd., flared rim, 400/138B	100.00
Vase, 6" diam., 400/198	250.00
Vase, 6" fan, 400/287 F	30.00
Vase, 7", ftd., bud, 400/186	225.00
Vase, 7", ftd., bud, 400/187	200.00
Vase, 7", ivy bowl, 400/74J	135.00
Vase, 7", rolled rim w/bead hdld., 400/87 R	35.00
Vase, 7", rose bowl, 400/142 K	210.00
Vase, 7¼", ftd., rose bowl, crimped top, 400/132C	395.00
Vase, 7½", ftd., rose bowl, 400/132	350.00
Vase, 8", fan, w/bead hdld., 400/87F	35.00
Vase, 8", flat, crimped edge, 400/143C	70.00
Vase, 8", fluted rim w/bead hdlds., 400/87C	27.50
Vase, 8½", bead ft., bud, 400/28C	75.00
Vase, 8½", bead ft., flared rim, 400/21	175.00
Vase, 8½", bead ft., inward rim, 400/27	175.00
Vase, 8½", hdld. (pitcher shape), 400/227	350.00
Vase, 10", bead ft., straight side, 400/22	150.00
Vase, 10", ftd., 400/193	165.00

CANDLEWICK

The Season's CANDLEWICK Best!

IMPERIAL GLASS CORPORATION
BELLAIRE, OHIO

Easter Dinner
IMPERIAL CANDLEWICK
Family Style

A beautiful table crystal to express your joy in living—and dining...to reflect the rich colors of the awakening season and help you make your table an invitation to good company as well as to complement your Easter cuisine. Each piece of this extensive and varied service is designed for functional use...superbly hand-crafted crystal for daily family appreciation as well as for your most memorable occasions.

Imperial Candlewick is an open stock pattern. Add to your collection as your need and budget permits, for a perfect, scintillating table service.

HAND-CRAFTED AT IMPERIAL GLASS CORPORATION, BELLAIRE, OHIO

CANTERBURY NO. 115, Duncan & Miller Glass Company, 1937

Color: crystal, Sapphire blue, Cape Cod blue, Chartreuse, Ruby, Cranberry pink, Jasmine yellow

Duncan's light blue was called Sapphire and the opalescent blue was dubbed Cape Cod blue. Yellow-green was named Chartreuse and the red was Ruby. Although not pictured, you may find opalescent pieces of Canterbury in pink called Cranberry pink. Jasmine yellow is the name of the opalescent tumbler shown on the bottom of page 37.

After adding Canterbury for the first time in the last book, I have had numerous letters thanking me for its inclusion. I have now learned that Chartreuse was also a Tiffin color name as well as Duncan. The tumbler and candlestick shown on the bottom of page 37 are most likely Tiffin manufactured from Duncan's moulds. I have accumulated several pieces that have the original Tiffin sticker on them. Prices for this color seem to be 10% to 20% higher than crystal. I have not found enough of the other colors to get a feel for their prices yet. Prices for opalescent seem to double prices for the crystal.

I have also added the 64 oz. water pitcher to the price listings. It was omitted in the last book even though it was pictured. Don't miss the four pages of catalog reprints on pages 40 – 43. These pages are to help identify individual pieces. If you know of additional pieces or wish to help in relating prices on colored pieces, just drop me a postcard!

	Crystal		Crystal
Ash tray, 3"	6.00	Bowl, 13" x 10" x 5", crimped, oval	37.50
Ash tray, 3", club	8.00	Bowl, 15" x 2¾", shallow salad	42.00
Ash tray, 4½", club	10.00	Candle, 3", low	12.50
Ash tray, 5"	12.00	Candle, 3½"	12.50
Ash tray, 5½", club	15.00	Candlestick, 6", 3 light	25.00
Basket, 3" x 3" x 3¼", oval, hdld.	20.00	Candlestick, 6"	22.50
Basket, 3" x 4", crimped, hdld.	27.50	Candlestick, 7", w/U prisms	45.00
Basket, 3½", crimped, hdld	30.00	Candy and cover, 8" x 3½", 3 hdld., 3 part	32.50
Basket, 3½", oval, hdld	25.00	Candy, 6½", w/5" lid	32.50
Basket, 4½" x 4¾" x 4¾", oval, hdld	35.00	Celery and relish, 10½" x 6¾" x 1¼", 2 hdld.,	
Basket, 4½" x 5" x 5", crimped, hdld.	40.00	2 part	30.00
Basket, 9¼" x 10" x 7¼"	60.00	Celery and relish, 10½" x 6¾" x 1¼", 2 hdld.,	
Basket, 10" x 4¼" x 7", oval, hdld.	65.00	3 part	32.50
Basket, 10" x 4½" x 8", oval, hdld.	70.00	Celery, 9" x 4" x 1¼", 2 hdld.	20.00
Basket, 11½", oval, hdld.	70.00	Cheese stand, 5½" x 3½" high	10.00
Bowl, 4¼" x 2", finger	9.00	Cigarette box w/cover, 3½" x 4½"	18.00
Bowl, 5" x 3¼", 2 part, salad dressing	12.50	Cigarette jar w/cover, 4"	20.00
Bowl, 5" x 3¼", salad dressing	12.50	Comport, high, 6" x 5½" high	20.00
Bowl, 5½" x 1¾", one hdld. heart	9.00	Comport, low, 6" x 4½" high	18.00
Bowl, 5½" x 1¾", one hdld. square	9.00	Creamer, 2¾", 3 oz., individual	9.00
Bowl, 5½" x 1¾", one hdld. star	10.00	Creamer, 3¾", 7 oz.	7.50
Bowl, 5½" x 1¾", one hdld., fruit	7.00	Cup	10.00
Bowl, 5½" x 1¾", one hdld., round	7.00	Decanter w/stopper, 12", 32 oz.	45.00
Bowl, 5", fruit nappy	8.00	Ice bucket or vase, 7"	37.50
Bowl, 6" x 2", 2 hdld., round	10.00	Ice bucket or vase, 6"	32.50
Bowl, 6" x 2", 2 hdld.., sweetmeat, star	15.00	Lamp, hurricane, w/prisms, 15"	75.00
Bowl, 6" x 3¼", 2 part, salad dressing	14.00	Marmalade, 4½" x 2¾", crimped	12.00
Bowl, 6" x 3¼", salad dressing	14.00	Mayonnaise, 5" x 3¼"	15.00
Bowl, 6" x 5¼" x 2¼", oval olive	10.00	Mayonnaise, 5½" x 3¼", crimped	17.50
Bowl, 7½" x 2¼", crimped	15.00	Mayonnaise, 6" x 3¼"	17.50
Bowl, 7½" x 2¼", gardenia	15.00	Pitcher, 9¼", 32 oz., hdld., martini	50.00
Bowl, 8" x 2¾", crimped	20.00	Pitcher, 9¼", 32 oz., martini	45.00
Bowl, 8" x 2½", flared	17.50	Pitcher, 64 oz.	195.00
Bowl, 8½" x 4"	22.00	Plate, 6½", one hdld., fruit	6.00
Bowl, 9" x 2", gardenia	25.00	Plate, 6", finger bowl liner	6.00
Bowl, 9" x 4¼", crimped	27.50	Plate, 7½"	9.00
Bowl, 9" x 6" x 3", oval	30.00	Plate, 7½", 2 hdld., mayonnaise	9.00
Bowl, 10" x 5", salad	30.00	Plate, 8½"	10.00
Bowl, 10" x 8½" x 5", oval	27.50	Plate, 11¼", dinner	27.50
Bowl, 10¾" x 4¾"	27.50	Plate, 11", 2 hdld. w/ring, cracker	20.00
Bowl, 10½" x 5", crimped	30.00	Plate, 11", 2 hdld., sandwich	22.00
Bowl, 11½" x 8¼", oval	30.00	Plate, 13½", cake, hdld.	25.00
Bowl, 12" x 2¾", gardenia	30.00	Plate, 14", cake	25.00
Bowl, 12" x 3½", flared	30.00	Relish, 6" x 2", 2 hdld., 2 part, round	12.00
Bowl, 12" x 3¾", crimped	32.50	Relish, 6" x 2", 2 hdld., 2 part, star	12.00
Bowl, 13" x 8½" x 3 ¼", oval, flared	35.00	Relish, 7" x 5¼" x 2¼", 2 hdld., 2 part, oval	15.00

CANTERBURY NO. 115

	Crystal		Crystal
Relish, 8" x 1¾", 3 hdld., 3 part	17.50	Tumbler, 4½", 9 oz., flat, table, straight	12.00
Relish, 9" x 1½", 3 hdld., 3 part	20.00	Tumbler, 4½", 10 oz., ftd., water, #5115	12.50
Rose bowl, 5"	20.00	Tumbler, 5½", 9 oz., ftd., luncheon goblet	12.50
Rose bowl, 6"	22.50	Tumbler, 5¾", 12 oz., ftd., ice tea, #5115	14.00
Salt and pepper	22.50	Tumbler, 6¼", 13 oz., flat, ice tea	15.00
Sandwich tray, 12" x 5¼", center handle	35.00	Tumbler, 6¼", 13 oz., ftd., ice tea	15.00
Saucer	3.00	Urn, 4½" x 4½"	15.00
Sherbet, crimped, 4½", 2¾" high	10.00	Vase, 3", crimped violet	15.00
Sherbet, crimped, 5½", 2¾" high	12.00	Vase, 3½", clover leaf	15.00
Stem, 3¾", 6 oz., ice cream	6.00	Vase, 3½", crimped	15.00
Stem, 4", 4½ oz., oyster cocktail	12.50	Vase, 3½", crimped violet	15.00
Stem, 4½", 6 oz., saucer champagne	9.00	Vase, 3½", oval	15.00
Stem, 4¼", 1 oz., cordial, #5115	25.00	Vase, 4", clover leaf	17.50
Stem, 4¼", 3½ oz., cocktail	10.00	Vase, 4", crimped	17.50
Stem, 5½", 5 oz., saucer champagne, #5115	12.00	Vase, 4", flared rim	17.50
Stem, 5¼", 3 oz., cocktail, #5115	14.00	Vase, 4", oval	17.50
Stem, 5", 4 oz., claret or wine	20.00	Vase, 4½" x 4¾"	15.00
Stem, 6¾", 5 oz., claret, #5115	25.00	Vase, 4½", clover leaf	17.50
Stem, 6", 3½ oz., wine, #5115	27.50	Vase, 4½", crimped violet	17.50
Stem, 6", 9 oz., water	14.00	Vase, 4½", oval	17.50
Stem, 7¼", 10 oz., water, #5115	17.50	Vase, 5" x 5", crimped	17.50
Sugar, 2½", 3 oz., individual	8.00	Vase, 5", clover leaf	20.00
Sugar, 3", 7 oz.	7.50	Vase, 5", crimped	17.50
Top hat, 3"	15.00	Vase, 5½", crimped	20.00
Tray, 9", individual cr/sug	10.00	Vase, 5½", flower arranger	27.50
Tray, 9" x 4" x 1¼", 2 part, pickle and olive	17.50	Vase, 6½", clover leaf	32.00
Tumbler, 2½", 5 oz., ftd., ice cream, #5115	10.00	Vase, 7", crimped	32.00
Tumbler, 3¼", 4 oz., ftd., oyster cocktail, #5115	15.00	Vase, 7", flower arranger	35.00
Tumbler, 3¾", 5 oz., flat, juice	8.00	Vase, 8½" x 6"	50.00
Tumbler, 4¼", 5 oz., ftd., juice	7.50	Vase, 12", flared	65.00
Tumbler, 4¼", 5 oz., ftd., juice, #5115	10.00		

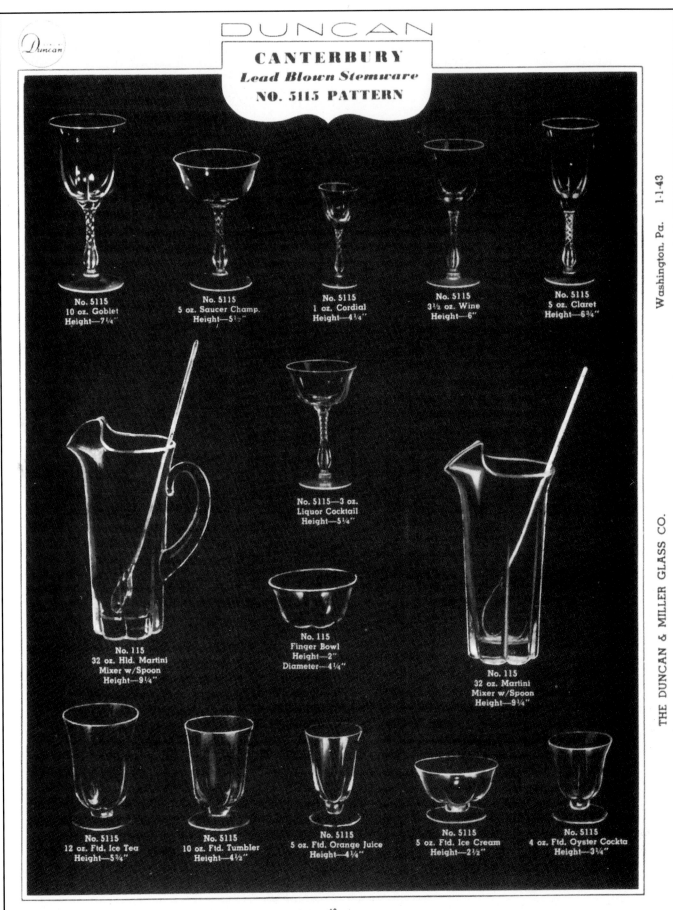

DUNCAN

CANTERBURY
Lead Blown Stemware
NO. 5115 PATTERN

No. 5115
10 oz. Goblet
Height—7¼"

No. 5115
5 oz. Saucer Champ.
Height—5½"

No. 5115
1 oz. Cordial
Height—4¼"

No. 5115
3½ oz. Wine
Height—6"

No. 5115
5 oz. Claret
Height—6¾"

Washington, Pa.   1-1-43

No. 5115—3 oz.
Liquor Cocktail
Height—5¼"

No. 115
32 oz. Hld. Martini
Mixer w/Spoon
Height—9¼"

No. 115
Finger Bowl
Height—2"
Diameter—4¼"

No. 115
32 oz. Martini
Mixer w/Spoon
Height—9¼"

THE DUNCAN & MILLER GLASS CO.

No. 5115
12 oz. Ftd. Ice Tea
Height—5¾"

No. 5115
10 oz. Ftd. Tumbler
Height—4½"

No. 5115
5 oz. Ftd. Orange Juice
Height—4¼"

No. 5115
5 oz. Ftd. Ice Cream
Height—2½"

No. 5115
4 oz. Ftd. Oyster Cockta
Height—3¼"

46

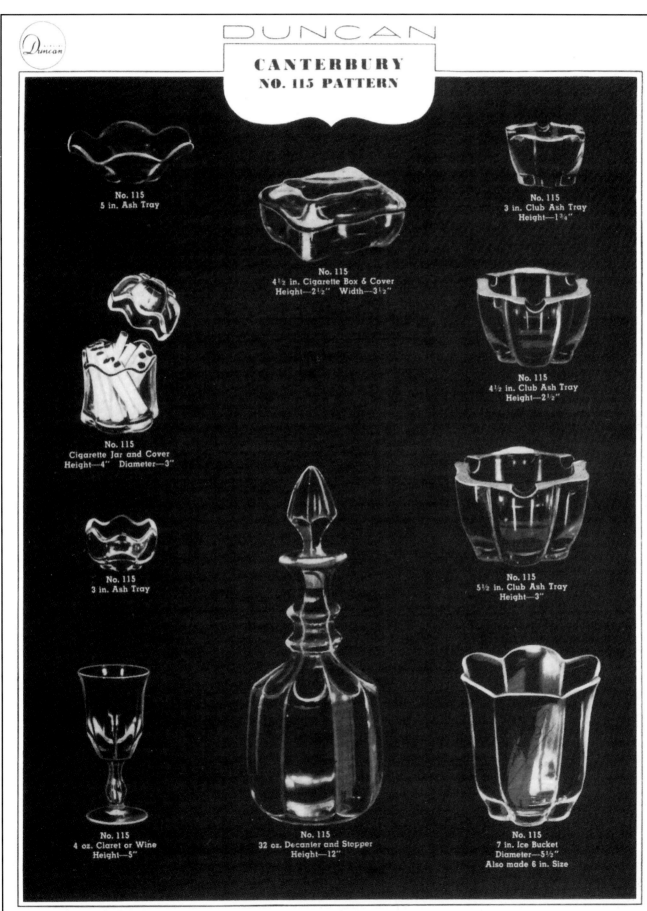

No. 115
5 in. Ash Tray

No. 115
4½ in. Cigarette Box & Cover
Height—2½" Width—3½"

No. 115
3 in. Club Ash Tray
Height—1¾"

No. 115
Cigarette Jar and Cover
Height—4" Diameter—3"

No. 115
4½ in. Club Ash Tray
Height—2½"

No. 115
3 in. Ash Tray

No. 115
5½ in. Club Ash Tray
Height—3"

No. 115
4 oz. Claret or Wine
Height—5"

No. 115
32 oz. Decanter and Stopper
Height—12"

No. 115
7 in. Ice Bucket
Diameter—5½"
Also made 6 in. Size

Washington, Pa.   1-1-43

THE DUNCAN & MILLER GLASS CO.

50

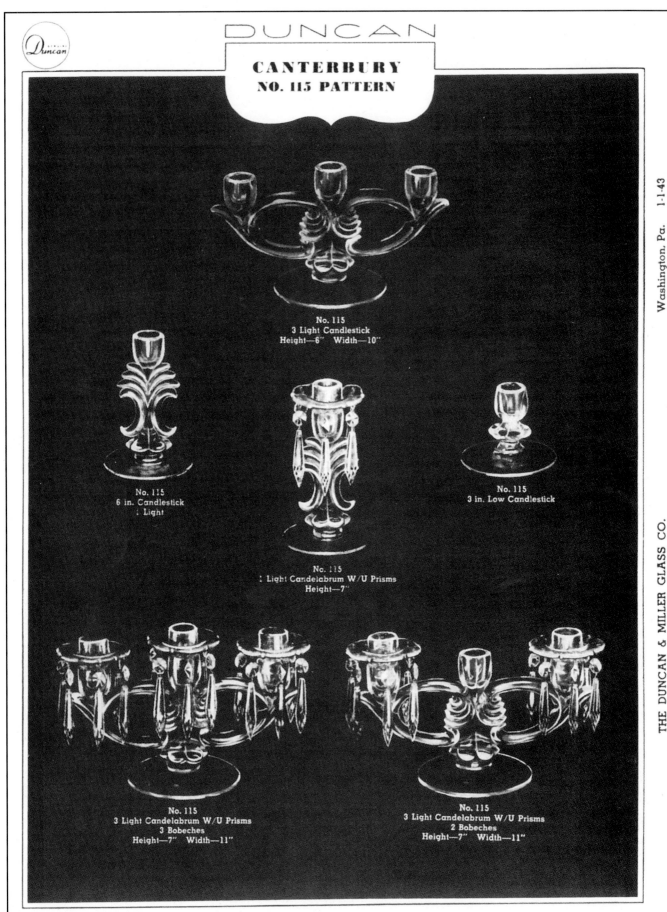

DUNCAN

CANTERBURY
NO. 115 PATTERN

No. 115
3 Light Candlestick
Height—6" Width—10"

No. 115
6 in. Candlestick
1 Light

No. 115
1 Light Candelabrum W/U Prisms
Height—7"

No. 115
3 in. Low Candlestick

No. 115
3 Light Candelabrum W/U Prisms
3 Bobeches
Height—7" Width—11"

No. 115
3 Light Candelabrum W/U Prisms
2 Bobeches
Height—7" Width—11"

Washington. Pa. 1-1-43

THE DUNCAN & MILLER GLASS CO.

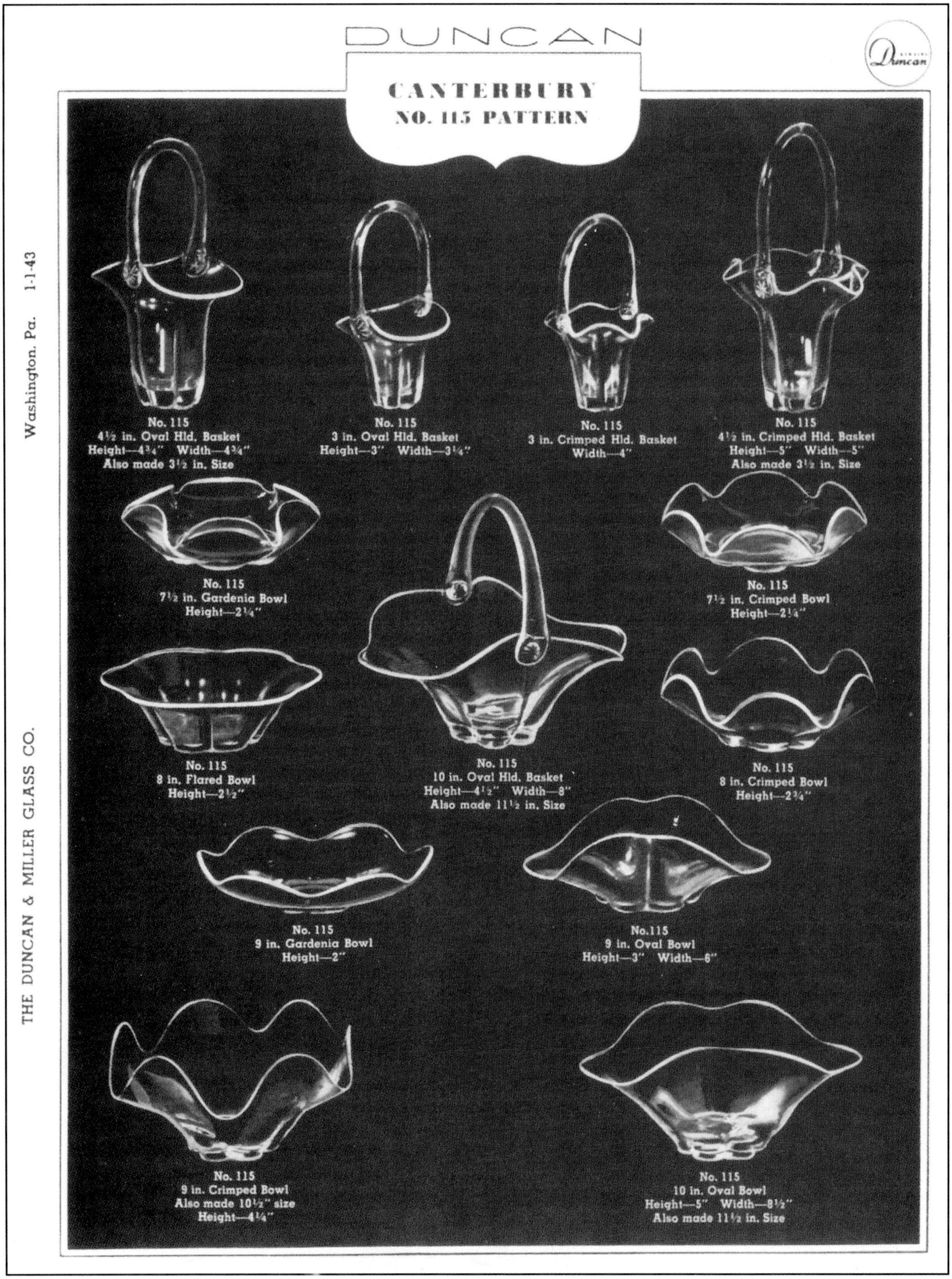

Washington, Pa.   1-1-43

THE DUNCAN & MILLER GLASS CO.

DUNCAN

CANTERBURY
NO. 115 PATTERN

Duncan

No. 115
4½ in. Oval Hld. Basket
Height—4¾"   Width—4¾"
Also made 3½ in. Size

No. 115
3 in. Oval Hld. Basket
Height—3"   Width—3¼"

No. 115
3 in. Crimped Hld. Basket
Width—4"

No. 115
4½ in. Crimped Hld. Basket
Height—5"   Width—5"
Also made 3½ in. Size

No. 115
7½ in. Gardenia Bowl
Height—2¼"

No. 115
7½ in. Crimped Bowl
Height—2¼"

No. 115
8 in. Flared Bowl
Height—2½"

No. 115
10 in. Oval Hld. Basket
Height—4½"   Width—9"
Also made 11½ in. Size

No. 115
8 in. Crimped Bowl
Height—2¾"

No. 115
9 in. Gardenia Bowl
Height—2"

No. 115
9 in. Oval Bowl
Height—3"   Width—6"

No. 115
9 in. Crimped Bowl
Also made 10½" size
Height—4¼"

No. 115
10 in. Oval Bowl
Height—5"   Width—8½"
Also made 11½ in. Size

CAPE COD, Imperial Glass Company, 1932 – 1984

Colors: amber, crystal, blue, cobalt blue, red, green, black, milk glass, pink

Cape Cod still takes a back seat to Candlewick even though both patterns were heavily promoted by Imperial. The advertisements shown on page 48 and 49 were taken from 1940's magazines. The demand generated for Cape Cod has never been as impassioned as for Candlewick.

Even non-aficionados of Cape Cod can recognize the spouted "Aladdin" style pieces shown in the third row of the next page. The smaller is a salad dressing and the larger is the gravy. Following the decanter in the bottom row is (in order) a 1602 cordial, 160 wine, 1602 wine, 1602 juice, 1602 claret, 1602 parfait, 1602 tea, and 1602 water goblet. Some collectors have trouble identifying the parfait from the juice in some patterns; so that should show the difference.

Colored Cape Cod has begun to titillate the interest of a few collectors. Most of these colors are shown on page 47. The top row shows Imperial's green called Verde; the darker green in row 2 was known as Evergreen. Imperial's pink, Azalea, is depicted in row 2. The blue color shown in rows 3 and 4 was called Antique blue. Row 3 also shows black, milk glass, and Ruby. Ritz blue (cobalt blue, not pictured) and Ruby are the colors that are most in demand. These two colors are selling 75% to 200% more than crystal, depending upon the piece. Prices for other colors are selling up to 50% more than crystal with most of them selling at reasonable prices — if at all! The Verde seems to be the slowest seller; now might be the time to buy some of it. There is a rising demand for Azalea; so be aware of that. If a consistent market is ever established for colors, I will try to list them.

A whimsy vase is on the bottom row of page 47. Evidently, some factory worker played around with a goblet. This unusual item now resides in a Texan's collection. Many collectors like to add a piece or two of one-of-a-kind items to their patterns.

	Crystal		Crystal
Ash tray, 4", 160/134/1	14.00	Bowl, 12", oval, 160/131B	70.00
Ash tray, 5½", 160/150	17.50	Bowl, 12", oval crimped, 160/131C	90.00
Basket, 9", handled, crimped, 160/221/0	175.00	Bowl, 12", punch, 160/20B	60.00
Basket, 11" tall, handled, 160/40	110.00	Bowl, 13", console, 160/75L	42.50
Bottle, bitters, 4 oz., 160/235	55.00	Bowl, 15", console, 1601/0L	75.00
Bottle, cologne, w/stopper, 1601	55.00	Butter, 5", w/cover, handled, 160/144	30.00
Bottle, condiment, 6 oz., 160/224	65.00	Butter, w/cover, ¼ lb., 160/161	45.00
Bottle, cordial, 18 oz., 160/256	115.00	Cake plate, 10", 4 toed, 160/220	90.00
Bottle, decanter, 26 oz., 160/244	115.00	Cake stand, 10½", footed, 160/67D	40.00
Bottle, ketchup, 14 oz., 160/237	195.00	Cake stand, 11", 160/103D	75.00
Bowl, 3", handled mint, 160/183	20.00	Candleholder, twin, 160/100	55.00
Bowl, 3", jelly, 160/33	12.00	Candleholder, 3", single, 160/170	17.50
Bowl, 4" finger, 1602	12.00	Candleholder, 4", 160/81	25.00
Bowl, 4½", finger, 1604½A	12.00	Candleholder, 4", Aladdin style, 160/90	125.00
Bowl, 4½", handled spider, 160/180	22.50	Candleholder, 4½", saucer, 160/175	22.50
Bowl, 4½", dessert, tab handled, 160/197	23.00	Candleholder, 5", 160/80	20.00
Bowl, 5", dessert, heart shape, 160/49H	17.50	Candleholder, 5", flower, 160/45B	60.00
Bowl, 5", flower, 1605N	25.00	Candleholder, 5½", flower, 160/45N	85.00
Bowl, 5½", fruit, 160/23B	10.00	Candleholder, 6", centerpiece, 160/48BC	70.00
Bowl, 5½", handled spider, 160/181	22.50	Candy, w/cover, 160/110	65.00
Bowl, 5½", tab handled, soup, 160/198	15.00	Carafe, wine, 26 oz., 160/185	165.00
Bowl, 6", fruit, 160/3F	10.00	Celery, 8", 160/105	30.00
Bowl, 6", baked apple, 160/53X	9.00	Celery, 10½", 160/189	55.00
Bowl, 6", handled, round mint, 160/51F	22.00	Cigarette box, 4½", 160/134	45.00
Bowl, 6", handled heart, 160/40H	20.00	Cigarette holder, ftd., 1602	12.50
Bowl, 6", handled mint, 160/51H	22.00	Cigarette holder, Tom & Jerry mug, 160/200	32.50
Bowl, 6", handled tray, 160/51T	20.00	Cigarette lighter, 1602	30.00
Bowl, 6½", handled portioned spider, 160/187	27.50	Coaster, w/spoon rest, 160/76	10.00
Bowl, 6½", handled spider, 160/182	32.50	Coaster, 3", square, 160/85	12.50
Bowl, 6½", tab handled, 160/199	25.00	Coaster, 4", round, 160/78	12.50
Bowl, 7", nappy, 160/5F	22.00	Coaster, 4½", flat, 160/1R	9.00
Bowl, 7½", 160/7F	22.00	Comport, 5¼", 160F	27.50
Bowl, 7½", 2-handled, 160/62B	27.50	Comport, 5¾", 160X	30.00
Bowl, 8¾", 160/10F	27.50	Comport, 6", 160/45	25.00
Bowl, 9", footed fruit, 160/67F	62.50	Comport, 6", w/cover, ftd., 160/140	70.00
Bowl, 9½", 2-handled, 160/145B	37.50	Comport, 7", 160/48B	35.00
Bowl, 9½", crimped, 160/221C	75.00	Comport, 11¼", oval, 1602, 6½" tall	175.00
Bowl, 9½", float, 160/221F	65.00	Creamer, 160/190	30.00
Bowl, 10", footed, 160/137B	70.00	Creamer, 160/30	8.00
Bowl, 10", oval, 160/221	75.00	Creamer, ftd., 160/31	15.00
Bowl, 11", flanged edge, 1608X	125.00	Cruet, w/stopper, 4 oz., 160/119	22.50
Bowl, 11", oval, 160/124	70.00	Cruet, w/stopper, 5 oz., 160/70	25.00
Bowl, 11", oval divided, 160/125	80.00	Cruet, w/stopper, 6 oz., 160/241	37.50
Bowl, 11", round, 1608A	65.00	Cup, tea, 160/35	7.00
Bowl, 11", salad, 1608D	40.00	Cup, coffee, 160/37	7.00
Bowl, 11¼", oval, 1602	70.00	Cup, bouillon, 160/250	30.00
Bowl, 12", 160/75B	40.00	Decanter, bourbon, 160/260	80.00

CAPE COD

	Crystal		Crystal
Decanter, rye, 160/260	75.00	Puff Box, w/cover, 1601	40.00
Decanter w/stopper, 30 oz., 160/163	65.00	Relish, 8", hdld., 2 part. 160/223	37.50
Decanter w/stopper, 24 oz., 160/212	75.00	Relish, 9½", 4 pt., 160/56	35.00
Egg cup, 160/225	32.50	Relish, 9½", oval, 3 part, 160/55	35.00
Epergne, 2 pc., plain center, 160/196	210.00	Relish, 11", 5 part, 160/102	55.00
Fork, 160/701	12.00	Relish, 11¼", 3 part, oval, 1602	70.00
Gravy bowl, 18 oz., 160/202	65.00	Salad dressing, 6 oz., hdld., spouted, 160/208	55.00
Horseradish, 5 oz. jar, 160/226	75.00	Salad set, 14" plate, 12" bowl, fork & spoon,	
Ice bucket, 6½", 160/63	165.00	160/75	95.00
Icer, 3 pc., bowl, 2 inserts, 160/53/3	50.00	Salt & pepper, individual, 160/251	15.00
Jar, 12 oz., hdld. peanut w/lid, 160/210	60.00	Salt & pepper, pr., ftd., 160/116	20.00
Jar, 10", "Pokal," 160/133	80.00	Salt & pepper, pr., ftd., stemmed, 160/243	35.00
Jar, 11", "Pokal," 160/128	85.00	Salt & pepper, pr., 160/96	15.00
Jar, 15", "Pokal," 160/132	135.00	Salt & pepper, pr. square, 160/109	20.00
Jar, candy w/lid, wicker hand., 5" h., 160/194	80.00	Salt dip, 160/61	15.00
Jar, cookie, w/lid, wicker hand., 6½" h., 160/195	100.00	Salt spoon, 1600	8.00
Jar, peanut butter w/lid, wicker hand., 4" h.,		Saucer, tea, 160/35	2.00
160/193	75.00	Saucer, coffee, 160/37	2.00
Ladle, marmalade, 160/130	10.00	Server, 12", ftd. or turned over, 160/93	85.00
Ladle, mayonnaise, 160/165	10.00	Spoon, 160/701	12.00
Ladle, punch	25.00	Stem, 1½ oz., cordial, 1602	10.00
Lamp, hurricane, 2 pc., 5" base, 160/79	85.00	Stem, 3 oz., wine, 1602	8.00
Lamp, hurricane, 2 pc., bowl-like base, 1604	115.00	Stem, 3½ oz., cocktail, 1602	8.00
Marmalade, 3 pc. set, 160/89/3	32.50	Stem, 5 oz., claret, 1602	14.00
Marmalade, 4 pc. set, 160/89	40.00	Stem, 6 oz., low sundae, 1602	7.00
Mayonnaise, 3 pc. set, 160/52H	37.50	Stem, 6 oz., parfait, 1602	12.00
Mayonnaise, 3 pc., 160/23	27.50	Stem, 6 oz., sherbet, 1600	15.00
Mayonnaise, 12 oz., hdld., spouted, 160/205	47.50	Stem, 6 oz., tall sherbet, 1602	8.50
Mug, 12 oz., handled, 160/188	42.50	Stem, 9 oz., water, 1602	9.50
Mustard, w/cover & spoon, 160/156	22.50	Stem, 10 oz., water, 1600	20.00
Nut dish, 3", hdld., 160/183	25.00	Stem, 11 oz., dinner goblet, 1602	10.00
Nut dish, 4", hdld., 160/184	25.00	Stem, 14 oz., goblet, magnum, 160	33.00
Pepper mill, 160/236	27.50	Stem, oyster cocktail, 1602	10.00
Pitcher, milk, 1 pt., 160/240	42.50	Sugar, 160/190	30.00
Pitcher, ice lipped, 40 oz., 160/19	75.00	Sugar, 160/30	7.00
Pitcher, martini, blown, 40 oz., 160/178	185.00	Sugar, ftd., 160/31	15.00
Pitcher, ice lipped, 2 qt., 160/239	90.00	Toast, w/cover, 160/123	145.00
Pitcher, 2 qt., 160/24	80.00	Tom & Jerry footed punch bowl, 160/200	335.00
Pitcher, blown, 5 pt., 160/176	150.00	Tray, square covered sugar & creamer,	
Plate, 4½" butter, 160/34	8.00	160/25/26	135.00
Plate, 6", cupped, (liner for 160/208 salad		Tray, 7", for creamer/sugar, 160/29	15.00
dressing), 160/209	20.00	Tray, 11", pastry, center handle, 160/68D	70.00
Plate, 6½", bread & butter, 160/1D	7.00	Tumbler, 2½ oz., whiskey, 160	12.50
Plate, 7", 160/3D	8.00	Tumbler, 6 oz., ftd., juice, 1602	9.00
Plate, 7", cupped (liner for 160/205 Mayo),		Tumbler, 6 oz., juice, 1600	10.00
160/206	32.00	Tumbler, 7 oz., old-fashioned, 160	12.50
Plate, 8", center handled tray, 160/149D	40.00	Tumbler, 10 oz., ftd., water, 1602	10.00
Plate, 8", crescent salad, 160/12	47.50	Tumbler, 10 oz., water, 160	10.00
Plate, 8", cupped, (liner for gravy), 160/203	37.50	Tumbler, 12 oz., ftd., ice tea, 1602	12.00
Plate, 8", salad, 160/5D	9.00	Tumbler, 12 oz., ftd., tea, 1600	19.00
Plate, 8½", 2-handled, 160/62D	30.00	Tumbler, 12 oz., ice tea, 160	12.50
Plate, 9", 160/7D	20.00	Tumbler, 14 oz., double old-fashioned, 160	25.00
Plate, 9½", 2 hdld., 160/62D	40.00	Tumbler, 16 oz., 160	32.00
Plate, 10", dinner, 160/10D	35.00	Vase, 6¼", ftd., 160/22	35.00
Plate, 11½", 2-handled, 160/145D	35.00	Vase, 6½", ftd., 160/110B	70.00
Plate, 12½" bread, 160/222	65.00	Vase, 7½", ftd., 160/22	40.00
Plate, 13", birthday, 72 candle holes, 160/72	335.00	Vase, 8", fan, 160/87F	125.00
Plate, 13", cupped torte, 1608V	35.00	Vase, 8½", flip, 160/143	50.00
Plate, 13", torte, 1608F	37.50	Vase, 8½", ftd., 160/28	42.50
Plate, 14", cupped, 160/75V	35.00	Vase, 10", cylinder, 160/192	80.00
Plate, 14", flat, 160/75D	35.00	Vase, 10½", hdld., urn, 160/186	150.00
Plate, 16", cupped, 160/20V	55.00	Vase, 11", flip, 1603	150.00
Plate, 17", 2 styles, 160/10D or 20D	50.00	Vase, 11½", ftd., 160/21	65.00
Platter, 13½", oval, 160/124D	50.00		

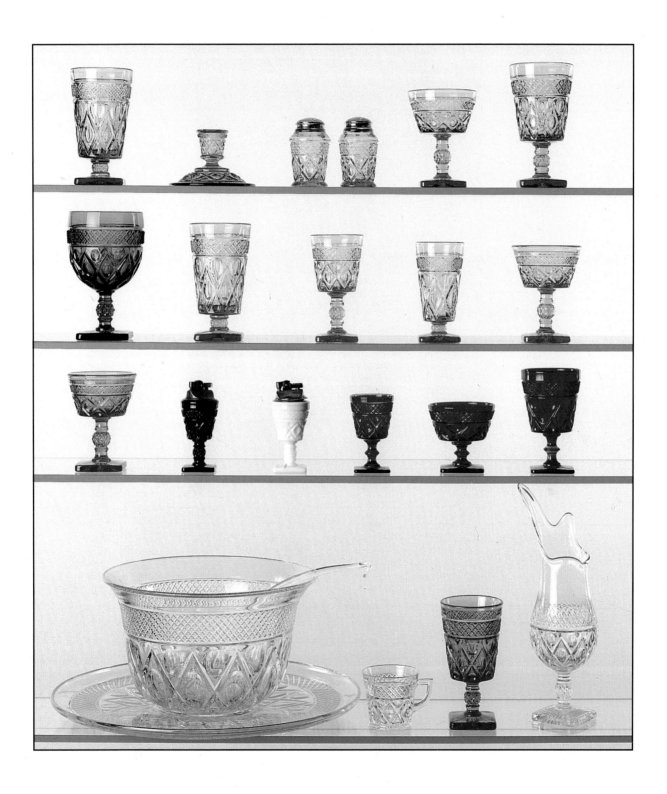

CAPE COD

MARTIN BRUEHL

Mission Accomplished

Farewell to the old order, hail to the new standard of fine things and a manner of joyous living! Captured prize for this, as for *every* happy occasion, is the diamond-like brilliance of our Cape Cod Crystal table service. There is a tradition in this design; it delighted your Grandmother and your great Grandmother when it graced proud tables of yesterdays. For *your* table today Imperial craftsmen have given the Cape Cod pattern a new grace, balance and sparkling fire as they blow, mould and finish each piece by hand. Cape Cod is crystal tableware to be proudly possessed, used every day, cherished always. Available in fine stores everywhere; crafted by THE IMPERIAL GLASS CORPORATION, BELLAIRE, OHIO.

MARTIN BRUEHL

A Bountiful

HARVEST TABLE

An American tradition, as old as Thanksgiving, but Imperial gives you a wonderful *new* way to serve it this year! Table crystal in the Cape Cod pattern, transparent in loveliness, sturdy for constant use. All these pieces and many, many more. A leading dealer near you will have everything you need for a complete table service, and for gifts, too! Cape Cod hand-crafted crystal is open stock, priced for budget keeping. Made skillfully by master crystal craftsmen and patent protected by the Imperial Glass Corporation, Bellaire, Ohio.

CAPRICE, Cambridge Glass Company, 1940's – 1957

Colors: crystal, Moonlight Blue, white, amber, amethyst, pink, emerald green, pink, cobalt blue, milk glass

I hear how nothing ever turns up at bargain prices in Caprice as it does in many other patterns. You just haven't been searching hard enough! Last spring, the pink pitcher (bottom 53) and six tumblers ran through an auction near Cincinnati, Ohio, for less than $300.00. A few months ago a blue mustard and marmalade were bought for $18.00 in an antique mall in central Florida! So, just keep looking; bargains do occasionally show up in Caprice!

Prices on more commonly found pieces are steady. Rarely found pieces continue to soar in price with some pieces being on everyone's want list. Clarets, moulded, straight side nine and twelve ounce tumblers and footed whiskeys seem to have been swallowed up into long-time collections; most beginners have never seen those. Blue bitters bottles and covered cracker jars are only in a few collections although most major collections have the Doulton pitcher. The supply of these has dwindled; the price scares off all but the serious.

Many newer collectors who resolved to collect pink Caprice have already surrendered that urge. There just isn't enough of the color now available to encourage them to continue. Prices for pink have caught up with those of blue in basic pieces and are selling above blue in harder-to-find pieces. Prices for pink are listed with the blue. Enough items were made in pink to assemble a basic set; yet a set of pink will lack many of the interesting pieces found in blue or crystal!

Caprice pieces with satinized panels are called Alpine. Several pieces are shown on the top of page 53. A few more collectors are soliciting these recently; others shun them. There are collectors for crystal Caprice and they are helped by more reasonable prices. Crystal candle reflectors and punch bowls are rarely found; but there is strong demand for them when they do turn up! A punch bowl was recently bought at a New Jersey auction for $200.00!

Other colors of Caprice are bought by collectors looking for novel additions to their sets of Caprice. As far as I know, colors other than blue, crystal, and pink cannot be collected in anything other than luncheon sets. Prices for most seldom seen colors of Caprice follow those of blue. There is little demand for amber or amethyst and those colored pieces are priced nearer to crystal.

The 50th anniversary plate shown on bottom of page 52 was bought a few years ago because both Cathy's and my parents were celebrating that milestone in 1992. Sadly, this plate was in our photography boxes and failed to be retrieved in time to present it to either one. These plates and the silver anniversary ones sell in the $30.00 to $40.00 range.

	Crystal	Blue, Pink		Crystal	Blue, Pink
Ash tray, 2¾", 3 ftd., shell, #213	8.00	14.00	*Spade, 6½", #172	30.00	90.00
* Ash tray, 3", #214	6.00	12.00	* Butterdish, ¼ lb., #52	235.00	
* Ash tray, 4", #215	8.00	16.00	Cake plate, 13", ftd., #36	150.00	350.00
* Ash tray, 5", #216	10.00	25.00	Candle reflector, #73	250.00	
Bonbon, 6", oval, ftd., #155	20.00	42.00	Candlestick, 2½", ea., #67	15.00	32.50
Bonbon, 6", sq., 2 hdld., #154	15.00	40.00	Candlestick, 2-lite, keyhole, 5", #647	20.00	65.00
Bonbon, 6", sq., ftd., #133	20.00	50.00	Candlestick, 3-lite, #74	40.00	125.00
Bottle, 7 oz., bitters, #186	175.00	395.00	Candlestick, 3-lite, keyhole #638	25.00	75.00
Bowl, 2", 4 ftd., almond #95	25.00	65.00	Candlestick, 3-lite, #1338	35.00	75.00
* Bowl, 5", 2 hdld., jelly, #151	15.00	35.00	Candlestick, 5-lite, #1577	125.00	
Bowl, 5", fruit, #18	30.00	75.00	Candlestick, 5", ea. keyhole, #646	20.00	35.00
Bowl, 5", fruit, crimped, #19	30.00	75.00	Candlestick, 6", 2-lite, ea., #72	40.00	95.00
Bowl, 8", 4 ftd., #49	40.00	115.00	Candlestick, 7", ea. w/prism, #70	25.00	65.00
Bowl, 8", sq., 4 ftd., #50	50.00	125.00	Candlestick, 7½", dbl., ea., #69	150.00	500.00
* Bowl, 8", 3 pt., relish, #124	20.00	45.00	Candy, 6", 3 ftd. w/cover, #165	42.50	110.00
Bowl, 9½", crimped, 4 ftd., #52	40.00	115.00	Candy, 6", w/cover (divided), #168	55.00	135.00
Bowl, 9", pickle, #102	25.00	60.00	Celery & relish, 8½", 3 pt., #124	20.00	45.00
Bowl, 10", salad, 4 ftd., #57	40.00	125.00	Cigarette box, w/cover, 3½" x 2¼", #207	20.00	50.00
Bowl, 10", sq., 4 ftd., #58	35.00	115.00	Cigarette box, w/cover, 4½" x 3½", #208	25.00	75.00
Bowl, 10½", belled, 4 ftd., #54	35.00	75.00	Cigarette holder, 2" x 2¼", triangular, #205	20.00	70.00
Bowl, 10½", crimped, 4 ftd., #53	40.00	110.00	Cigarette holder, 3" x 3", triangular, #204	22.00	55.00
Bowl, 11", crimped, 4 ftd., #60	35.00	115.00	Coaster, 3½", #13	15.00	35.00
* Bowl, 11", 2 hdld., oval, 4 ftd., #65	40.00	115.00	Comport, 6", low ftd., #130	22.00	50.00
Bowl, 11½", shallow, 4 ftd., #81	35.00	100.00	Comport, 7", low ftd., #130	24.00	50.00
* Bowl, 12", 4 pt. relish, oval, #126	80.00	225.00	Comport, 7", tall, #136	40.00	100.00
* Bowl, 12", relish, 3 pt., rect., #125	50.00	150.00	Cracker jar & cover, #202	250.00	1,000.00
Bowl, 12½", belled, 4 ftd., #62	35.00	90.00	* Creamer, large, #41	13.00	30.00
Bowl, 12½", crimped, 4 ftd., #61	35.00	100.00	* Creamer, medium, #38	11.00	22.00
Bowl, 13", cupped, salad, #80	75.00	175.00	* Creamer, ind., #40	12.00	27.50
Bowl, 13", crimped, 4 ftd., #66	40.00	125.00	Cup, #17	14.00	35.00
Bowl, 13½", 4 ftd., shallow cupped #82	40.00	110.00	Decanter, w/stopper, 35 oz., #187	150.00	425.00
Bowl, 15", salad, shallow, #84	55.00	155.00	Finger bowl & liner, #16	40.00	125.00
Bridge set:			Finger bowl and liner, blown, #300	45.00	125.00
*Cloverleaf, 6½", #173	30.00	90.00	Ice bucket, #201	60.00	175.00
*Club, 6½", #170	30.00	90.00	Marmalade, w/cover, 6 oz., #89	65.00	210.00
Diamond, 6½", #171	30.00	90.00	* Mayonnaise, 6½", 3 pc. set, #129	42.00	115.00
*Heart, 6½", #169	35.00	100.00			

CAPRICE

	Crystal	Blue, Pink
* Mayonnaise, 8", 3 pc. set, #106	50.00	120.00
Mustard, w/cover, 2 oz., #87.............	55.00	165.00
Nut Dish, 2½", #93..........................	22.00	55.00
Nut Dish, 2½", divided, #94.............	25.00	60.00
* Oil, 3 oz., w/stopper, #101	30.00	90.00
* Oil, 5 oz., w/stopper, #100	70.00	210.00
Pitcher, 32 oz., ball shape, #179	115.00	325.00
Pitcher, 80 oz., ball shape, #183	100.00	320.00
Pitcher, 90 oz., tall Doulton style, #178..	750.00	3,995.00
Plate, 5½", bread & butter, #20..........	12.00	27.50
Plate, 6½", bread & butter, #21..........	11.00	24.00
Plate, 6½", hdld., lemon, #152..........	11.00	20.00
Plate, 7½", salad, #23......................	15.00	27.50
Plate, 8½", luncheon, #22................	14.00	32.50
* Plate, 9½", dinner, #24...................	40.00	130.00
Plate, 11", cabaret, 4 ftd., #32........	30.00	70.00
Plate, 11½", cabaret, #26................	30.00	70.00
Plate, 14", cabaret, 4 ftd., #33........	35.00	85.00
Plate, 14", 4 ftd., #28	35.00	85.00
Plate, 16", #30............................	40.00	110.00
Punch bowl, ftd., #498	2,200.00	
* Salad dressing, 3 pc., ftd. & hdld., 2 spoons, #112	190.00	465.00
Salt & pepper, pr., ball, #91.............	40.00	115.00
* Salt & pepper, pr., flat, #96	28.00	100.00
Salt & pepper, indiv., ball, pr., #90 ...	45.00	145.00
Salt & pepper, indiv., flat, pr., #92....	40.00	135.00
Salver, 13", 2 pc. (cake atop pedestal), #31	165.00	500.00
Saucer, #17	2.50	5.50
Stem, #300, blown, 1 oz., cordial.......	42.00	130.00
Stem, #300, blown, 2½ oz., wine......	27.50	62.50
Stem, #300, blown, 3 oz., cocktail....	22.00	45.00
Stem, #300, blown, 4½ oz., claret	70.00	225.00
Stem, #300, blown, 4½ oz., low oyster cocktail	20.00	50.00
Stem, #300, blown, 5 oz., parfait......	80.00	210.00
Stem, #300, blown, 6 oz., low sherbet..	11.00	18.00
Stem, #300, blown, 6 oz., tall sherbet ..	12.00	27.50
Stem, #300, blown, 9 oz. water........	18.00	38.00
Stem, #301, blown, 1 oz., cordial	37.50	
Stem, #301, blown, 2½ oz., wine......	27.50	
Stem, #301, blown, 3 oz., cocktail....	20.00	
Stem, #301, blown, 4½ oz., claret.....	45.00	
Stem, #301, blown, 6 oz., sherbet.....	13.00	
Stem, #301, blown, 9 oz., water........	17.50	
* Stem, 3 oz., wine, #6	38.00	125.00
* Stem, 3½ oz., cocktail, #3	25.00	55.00
* Stem, 4½ oz., claret, #5	65.00	225.00
Stem, 4½ oz., fruit cocktail, #7	35.00	100.00
Stem, 5 oz., low sherbet, #4	25.00	85.00
* Stem, 7 oz., tall sherbet, #2	17.50	36.00
Stem, 10 oz., water, #1	27.50	47.50
* Sugar, large, #41	12.50	25.00
* Sugar, medium, #38	10.00	22.50
* Sugar, indiv., #40	12.00	25.00
* Tray, for sugar & creamer, #37...........	17.50	40.00
Tray, 9" oval, #42	22.00	50.00
* Tumbler, 2 oz., flat, #188	22.00	65.00
Tumbler, 3 oz., ftd., #12	27.50	75.00
Tumbler, 5 oz., ftd., #11	20.00	50.00
Tumbler, 5 oz., flat, #180	22.00	50.00
Tumbler, #300, 2½ oz., whiskey	40.00	210.00
Tumbler, #300, 5 oz., ftd., juice	18.00	37.50

	Crystal	Blue, Pink
Tumbler, #300, 10 oz., ftd. water	20.00	40.00
Tumbler, #300, 12 oz., ftd. tea	20.00	40.00
Tumbler, #301, blown, 4½ oz., low oyster cocktail	17.50	
Tumbler, #301, blown, 5 oz., juice ...	15.00	
Tumbler, #301, blown, 12 oz., tea.....	20.00	
* Tumbler, 9 oz., straight side, #14......	40.00	105.00
* Tumbler, 10 oz., ftd., #10	20.00	40.00
Tumbler, 12 oz., flat, #184	25.00	50.00
Tumbler, 12 oz., ftd., #9	22.50	47.50
* Tumbler, 12 oz., straight side, #15....	37.50	95.00
Tumbler, #310, 5 oz., flat, juice	25.00	75.00
Tumbler, #310, 7 oz., flat, old-fashioned	35.00	125.00
Tumbler, #310, 10 oz., flat, table	25.00	65.00
Tumbler, #310, 11 oz., flat, tall, 4¹³⁄₁₆"	25.00	80.00
Tumbler, #310, 12 oz., flat, tea.........	30.00	125.00
Vase, 3½", #249..........................	70.00	195.00
Vase, 4", blown, #251, blown............	70.00	195.00
Vase, 4¼", #241, ball.....................	45.00	115.00
Vase, 4½", #237, ball.....................	60.00	150.00
Vase, 4½", #252, blown	55.00	160.00
Vase, 4½", #337, crimped top............	55.00	110.00
Vase, 4½", #344, crimped top............	85.00	185.00
Vase, 4½", #244............................	60.00	150.00
Vase, 5", ivy bowl #232	60.00	225.00
Vase, 5½", #245..........................	65.00	165.00
Vase, 5½", #345, crimped top..........	65.00	210.00
Vase, 6", #242, ftd.	35.00	140.00
Vase, 6", blown, #254	175.00	350.00
Vase, 6", #342, crimped top	95.00	200.00
Vase, 6", #235, ftd., rose bowl	75.00	150.00
Vase, 6½", #238, ball.....................	65.00	165.00
Vase, 6½", #338, crimped top..........	100.00	225.00
Vase, 7½", #246...........................	65.00	185.00
Vase, 7½", #346, crimped top..........	110.00	250.00
Vase, 8", #236, ftd., rose bowl..........	100.00	210.00
Vase, 8½", #243................................	110.00	225.00
Vase, 8½", #239, ball........................	95.00	210.00
Vase, 8½", #339, crimped top............	85.00	225.00
Vase, 8½", #343, crimped top............	140.00	325.00
Vase, 9¼" #240, ball........................	140.00	295.00
Vase, 9½" #340, crimped top.............	160.00	375.00

*Moulds owned by Summit Art Glass and many of these pieces have been reproduced.

CARIBBEAN, Line #112, Duncan Miller Glass Company, 1936 – 1955

Colors: blue, crystal, amber, red

Blue Caribbean dinnerware pieces such as dinner plates, cups, and saucers have almost vanished from the collecting scene. I have not heard from anyone having blue cordials since I mentioned how I came by mine in the last book. Doesn't anyone have a few of these stashed away? Some collectors have begun buying crystal Caribbean since they are becoming discouraged trying to finish sets in blue. Blending colors and patterns is becoming the "in" thing with today's collector. In the past that was unheard of except by a few odd collectors who combined pieces they liked regardless of the pattern or color. Now, it's fast becoming a trend! There is even a name for it..."Rainbow Collections."

Notice the cordial dispenser in the top row on the next page. The bottle is threaded to fit the metal threads of the dispenser. Four cordials fit on the metal tray. The last item in row three was a cup that had the handle ground off to make a sherbet. What makes this interesting is that several of these were found in a home in the Chicago area and were truly thought to be sherbets!

The crystal punch set with colored handled cups and ladle sells for about $50.00 more than the plain crystal set. Red and cobalt blue handled pieces are more desirable than amber! Several collectors have mentioned how they have used a mixture of colored handles on their cups in punch sets. This makes sense and it would be easier to obtain four of each color cup; the colored handle on the ladle could then be any color and still look fine.

Since most of this pattern turns up in western Pennsylvania, that is the best place to find it as well as to check prices. Caribbean is the most difficult pattern to price in this book since there is never enough seen at shows to establish a representative price! My price advisers on this pattern always have very divergent ideas!

	Crystal	Blue
Ash tray, 6", 4 indent	15.00	32.50
Bowl, 3¾" x 5", folded side, hdld.	16.00	35.00
Bowl, 4½", finger	16.00	32.00
Bowl, 5", fruit nappy (takes liner), hdld.	12.00	25.00
Bowl, 5" x 7", folded side, hdld.	16.00	37.50
Bowl, 6½", soup (takes liner)	16.00	37.50
Bowl, 7", hdld.	25.00	45.00
Bowl, 7¼", ftd., hdld., grapefruit	20.00	45.00
Bowl, 8½"	27.50	70.00
Bowl, 9", salad	30.00	75.00
Bowl, 9¼", veg., flared edge	30.00	65.00
Bowl, 9¼", veg., hdld.	30.00	75.00
Bowl, 9½", epergne, flared edge	37.50	95.00
Bowl, 10", 6¼ qt., punch	90.00	450.00
Bowl, 10", 6¼ qt. punch, flared top (catalog lists as salad)	90.00	400.00
Bowl, 10¾", oval, flower, hdld.	35.00	80.00
Bowl, 12", console, flared edge	40.00	90.00
Candelabrum, 4¾", 2-lite	40.00	80.00
Candlestick, 7¼", 1-lite, w/bl. prisms	65.00	165.00
Candy dish w/cover, 4" x 7"	40.00	95.00
Cheese/cracker crumbs, 3½" h., plate 11", hdld.	40.00	85.00
Cigarette holder, (stack ash tray top)	35.00	80.00
Cocktail shaker, 9", 33 oz.	85.00	185.00
Creamer	14.00	25.00
Cruet	37.50	85.00
Cup, tea	15.00	60.00
Cup, punch	8.00	22.50
Epergne, 4 pt., flower (12" bowl; 9½" bowl; 7¾" vase; 14" plate)	190.00	425.00
Ice bucket, 6½", hdld.	75.00	165.00
Ladle, punch	32.50	95.00
Mayonnaise, w/liner, 5¾", 2 pt., 2 spoons, hdld.	42.50	95.00
Mayonnaise, w/liner, 5¾", hdld., 1 spoon	35.00	80.00
Mustard, 4", w/slotted cover	35.00	65.00
Pitcher, 4¼", 9 oz., syrup	65.00	145.00
Pitcher, 4¾" 16 oz., milk	95.00	235.00

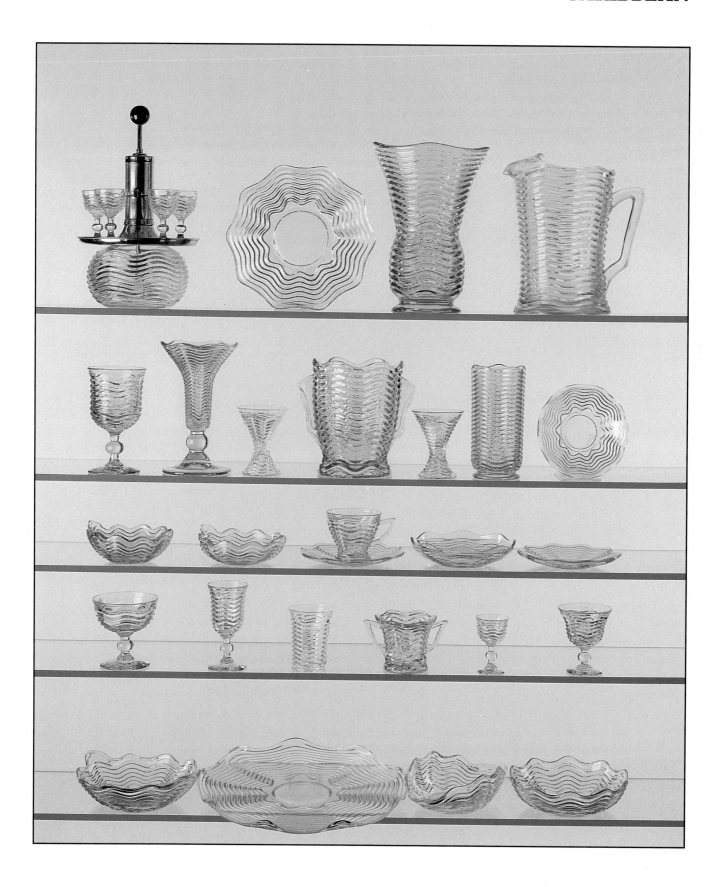

CARIBBEAN

	Crystal	Blue
Pitcher, w/ice lip, 9", 72 oz., water	195.00	550.00
Plate, 6", hdld., fruit nappy liner	4.00	12.00
Plate 6¼", bread/butter	5.00	12.00
Plate, 7¼", rolled edge, soup liner	5.00	12.50
Plate, 7½", salad	10.00	20.00
Plate, 8", hdld., mayonnaise liner	6.00	14.00
Plate, 8½", luncheon	15.00	35.00
Plate, 10½", dinner	50.00	125.00
Plate, 11", hdld., cheese/cracker liner	20.00	42.50
Plate, 12", salad liner, rolled edge	22.00	55.00
Plate, 14"	25.00	70.00
Plate, 16", torte	35.00	85.00
Plate, 18", punch underliner	40.00	95.00
Relish, 6", round, 2 pt.	12.00	25.00
Relish, 9½", 4 pt., oblong	30.00	65.00
Relish, 9½", oblong	27.50	60.00
Relish, 12¾", 5 pt., rnd.	40.00	90.00
Relish, 12¾", 7 pt., rnd.	40.00	90.00
Salt dip, 2½"	10.00	23.00
Salt & pepper, 3", metal tops	32.00	80.00
Salt & pepper, 5", metal tops	37.50	95.00
Saucer	4.00	8.00
Server, 5¾", ctr. hdld.	13.00	45.00
Server, 6½", ctr. hdld.	22.00	50.00
Stem, 3", 1 oz., cordial	67.50	225.00
Stem, 3½", 3½ oz., ftd., ball stem, wine	20.00	40.00
Stem, 3⅝", 2½ oz., wine (egg cup shape)	22.50	35.00
Stem, 4", 6 oz., ftd., ball stem, champagne	14.00	27.50
Stem, 4¼", ftd., sherbet	8.00	17.50
Stem, 4¾", 3 oz., ftd., ball stem, wine	20.00	50.00
Stem, 5¾", 8 oz., ftd., ball stem	18.00	42.50
Sugar	11.00	22.00
Syrup, metal cutoff top	80.00	175.00
Tray, 6¼", hand., mint, div.	14.00	30.00
Tray, 12¾", rnd.	25.00	50.00
Tumbler, 2¼", 2 oz., shot glass	25.00	55.00
Tumbler, 3½", 5 oz., flat	20.00	40.00
Tumbler, 5¼" 11½ oz., flat	20.00	40.00
Tumbler, 5½", 8½ oz., ftd.	22.00	45.00
Tumbler, 6½", 11 oz., ftd., ice tea	27.50	55.00
Vase, 5¾", ftd., ruffled edge	22.00	55.00
Vase, 7¼", ftd., flared edge, ball	27.50	60.00
Vase, 7½", ftd., flared edge, bulbous	32.50	70.00
Vase, 7¾", flared edge, epergne	35.00	100.00
Vase, 8", ftd., straight side	40.00	85.00
Vase, 9", ftd., ruffled top	50.00	175.00
Vase, 10", ftd.	55.00	135.00

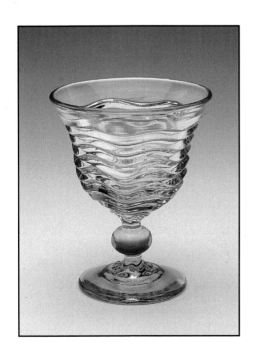

CHANTILLY, Cambridge Glass Company, Late 1940's – Early 1950's

Colors: crystal, Ebony (gold encrusted)

A couple of pieces of Chantilly have been highlighted on the opposite page. We have done that, along with the bowl of the stem at right, to give a better view of the pattern. There is a more comprehensive listing for Cambridge patterns under Rose Point in this book. Many pieces found in Chantilly are not yet listed here. There are several blanks and hundreds of items that can be collected in Chantilly. Let me know what you find that isn't in my listing. Remember that prices for Rose Point items are 20% to 30% higher than those of Chantilly due to collector demand!

The oil bottle's stopper is missing in the bottom photo. Take note of the syrup in that photo. It is rarely seen!

Cambridge's Chantilly is most often collected on stemware line #3625. This stem is depicted on page 229 where I have shown most of the popular Cambridge stemware lines.

	Crystal		Crystal
Bowl, 7", bonbon, 2 hdld., ftd.	17.50	Saucer	3.00
Bowl, 7", relish/pickle, 2 pt.	18.00	Stem, #3600, 1 oz., cordial	52.50
Bowl, 7", relish/pickle	20.00	Stem, #3600, 2½ oz., cocktail	24.00
Bowl, 9", celery/relish, 3 pt.	25.00	Stem #3600, 2½ oz., wine	32.00
Bowl, 10", 4 ftd., flared	40.00	Stem, #3600, 4½ oz., claret	40.00
Bowl, 11", tab hdld.	35.00	Stem, #3600, 4½ oz., low oyster cocktail	15.00
Bowl, 11½", tab hdld. ftd.	35.00	Stem, #3600, 7 oz., tall sherbet	17.50
Bowl, 12", celery/relish, 3 pt.	35.00	Stem, #3600, 7 oz., low sherbet	15.00
Bowl, 12", 4 ftd., flared	35.00	Stem, #3600, 10 oz., water	20.00
Bowl, 12", 4 ftd., oval	40.00	Stem, #3625, 1 oz., cordial	52.50
Bowl, 12", celery/relish, 5 pt.	45.00	Stem, #3625, 3 oz., cocktail	27.50
Butter, w/cover, round	135.00	Stem, #3625, 4½ oz., claret	40.00
Butter, ¼ lb.	225.00	Stem, #3625, 4½ oz., low oyster cocktail	16.00
Candlestick, 5"	17.50	Stem, #3625, 7 oz., low sherbet	16.00
Candlestick, 6", 2-lite, "fleur-de-lis"	35.00	Stem, #3625, 7 oz., tall sherbet	18.00
Candlestick, 6", 3-lite	40.00	Stem, #3625, 10 oz., water	25.00
Candy box, w/cover, ftd.	145.00	Stem, #3775, 1 oz., cordial	52.50
Candy box, w/cover, rnd.	75.00	Stem, #3775, 2½ oz., wine	32.00
Cocktail icer, 2 pc.	60.00	Stem, #3775, 3 oz., cocktail	25.00
Comport, 5½"	30.00	Stem, #3775, 4½ oz., claret	40.00
Comport, 5⅜", blown	37.50	Stem, #3775, 4½ oz., oyster cocktail	15.00
Creamer	14.50	Stem, #3775, 6 oz., low sherbet	15.00
Creamer, indiv., #3900, scalloped edge	12.50	Stem, #3775, 6 oz., tall sherbet	17.50
Cup	17.50	Stem, #3779, 1 oz., cordial	62.50
Decanter, ftd.	155.00	Stem, #3779, 2½ oz., wine	32.00
Decanter, ball	195.00	Stem, #3779, 3 oz., cocktail	25.00
Hat, small	175.00	Stem, #3779, 4½ oz., claret	40.00
Hat, large	225.00	Stem, #3779, 4½ oz., low oyster cocktail	15.00
Hurricane lamp, candlestick base	115.00	Stem, #3779, 6 oz., tall sherbet	17.50
Hurricane lamp, keyhole base w/prisms	165.00	Stem, #3779, 6 oz., low sherbet	15.00
Ice bucket, w/chrome handle	70.00	Stem, #3779, 9 oz., water	20.00
Marmalade & cover	55.00	Sugar	13.50
Mayonnaise, (sherbet type bowl w/ladle)	25.00	Sugar, indiv., #3900, scalloped edge	11.00
Mayonnaise, div. w/liner & 2 ladles	40.00	Tumbler, #3600, 5 oz., ftd., juice	17.00
Mayonnaise, w/liner & ladle	37.50	Tumbler, #3600, 12 oz., ftd., tea	22.00
Mustard & cover	65.00	Tumbler, #3625, 5 oz., ftd., juice	15.00
Oil, 6 oz., hdld., w/stopper	75.00	Tumbler, #3625, 10 oz., ftd., water	17.50
Pitcher, ball	120.00	Tumbler, #3625, 12 oz., ftd., tea	24.00
Pitcher, Doulton	275.00	Tumbler, #3775, 5 oz., ftd., juice	15.00
Pitcher, upright	185.00	Tumbler, #3775, 10 oz., ftd., water	15.00
Plate, crescent, salad	100.00	Tumbler, #3775, 12 oz., ftd., tea	20.00
Plate, 6½", bread/butter	6.50	Tumbler, #3779, 5 oz., ftd., juice	17.00
Plate, 8", salad	12.50	Tumbler, #3779, 12 oz., ftd., tea	22.00
Plate, 8", tab hdld., ftd., bonbon	15.00	Tumbler, 13 oz.	24.00
Plate, 10½", dinner	57.50	Vase, 5", globe	35.00
Plate, 12", 4 ftd., service	30.00	Vase, 6", high ftd., flower	30.00
Plate, 13", 4 ftd.	30.00	Vase, 8", high ftd., flower	35.00
Plate 13½", tab hdld., cake	32.50	Vase, 9", keyhole base	40.00
Plate, 14", torte	35.00	Vase, 10", bud	35.00
Salad dressing bottle	100.00	Vase, 11", ftd., flower	60.00
Salt & pepper, pr., flat	27.50	Vase, 11", ped. ftd., flower	65.00
Salt & pepper, footed	30.00	Vase, 12", keyhole base	65.00
Salt & pepper, handled	30.00	Vase, 13", ftd., flower	95.00

Note: See pages 228 – 229 for stem identification.

CHARTER OAK, #3362, A.H. Heisey Co., 1926 – 1935

Colors: crystal, Flamingo, Moongleam, Hawthorne, Marigold

Charter Oak has been included here for four years, but no new pieces or information have been forthcoming. I did have several letters thanking me for identifying this "mystery" pattern. Prices have remained steady. The only problem has been that more people now recognize this as a Heisey pattern and bargains are not as easily found. The only pieces I have seen recently have been stems; but they were all priced so I could not buy them for resale. Those acorns remind me of an elementary school friend who used to argue with me that the trees were "acorn trees" and not oaks! Isn't it amazing what pops in your mind... forty years later?

I have only shown Flamingo (pink), but there are several other colors of Charter Oak that can be collected. Yeoman cups and saucers are often used with this set since there were no cups and saucers made. A Yeoman set is pictured here, but only priced under that pattern. I mention that since several collectors have wanted to know why I didn't price a cup and saucer in my listing.

The #4262 Charter Oak lamp was produced from 1928 to 1931. It looks like a blown comport with an acorn in the stem. It has a diamond optic font that was filled with water to magnify the design and to stabilize the lamp. This is the choice Charter Oak piece to own!

The #130 one lite candleholder base is an oak leaf with stem curled up having an acorn for the candle cup! Find me one of those to picture!

	Crystal	Flamingo	Moongleam	Hawthorne	Marigold
Bowl, 11" floral #116 (oak leaf)	30.00	45.00	47.50	75.00	
Bowl, finger #3362	10.00	17.50	20.00		
Candleholder, 1-lite, #130 "Acorn"	100.00	125.00	135.00		
Candlestick, 3",#116 (oak leaf)	25.00	30.00	35.00	125.00	
Candlestick, 5", 3-lite, #129 "Tricorn"		65.00	85.00	125.00	150.00
Comport, 6" low ft., #3362	45.00	50.00	55.00	70.00	100.00
Comport, 7" ftd., #3362	50.00	55.00	60.00	160.00	175.00
Lamp #4262 (blown comport/water filled to magnify design & stabilize lamp)	400.00	700.00	850.00		
Pitcher, flat #3362		85.00	95.00		
Plate, 6" salad #1246 (Acorn & Leaves)	5.00	10.00	12.50	20.00	
Plate, 7" luncheon/salad #1246 (Acorn & Leaves)	8.00	12.00	17.50	22.50	
Plate, 8" luncheon #1246 (Acorn & Leaves)	10.00	15.00	20.00	25.00	
Plate, 10½" dinner #1246 (Acorn & Leaves)	27.50	35.00	45.00	65.00	
Stem, 3 oz. cocktail #3362	10.00	15.00	20.00	45.00	40.00
Stem, 3½ oz. low ft., oyster cocktail #3362	8.00	10.00	15.00	40.00	35.00
Stem, 4½ oz parfait #3362	15.00	25.00	30.00	60.00	50.00
Stem, 6 oz. saucer champagne #3362	10.00	15.00	20.00	50.00	40.00
Stem, 6 oz. sherbet, low ft. #3362	10.00	15.00	20.00	50.00	40.00
Stem, 8 oz. goblet, high ft. #3362	15.00	30.00	35.00	95.00	60.00
Stem, 8 oz. luncheon goblet, low ft. #3362	15.00	30.00	35.00	95.00	60.00
Tumbler, 10 oz. flat #3362	10.00	15.00	20.00	35.00	30.00
Tumbler, 12 oz. flat #3362	12.50	17.50	22.50	40.00	35.00

CHEROKEE ROSE, Tiffin Glass Company, 1940's – 1950's

Colors: crystal

Cherokee Rose shakers have finally appeared! Can cup and saucers be far behind? I saw a large set for sale in an antique mall recently. It was priced by the set and not by the piece. Some dealers do not seem to realize that few collectors will buy a whole set at one time. About the only person who will buy several thousand dollars worth of glass at once is another dealer; and they are not going to buy a set for 10% off retail. Marketing merchandise is a concept that dealers also need to heed.

As with most Tiffin patterns, stems are the pieces most often seen. In my travels around the country, I see mostly stemware line #17399. This is the tear drop style that is shown on most of the stemware in the top picture. The other #17403 stem style is represented by the cordial on the far right and the wine on the left in the lower photo. There is no distinction in stemware line prices at this time, but I am asked for #17399 tear drop most often.

I was happy to find the icer even without a liner for it. It is not as flamboyant as the one in Fuchsia, but it will do as a newly found piece of Cherokee Rose.

	Crystal		Crystal
Bowl, 5", finger.	25.00	Stem, 1 oz., cordial	50.00
Bowl, 6", fruit or nut	22.00	Stem, 2 oz., sherry	35.00
Bowl, 7", salad	35.00	Stem, 3½ oz., cocktail	20.00
Bowl, 10", deep salad	50.00	Stem, 3½ oz., wine	35.00
Bowl, 10½", celery, oblong	35.00	Stem, 4 oz., claret	50.00
Bowl, 12", crimped	50.00	Stem, 4½ oz., parfait	45.00
Bowl, 12½" centerpiece, flared	50.00	Stem, 5½ oz., sherbet/champagne	20.00
Bowl, 13", centerpiece	60.00	Stem, 9 oz., water	25.00
Cake plate, 12½", center hdld.	45.00	Sugar	20.00
Candlesticks, pr., double branch	85.00	Table bell	75.00
Comport, 6"	35.00	Tumbler, 4½ oz., oyster cocktail	22.00
Creamer	20.00	Tumbler, 5 oz., ftd., juice	22.00
Icer	40.00	Tumbler, 8 oz., ftd., water	22.50
Mayonnaise, liner and ladle	55.00	Tumbler, 10½ oz., ftd., ice tea	35.00
Pitcher	325.00	Vase, 6", bud	25.00
Plate, 6", sherbet	6.00	Vase, 8", bud	35.00
Plate, 8", luncheon	12.50	Vase, 8½", tear drop	65.00
Plate, 13½", turned-up edge, lily	35.00	Vase, 9¼", tub	85.00
Plate, 14", sandwich	35.00	Vase, 10", bud	40.00
Relish, 6½", 3 pt.	25.00	Vase, 11", bud	45.00
Relish, 12½", 3 pt.	45.00	Vase, 11", urn	100.00
Shaker, pr.	65.00	Vase, 12", flared	110.00

CHINTZ, #1401 (Empress Blank) and CHINTZ #3389 (Duquesne Blank), A.H. Heisey Co., 1931 – 1938

Colors: crystal, "Sahara" yellow, "Moongleam" green, "Flamingo" pink, and "Alexandrite" orchid

Previously overlooked Chintz salt and pepper shakers have been added to the listing! It amazes me how some items slip by for years until someone asks me why an item is not listed. If you have pieces that are not in this listing, please let me know.

A set of Alexandrite Chintz surfaced a few years ago. It did not take long for these wonderful pieces to vanish into collections.

Pieces with the encircled flowers are known as "formal" Chintz. The piece in the pattern shot, one cream soup and the individual sugar are all "formal" Chintz. Personally, I prefer this more detailed design.

Don't confuse this pattern with Fostoria's Chintz; and learn that you must also specify the company name when you ask for a pattern named Chintz. It was a popular name that was used by several glass companies for their wares.

	Crystal	Sahara
Bowl, finger, #4107	8.00	15.00
Bowl, 5½", ftd., preserve, hdld	15.00	27.00
Bowl, 6", ftd., mint	18.00	30.00
Bowl, 6", ftd., 2 hdld., jelly	15.00	30.00
Bowl, 7", triplex relish	16.00	35.00
Bowl, 7½", Nasturtium	16.00	30.00
Bowl, 8½", ftd., 2 hdld., floral	32.00	65.00
Bowl, 11", dolphin ft., floral	40.00	110.00
Bowl, 13", 2 pt., pickle & olive	15.00	35.00
Comport, 7", oval	40.00	85.00
Creamer, 3 dolphin ft.	20.00	45.00
Creamer, individual	12.00	25.00
Grapefruit, ftd., #3389, Duquesne	30.00	60.00
Ice bucket, ftd.	85.00	135.00
Mayonnaise, 5½", dolphin ft.	35.00	65.00
Oil, 4 oz.	60.00	125.00
Pitcher, 3 pint, dolphin ft.	125.00	235.00
Plate, 6", square, bread	6.00	15.00
Plate, 7", square, salad	8.00	18.00
Plate, 8", square, luncheon	10.00	22.00
Plate, 10½", square, dinner	40.00	85.00
Plate, 12", two hdld.,	25.00	45.00
Plate, 13", hors d' oeuvre, two hdld.	20.00	37.50
Platter, 14", oval	30.00	65.00
Salt and pepper, pr.	35.00	80.00
Stem, #3389, Duquesne, 1 oz., cordial	115.00	235.00
Stem, #3389, 2½ oz., wine	17.50	45.00
Stem, #3389, 3 oz., cocktail	15.00	35.00
Stem, #3389, 4 oz., claret	20.00	45.00
Stem, #3389, 4 oz., oyster cocktail	10.00	20.00
Stem, #3389, 5 oz., parfait	14.00	35.00
Stem, #3389, 5 oz., saucer champagne	11.00	22.50
Stem, #3389, 5 oz., sherbet	8.00	17.50
Stem, #3389, 9 oz., water	15.00	30.00
Sugar, 3 dolphin ft.	20.00	42.50
Sugar, individual	12.00	28.00
Tray, 10", celery	14.00	27.50
Tray, 12", sq., ctr. hdld., sandwich	35.00	65.00
Tray, 13", celery	18.00	26.00
Tumbler, #3389, 5 oz., ftd., juice	12.00	22.00
Tumbler, #3389, 8 oz., soda	13.00	24.00
Tumbler, #3389, 10 oz., ftd., water	14.00	25.00
Tumbler, #3389, 12 oz., iced tea	16.00	30.00
Vase, 9", dolphin ft.	95.00	185.00

CLASSIC, Tiffin Glass Company, 1913 – 1930's

Colors: crystal, pink

I have two reports from Texas about handled 14 oz. iced teas in Classic. This is a new listing. Classic stems abound. We, personally, have found few serving pieces. You will undoubtedly find additional pieces of Classic; let me hear what you discover so I get them in the listing.

Pink stems are found on the #17024 line that is also seen in Tiffin's Flanders pattern. Crystal stemmed items seem to occur on the #14185 line. There are some size inconsistencies within these stemware lines. We have measured both colors and noted the discrepancies in these price listings. Remember that the pitcher cover is plain; no pattern is etched on it.

	Crystal	Pink
Bowl, 2 hdld., 8"x9¼"	110.00	
Comport, 6" wide, 3¼" tall...................................	50.00	
Creamer, flat	35.00	55.00
Creamer,. ftd.	35.00	
Finger bowl, ftd..	17.50	27.50
Pitcher, 61 oz...	250.00	395.00
Pitcher, 61 oz., w/cover	325.00	495.00
Plate, 6⅜", champagne liner	10.00	
Plate, 8"..	12.50	15.00
Plate, 10", dinner...	75.00	
Sherbet, 3⅛", 6½ oz., short...................................	17.50	27.50
Stem, 3⅞", 1 oz., cordial	45.00	
Stem, 4¹⁵⁄₁₆", 3 oz., wine.....................................	32.50	47.50
Stem, 4⅞", 3¾ oz., cocktail	40.00	
Stem, 4⅞", 4 oz., cocktail	27.50	
Stem, 6½", 5 oz., parfait	35.00	50.00
Stem, 6", 7½ oz., saucer champagne......................	22.50	32.50
Stem, 8¼", 9 oz., water..	30.00	45.00
Sugar, flat..	35.00	55.00
Sugar, ftd.	35.00	
Tumbler, 3½", 5 oz., ftd., juice	17.50	
Tumbler, 4½", 8½ oz., ftd., water	20.00	35.00
Tumbler, 4⅛", 10½ oz., flat, water	25.00	
Tumbler, 5⁹⁄₁₆", 14 oz., ftd., tea	30.00	
Tumbler, 6", 13 oz., ftd., iced tea		45.00
Tumbler, 6¹⁄₁₆", 14 oz., ftd., iced tea	30.00	
Tumbler, 6¼", 6½ oz., ftd., Pilsner........................	32.50	
Vase, bud, 6½"	27.50	
Vase, bud, 10½"	42.50	

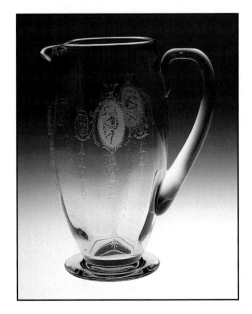

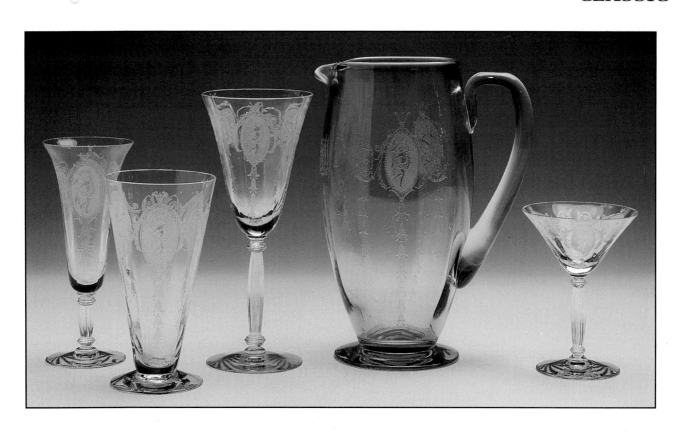

CLEO, Cambridge Glass Company, Introduced 1930

Colors: amber, blue, crystal, green, pink, yellow

I have often stated that Cleo can be collected in sets of pink or green. Several new collectors are trying to accomplish that in blue; be aware that collectors who have amassed large sets of blue have taken years to do that! One collector has found two different pitchers in blue in the last year. One of these is pictured in the upcoming *Very Rare Glassware of the Depression Years, Fifth Series.*

An array of pieces were made in Cleo, but it seems that most unusual items are discovered in amber instead of blue, pink, or green. A pink grill plate is pictured on the bottom of page 70. These are quite rare in Cleo. In fact, grill plates are rather uncommon in all Elegant patterns. Both Cambridge and Fostoria made them, but I can think of no pattern in which they would be considered common unlike most Depression glass patterns. I have never seen a colored icer like the crystal one in that picture. You could put beaucoup jumbo shrimp in that!

	Blue	Pink/ Green/ Yellow/ Amber		Blue	Pink/ Green/ Yellow/ Amber
Almond, 2½", individual	95.00	75.00	Cup, DECAGON	25.00	15.00
Basket, 7", 2 hdld. (upturned sides) DECAGON	40.00	22.00	Decanter, w/stopper		235.00
Basket, 11", 2 hdld. (upturned sides) DECAGON	50.00	30.00	Gravy boat, w/liner plate, DECAGON	295.00	185.00
Bouillon cup, w/saucer, 2 hdld., DECAGON	50.00	35.00	Ice pail	150.00	65.00
Bowl, 2 pt., relish	40.00	22.00	Ice tub	125.00	60.00
Bowl, 5½", fruit	30.00	18.00	Mayonnaise, w/liner and ladle, DECAGON	95.00	45.00
Bowl, 5½" 2 hdld., bonbon, DECAGON	30.00	20.00	Mayonnaise, ftd.	55.00	35.00
Bowl, 6", 4 ft., comport	50.00	35.00	Oil, 6 oz., w/stopper, DECAGON		145.00
Bowl, 6", cereal, DECAGON	40.00	25.00	Pitcher, 3½ pt., #38		195.00
Bowl, 6½", 2 hdld., bonbon DECAGON	35.00	22.00	Pitcher, w/cover, 22 oz.		175.00
Bowl, 6½", cranberry	45.00	30.00	Pitcher, w/cover, 60 oz., #804		250.00
Bowl, 7½", tab hdld., soup	50.00	33.00	Pitcher, w/cover, 62 oz., #955		250.00
Bowl, 8", miniature console		145.00	Pitcher, w/cover, 63 oz., #3077		275.00
Bowl, 8½"	65.00	40.00	Pitcher, w/cover, 68 oz., #937		295.00
Bowl, 8½" 2 hdld., DECAGON	70.00	40.00	Plate, 7"	15.00	12.00
Bowl, 9", covered vegetable		165.00	Plate, 7", 2 hdld., DECAGON	20.00	14.00
Bowl, 9½", oval veg., DECAGON	100.00	45.00	Plate, 8½", luncheon, DECAGON	30.00	20.00
Bowl, 9", pickle, DECAGON	60.00	30.00	Plate, 9½", dinner, DECAGON	100.00	65.00
Bowl, 10", 2 hdld., DECAGON	75.00	40.00	Plate, 9½", grill		100.00
Bowl, 11", oval	110.00	40.00	Plate, 11", 2 hdld., DECAGON	120.00	30.00
Bowl, 11½", oval	110.00	40.00	Platter, 12"	160.00	100.00
Bowl, 12", console	85.00	40.00	Platter, 15"	295.00	185.00
Bowl, 15½", oval, DECAGON		185.00	Platter, w/cover, oval (toast)		350.00
Bowl, cream soup w/saucer, 2 hdld., DECAGON	50.00	30.00	Platter, asparagus, indented, w/sauce & spoon		325.00
Bowl, finger w/liner, #3077	50.00	30.00	Salt dip, 1½"	110.00	75.00
Bowl, finger w/liner, #3115	50.00	30.00	Saucer, DECAGON	5.00	3.00
Candlestick, 1-lite, 2 styles	35.00	22.00	Server, 12", ctr. hand.	65.00	35.00
Candlestick, 2-lite	85.00	35.00	Stem, #3077, 1 oz., cordial	175.00	135.00
Candlestick, 3-lite	110.00	70.00	Stem, #3077, 2½ oz., cocktail	45.00	27.50
Candy box w/lid		125.00	Stem, #3077, 3½ oz., wine	95.00	60.00
Candy & cover, tall		155.00	Stem, #3077, 6 oz., low sherbet	27.50	15.00
Comport, 7", tall, #3115	75.00	40.00	Stem, #3077, 6 oz., tall sherbet	35.00	17.50
Creamer, DECAGON	27.50	17.50	Stem, #3115, 9 oz.		30.00
Creamer, ewer style, 6"		85.00	Stem, #3115, 3½ oz., cocktail		25.00
Creamer, ftd.	30.00	20.00	Stem, #3115, 6 oz., fruit		15.00
			Stem, #3115, 6 oz., low sherbet		15.00
			Stem, #3115, 6 oz., tall sherbet		17.00
			Stem, #3115, 9 oz., water		27.50

CLEO

	Blue	Pink/Green/Yellow/Amber		Blue	Pink/Green/Yellow/Amber
Sugar cube tray		185.00	Tumbler, #3077, 8 oz., ftd.	50.00	25.00
Sugar, DECAGON	25.00	17.50	Tumbler, #3077, 10 oz., ftd.	60.00	27.50
Sugar, ftd.	30.00	20.00	Tumbler, #3022, 12 oz., ftd.	85.00	35.00
Sugar sifter, ftd., 6¾"		295.00	Tumbler, #3115, 2½ oz., ftd.		55.00
Syrup pitcher, drip cut		160.00	Tumbler, #3115, 5 oz., ftd.		25.00
Syrup pitcher, glass lid		175.00	Tumbler, #3115, 8 oz., ftd.		25.00
Toast & cover, round		375.00	Tumbler, #3115, 10 oz., ftd.		37.50
Tobacco humidor		375.00	Tumbler, #3115, 12 oz., ftd.		35.00
Tray, 12", handled serving		155.00	Tumbler, 12 oz., flat		35.00
Tray, 12", oval service DECAGON	195.00	145.00	Vase, 5½"		75.00
Tray, creamer & sugar, oval		50.00	Vase, 9½"		125.00
Tumbler, #3077, 2½ oz., ftd.	110.00	65.00	Vase, 11"		135.00
Tumbler, #3077, 5 oz., ftd.	50.00	20.00	Wafer tray		225.00

COLONY, Line #2412, Fostoria Glass Company, 1930's – 1983

Colors: crystal; some yellow, blue, green, white amber, red in 1980's as Maypole

Colony has several rarely seen pieces even though Fostoria produced it for half a century. Cream soups, cigarette boxes, 48 oz., ice lipped pitchers, flat teas, and the 12" vase all persist in being hard to uncover. Mint condition dinner plates (without scratched centers) also aggravate collectors wanting perfect pieces. This pattern was very durable and more of it seems to be emerging of late, a hopeful sign for collectors.

The Colony patterned foot, but plain bowled stemware sold to go with this pattern was called Colonial Dame just as the plain stemware sold to go with American was called American Lady. This type stem has yet to be widely accepted by collectors and may often be confused with one of Anchor-Hocking's lines of the same time. Be aware of its existence, however.

Colony evolved from an earlier Fostoria pattern called Queen Ann and then gave way to a colored version under the new name "Maypole" in the 1980's. The candlesticks and oval bowl shown on top of page 73 were made in the early 1980's under "Maypole." Red vases, candlesticks, and bowls being seen were a product of Viking made for Fostoria in the early 1980's. We may see these again since Dalzell Viking is currently making red for Lancaster Colony who now owns the Fostoria name.

	Crystal
Ash tray, 2⅞", sq.	7.00
Ash tray, 3", round	7.00
Ash tray, 3½", sq.	10.00
Ash tray, 4½", round	12.50
Ash tray, 6", round	17.50
Bowl, 2¾" ftd., almond	15.00
Bowl, 4½", rnd.	7.00
Bowl, 4¾", finger	15.00
Bowl, 4¾", hdld.	8.00
Bowl, 5", bonbon	9.00
Bowl, 5", cream soup	45.00
Bowl, 5", hdld.	9.00
Bowl, 5½", sq.	10.00
Bowl, 5¾", high ft.	15.00
Bowl, 5", rnd.	12.00
Bowl, 6", rose	25.00
Bowl, 7", bonbon, 3 ftd.	12.00
Bowl, 7", olive, oblong	12.00
Bowl, 7¾", salad	22.50
Bowl, 8", cupped	35.00
Bowl, 8", hdld.	35.00
Bowl, 9", rolled console	35.00
Bowl, 9½", pickle	16.00
Bowl, 9¾", salad	37.50
Bowl, 10", fruit	35.00
Bowl, 10½", low ft.	75.00
Bowl, 10½", high ft.	95.00
Bowl, 10½", oval	32.00
Bowl, 10½", oval, 2 part	32.50
Bowl, 11", oval, ftd.	40.00
Bowl, 11", flared	35.00
Bowl, 11½", celery	30.00
Bowl, 13", console	35.00
Bowl, 13¼", punch, ftd.	365.00
Bowl, 14", fruit	42.00
Butter dish, ¼ lb.	35.00
Candlestick, 3½"	11.00
Candlestick, 6½", double	25.00
Candlestick, 7"	22.00
Candlestick, 7½", w/8 prisms	60.00
Candlestick, 9"	30.00
Candlestick, 9¾", w/prisms	80.00
Candlestick, 14½", w/10 prisms	150.00
Candy w/cover, 6½"	45.00
Candy, w/cover, ftd., ½ lb.	75.00
Cheese & cracker	50.00
Cigarette box	45.00
Comport, 4"	15.00

	Crystal
Comport, cover, 6½"	35.00
Creamer, 3¼" indiv.	6.50
Creamer, 3¾"	6.00
Cup, 6 oz., ftd.	7.50
Cup, punch	12.50
Ice bucket	70.00
Ice bucket, plain edge	125.00
Lamp, electric	145.00
Mayonnaise, 3 pc.	35.00
Oil w/stopper, 4½ oz.	37.50
Pitcher, 16 oz., milk	70.00
Pitcher, 48 oz., ice lip	195.00
Pitcher, 2 qt., ice lip	110.00
Plate, ctr. hdld., sandwich	30.00
Plate, 6", bread & butter	4.00
Plate, 6½", lemon, hdld.	12.00
Plate, 7", salad	8.00
Plate, 8", luncheon	10.00
Plate, 9", dinner	27.50
Plate, 10", hdld., cake	22.00
Plate, 12", ftd., salver	65.00
Plate, 13", torte	30.00
Plate, 15", torte	55.00
Plate, 18", torte	85.00
Platter, 12"	45.00
Relish, 10½", hdld., 3 part	20.00
Salt, 2½" indiv.	12.00
Salt & pepper, pr., 3⅝"	15.00
Saucer	2.00
Stem, 3⅜", 4 oz., oyster cocktail	12.00
Stem, 3⅝", 5 oz., sherbet	9.00
Stem, 4", 3½ oz., cocktail	12.00
Stem, 4¼", 3¼ oz., wine	27.00
Stem, 5¼", 9 oz., goblet	17.00
Sugar, 2¾", indiv.	6.00
Sugar, 3½"	5.00
Tray for indiv. sugar/cream	10.00
Tumbler, 3⅝", 5 oz., juice	20.00
Tumbler, 3⅞", 9 oz., water	16.00
Tumbler, 4⅞", 12 oz., tea	27.50
Tumbler, 4½", 5 oz., ftd.	16.00
Tumbler, 5¾", 12 oz., ftd.	20.00
Vase, 6", bud, flared	14.00
Vase, 7", cupped	35.00
Vase, 7½", flared	40.00
Vase, 9", cornucopia	60.00
Vase, 12", straight	185.00

COLONY

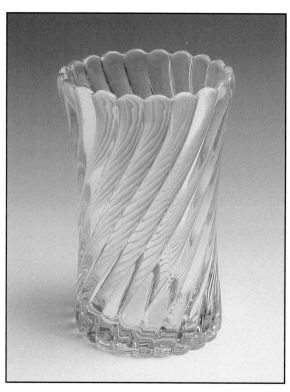

CRYSTOLITE, Blank #1503, A.H. Heisey & Co.

Colors: crystal, Zircon/Limelight, Sahara, and rare in amber

Crystolite is an easily recognized pattern and since most pieces are marked, you will rarely find a bargain. Prices on many pieces of Crystolite are edging upward. Several of the rarer pieces are rising even faster than in the past. Dealers are having a difficult time finding merchandise for resale; and when they do, the price always seems to be higher. This cost gets passed on to the consumer.

The cocktail shaker pictured here is missing from many collections. Accessory pieces rarely seen are the 6" basket, rye bottle, and pressed tumblers; but other items are also beginning to disappear. Notice the lack of pressed tumblers in the picture, but blown tumblers are so common that they found themselves in both photographs! Unfortunately, I was in the process of sorting and labeling over eight hundred cordials outside the studio when this was shot; so, slip-ups occurred occasionally. Although the punch set is not rare, it is a practical piece for people to use and display!

	Crystal
Ash tray, 3½", square	5.00
Ash tray, 4½", square	8.00
Ash tray, 5", w/book match holder	45.00
Ash tray (coaster), 4", rnd.	6.00
Basket, 6", hdld.	450.00
Bonbon, 7", shell	22.00
Bonbon, 7½", 2 hdld.	15.00
Bottle, 1 qt., rye, #107 stopper	300.00
Bottle, 4 oz., bitters, w/short tube	175.00
Bottle, 4 oz., cologne w/#108 stopper	65.00
w/drip stop	150.00
Bottle, syrup w/drip & cut top	120.00
Bowl, 7½ quart, punch	120.00
Bowl, 2", indiv. swan nut (or ash tray)	18.00
Bowl, 3", indiv. nut, hdld.	15.00
Bowl, 4½", dessert (or nappy)	14.00
Bowl, 5", preserve	20.00
Bowl, 5", 1000 island dressing, ruffled top	30.00
Bowl, 5½", dessert	14.00
Bowl, 6", oval jelly, 4 ft.	22.00
Bowl, 6", preserve, 2 hdld.	18.00
Bowl, 7", shell praline	35.00
Bowl, 8", dessert (sauce)	30.00
Bowl, 8", 2 pt. conserve, hdld.	55.00
Bowl, 9", leaf pickle	30.00
Bowl, 10", salad, rnd.	50.00
Bowl, 11", w/attached mayonnaise (chip 'n dip)	225.00
Bowl, 12", gardenia, shallow	50.00
Bowl, 13", oval floral, deep	55.00
Candle block, 1-lite, sq.	18.00
Candle block, 1-lite, swirl	20.00
Candlestick, 1-lite, ftd.	25.00
Candlestick, 1-lite, w/#4233, 5", vase	35.00
Candlestick, 2-lite	30.00
Candlestick, 2-lite, bobeche & 10 "D" prisms	65.00
Candlestick sans vase, 3-lite	30.00
Candlestick w/#4233, 5", vase, 3-lite	55.00
Candy, 6½", swan	45.00
Candy box, w/cover, 5½"	50.00
Candy box, w/cover, 7"	60.00
Cheese, 5½", ftd.	27.00
Cigarette box, w/cover, 4"	17.00
Cigarette box, w/cover, 4½"	20.00
Cigarette holder, ftd.	25.00
Cigarette holder, oval	25.00
Cigarette holder, rnd.	20.00
Cigarette lighter	30.00
Coaster, 4"	10.00
Cocktail shaker, 1 qt. w/#1 strainer; #86 stopper	325.00
Comport, 5", fed., deep, #5003, blown rare	275.00
Creamer, indiv.	17.00
Creamer, reg.	30.00
Creamer, round	40.00
Cup	20.00
Cup, punch or custard	7.00
Hurricane block, 1-lite, sq.	35.00
Hurricane block, w/#4061, 10" plain globe, 1-lite, sq.	90.00
Ice tub, w/silver plate handle	110.00

	Crystal
Jar, covered cherry	90.00
Jam jar, w/cover	50.00
Ladle, glass, punch	25.00
Ladle, plastic	7.50
Mayonnaise, 5½", shell, 3 ft.	32.00
Mayonnaise, 6", oval, hdld.	40.00
Mayonnaise ladle	9.00
Mustard & cover	40.00
Oil bottle, 3 oz.	40.00
Oil bottle, w/stopper, 2 oz.	30.00
Oval creamer, sugar, w/tray, set	47.50
Pitcher, ½ gallon, ice, blown	120.00
Pitcher, 2 quart swan, ice lip	700.00
Plate, 7", salad	15.00
Plate, 7", shell	24.00
Plate, 7", underliner for 1000 island dressing bowl	20.00
Plate, 7½", coupe	35.00
Plate, 8", oval, mayonnaise liner	16.00
Plate, 8½", salad	20.00
Plate, 10½", dinner	95.00
Plate, 11", ftd., cake salver	300.00
Plate, 11", torte	40.00
Plate, 12", sand.	45.00
Plate, 13", shell torte	90.00
Plate, 14", sand.	50.00
Plate, 14", torte	45.00
Plate, 20", buffet or punch liner	125.00
Puff box, w/cover, 4¾"	65.00
Salad dressing set, 3 pc.	38.00
Salt & pepper, pr.	30.00
Saucer	5.00
Stem, 1 oz., cordial, wide optic, blown, #5003	130.00
Stem, 3½ oz., cocktail, w.o., blown, #5003	24.00
Stem, 3½ oz., claret, w.o., blown, #5003	35.00
Stem, 3½ oz., oyster cocktail, w.o. blown, #5003	18.00
Stem, 6 oz., sherbet/saucer champagne, #5003	16.00
Stem, 10 oz., water, #1503, pressed	500.00
Stem, 10 oz., w.o., blown, #5003	28.00
Sugar, indiv.	17.00
Sugar, reg.	30.00
Sugar, round	40.00
Syrup pitcher, drip cut	135.00
Tray, 5½", oval, liner indiv. creamer/sugar set	40.00
Tray, 9", 4 pt., leaf relish	40.00
Tray, 10", 5 pt., rnd. relish	45.00
Tray, 12", 3 pt., relish, oval	35.00
Tray, 12", rect., celery	38.00
Tray, 12", rect., celery/olive	35.00
Tumbler, 5 oz., ftd., juice, w.o., blown, #5003	32.00
Tumbler, 8 oz., pressed, #5003	60.00
Tumbler, 10 oz., pressed	70.00
Tumbler, 10 oz., iced tea, w.o., blown, #5003	30.00
Tumbler, 12 oz., ftd., iced tea, w.o., blown #5003	27.00
Urn, 7", flower	75.00
Vase, 3", short stem	35.00
Vase, 6", ftd.	30.00
Vase, 12"	225.00

DECAGON, Cambridge Glass Company, 1930's – 1940's

Colors: Emerald green, Peach-Blo, Carmen, Royal blue, Amber, Moonlight blue, Ebony

Decagon is the Cambridge blank on which many of its famous etchings are found. This ten-sided pattern is keeping company with Fostoria's Baroque or Fairfax blanks in that respect. Cleo, Rosalie, and Imperial Hunt Scene patterns are better known than this Decagon blank on which they are all etched! However, there are some very ardent collectors of this plain, unetched Decagon "pattern."

The blue dresser set shown atop the next page only has Decagon lids, but a very happy Decagon collector bought it the first time it was offered for sale. The off-center snack plate and the flat soup are also uncommon blue pieces. I need one blue relish insert to finish that tray pictured unless some collector wants it missing a piece. An insert was broken twelve years ago and I have never spotted another!

Royal blue (cobalt) and Moonlight blue are the colors most collected although others are more plentiful. Pattern availability is only one determining factor in collecting! Color plays another major role; and blue usually wins out.

	Pastel Colors	Red Blue		Pastel Colors	Red Blue
Basket, 7", 2 hdld. (upturned sides)	15.00	25.00	Mayonnaise, w/liner & ladle	18.00	50.00
Bowl, bouillon, w/liner	7.50	25.00	Oil, 6 oz., tall, w/hdld. & stopper	50.00	95.00
Bowl, cream soup, w/liner	20.00	30.00	Plate, 6¼", bread/butter	3.00	5.00
Bowl, 2½", indiv., almond	22.00	38.00	Plate, 7", 2 hdld.	9.00	15.00
Bowl, 3¾", flat rim, cranberry	17.00	26.00	Plate, 7½"	4.00	10.00
Bowl, 3½" belled, cranberry	17.00	25.00	Plate, 8½", salad	6.00	15.00
Bowl, 5½", 2 hdld., bonbon	10.00	20.00	Plate, 9½", dinner	25.00	45.00
Bowl, 5½", belled, fruit	5.50	15.00	Plate, 10", grill	12.00	25.00
Bowl, 5¾", flat rim, fruit	8.00	15.00	Plate, 10", service	25.00	30.00
Bowl, 6", belled, cereal	15.00	25.00	Plate, 12½", service	9.00	35.00
Bowl, 6", flat rim, cereal	15.00	25.00	Relish, 6 inserts	75.00	125.00
Bowl, 6", ftd., almond	25.00	45.00	Salt dip, 1½", ftd.	17.00	25.00
Bowl, 6¼", 2 hdld., bonbon	12.00	20.00	Sauce boat & plate	45.00	85.00
Bowl, 8½", flat rim, soup "plate"	18.00	35.00	Saucer	1.50	3.00
Bowl, 9", rnd., veg.	20.00	40.00	Server, center hdld.	20.00	30.00
Bowl, 9", 2 pt., relish	12.00	20.00	Stem, 1 oz., cordial	40.00	65.00
Bowl, 9½", oval, veg.	15.00	32.00	Stem, 3½ oz., cocktail	14.00	22.00
Bowl, 10", berry	15.00	30.00	Stem, 6 oz., low sherbet	10.00	16.00
Bowl, 10½", oval, veg.	20.00	35.00	Stem, 6 oz., high sherbet	12.00	22.00
Bowl, 11", rnd. veg.	20.00	35.00	Stem, 9 oz., water	17.00	30.00
Bowl, 11", 2 pt., relish	12.00	25.00	Sugar, lightning bolt handles	7.00	12.00
Comport, 5¾"	15.00	22.00	Sugar, ftd.	9.00	20.00
Comport, 6½", low ft.	16.00	27.00	Sugar, scalloped edge	9.00	20.00
Comport, 7", tall	22.00	40.00	Sugar, tall, lg. ft.	8.00	18.00
Creamer, ftd.	10.00	20.00	Tray, 8", 2 hdld., flat pickle	14.00	25.00
Creamer, scalloped edge	9.00	18.00	Tray, 9", pickle	12.00	25.00
Creamer, lightning bolt handles	7.00	12.00	Tray, 11", oval, service	12.00	25.00
Creamer, tall, lg. ft.	10.00	22.00	Tray, 11", celery	12.00	25.00
Cup	6.00	10.00	Tray, 12", center handled	16.00	30.00
French dressing bottle, "Oil/Vinegar"	70.00	110.00	Tray, 12", oval, service	10.00	30.00
Gravy boat, w/2 hdld. liner (like spouted cream soup)	70.00	110.00	Tray, 13", 2 hdld., service	20.00	35.00
Ice bucket	35.00	60.00	Tray, 15", oval, service	20.00	45.00
Ice tub	35.00	50.00	Tumbler, 2½ oz., ftd.	15.00	25.00
Mayonnaise, 2 hdld., w/2 hdld. liner and ladle	27.00	45.00	Tumbler, 5 oz., ftd.	10.00	18.00
			Tumbler, 8 oz., ftd.	12.00	22.00
			Tumbler, 10 oz., ftd.	15.00	25.00
			Tumbler, 12 oz., ftd.	20.00	35.00

"DEERWOOD" or "BIRCH TREE," U.S. Glass Company, Late 1920's – Early 1930's

Colors: light amber, green, pink, black, crystal

Review the Black Forest pattern shot if you confuse these two patterns. Deer and trees are the predominant theme of Deerwood, whereas Black Forest depicts moose and trees.

Gold decorated, black "Deerwood" is rapidly being bought by people who are not necessarily collectors, but just like its looks. Not much of this is being found, but gold decorated pieces really make the pattern stand out... and photography easier! Of course, the photographer still fusses about the difficulties of light reflection on the shiny black surfaces.

That flat, three-part pink candy looks more like a Paden City blank than it does U.S. Glass. There is some catalog documentation for "Deerwood" which is not the case with Black Forest. I wonder if some other company did some etchings of "Deerwood." It definitely was produced by Tiffin, but maybe some of the contracts were sublet. The reason I say this is because a collector friend met a man who told her his job used to be running moulds back and forth between different glass factories. He said he moved them as many as three days a week and because of the cost of the moulds, he had to be bonded to get the job. He also said that, "Sometimes the other companies changed the mould a bit; but, often as not, they just ran it as it was." It probably won't make purists very happy, but that would explain a lot of "mysteries" of glass production!

There is no mayonnaise listed although I have had several reports of one. It was listed in old catalogs as a whipped cream pail instead of a mayonnaise. Terminology of the old glass companies often differs.

	*Black	Amber	Green	Pink
Bowl, 10", straight edge				45.00
Bowl, 12", console			55.00	60.00
Bowl, 10", footed	125.00			
Cake plate, low pedestal			60.00	60.00
Candlestick, 2½"	55.00		35.00	
Candlestick, 4"				45.00
Candy dish, w/cover, 3 part, flat				100.00
Candy jar, w/cover, ftd. cone			110.00	110.00
Celery, 12"			60.00	
Cheese and cracker			95.00	95.00
Comport, 10", low, ftd., flared	110.00			55.00
Creamer, 2 styles	60.00		40.00	40.00
Cup				70.00
Plate, 5½"			12.00	12.00
Plate, 7½", salad				22.00
Plate, 9½", dinner				65.00
Plate, 10¼", 2 hdld.	125.00			
Saucer				20.00
Server, center hdld.			40.00	40.00
Stem, 2 oz., wine, 4½"				35.00
Stem, 6 oz., sherbet, 4¾"			27.50	
Stem, 6 oz., cocktail, 5"			32.50	
Stem, 9 oz., water, 7"	110.00		45.00	45.00
Sugar, 2 styles	60.00		40.00	40.00
Tumbler, 9 oz.			37.50	37.50
Tumbler, 12 oz., tea, 5½"		45.00		
Vase, 7", sweet pea, rolled edge			95.00	95.00
Vase, 10", ruffled top			100.00	90.00
Vase, 12", 2 handles	125.00			
Whipped cream pail, w/ladle			45.00	45.00

*Add 20% for gold decorated

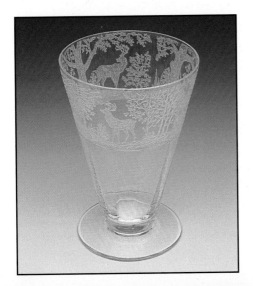

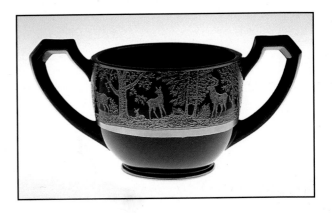

78

DIANE, Cambridge Glass Company, 1934 – Early 1950's

Colors: crystal; some pink, yellow, blue, Heatherbloom, Emerald green, amber, Crown Tuscan

Diane is one Cambridge pattern that comes in a multitude of colors; but it is almost impossible to obtain a set except in crystal. With luck, you might find a luncheon set in any of the colors pictured; but colored Diane appears irregularly. I had that dark, Emerald green candy lid for a dozen years looking for the bottom. Unfortunately, during our last move of glassware from storage, that lid hit a concrete floor!

Gold decorated Crown Tuscan pieces shown at the bottom of page 82 are sought both by Diane collectors and by connoisseurs of the Crown Tuscan color. At such an antique show, I saw the highest priced Crown Tuscan "almost" Diane lamps ever... $850.00 each. They were "almost" Diane due to half the design having been scrubbed off!

A few pieces of dark Emerald green, blue, and Heatherbloom have surfaced; notice my saucer-less Heatherbloom cup.

That's the martini pitcher or cocktail beverage mixer at top of the next page. The decanter set with Faberware holders and tray is an unusual find! You normally see these unetched.

The crystal item in the right foreground of page 82 is a cigarette holder. The stems on the bottom of page 83 are Regency stems. Unfortunately, they were utilized in only a couple of etched lines.

	Crystal		Crystal
Basket, 6", 2 hdld., ftd.	20.00	Comport, 5½"	27.50
Bottle, bitters	135.00	Comport, 5⅜", blown	37.50
Bowl, #3106, finger, w/liner	37.50	Creamer	14.00
Bowl, #3122	25.00	Creamer, indiv. #3500 (pie crust edge)	15.00
Bowl, #3400, cream soup, w/liner	35.00	Creamer, indiv. #3900, scalloped edge	15.00
Bowl, 3", indiv. nut, 4 ftd.	50.00	Creamer, scroll handle, #3400	15.00
Bowl, 5", berry	20.00	Cup	20.00
Bowl, 5¼" 2 hdld., bonbon	20.00	Decanter, ball	195.00
Bowl, 6", 2 hdld., ftd., bonbon	20.00	Decanter, lg. ftd.	175.00
Bowl, 6", 2 pt., relish	20.00	Decanter, short ft., cordial	210.00
Bowl, 6", cereal	27.50	Hurricane lamp, candlestick base	125.00
Bowl, 6½", 3 pt. relish	25.00	Hurricane lamp, keyhole base w/prisms	215.00
Bowl, 7", 2 hdld., ftd., bonbon	25.00	Ice bucket, w/chrome hand	65.00
Bowl, 7", 2 pt., relish	22.00	Mayonnaise, div., w/liner & ladles	45.00
Bowl, 7", relish or pickle	25.00	Mayonnaise (sherbet type w/ladle)	35.00
Bowl, 9", 3 pt., celery or relish	35.00	Mayonnaise, w/liner, ladle	40.00
Bowl, 9½", pickle (like corn)	25.00	Oil, 6 oz., w/stopper	125.00
Bowl, 10", 4 ft., flared	45.00	Pitcher, ball	150.00
Bowl, 10", baker	45.00	Pitcher, Doulton	300.00
Bowl, 11", 2 hdld.	40.00	Pitcher, martini	600.00
Bowl, 11", 4 ftd.	45.00	Pitcher, upright	175.00
Bowl, 11½" tab hdld., ftd.	45.00	Plate, 6", 2 hdld., plate.	7.00
Bowl, 12", 3 pt., celery & relish	35.00	Plate, 6", sq., bread/butter	5.00
Bowl, 12", 4 ft.	42.00	Plate, 6½", bread/butter	5.00
Bowl, 12", 4 ft., flared	42.00	Plate, 8", 2 hdld., ftd., bonbon	11.00
Bowl, 12", 4 ft., oval	45.00	Plate, 8", salad	10.00
Bowl, 12", 4 ft., oval, w/"ears" hdld.	55.00	Plate, 8½"	11.00
Bowl, 12", 5 pt., celery & relish	37.50	Plate, 10½", dinner	65.00
Butter, rnd.	135.00	Plate, 12", 4 ft., service	40.00
Cabinet flask	250.00	Plate, 13", 4 ft., torte	40.00
Candelabrum, 2-lite, keyhole	27.50	Plate, 13½", 2 hdld.	35.00
Candelabrum, 3-lite, keyhole	35.00	Plate, 14", torte	45.00
Candlestick, 1-lite, keyhole	20.00	Platter, 13½"	70.00
Candlestick, 5"	20.00	Salt & pepper, ftd., w/glass tops, pr.	35.00
Candlestick, 6", 2-lite, "fleur-de-lis"	32.50	Salt & pepper, pr., flat	35.00
Candlestick, 6", 3-lite	40.00	Saucer	5.00
Candy box, w/cover, rnd.	85.00	Stem, #1066, 1 oz., cordial	55.00
Cigarette urn	45.00	Stem, #1066, 3 oz., cocktail	16.00
Cocktail shaker, glass top	150.00	Stem, #1066, 3 oz., wine	28.00
Cocktail shaker, metal top	95.00	Stem, #1066, 3½ oz., tall cocktail	17.50
Cocktail icer, 2 pc.	65.00	Stem, #1066, 4½ oz., claret	40.00

DIANE

	Crystal		Crystal
Stem, #1066, 5 oz., oyster/cocktail	15.00	Tumbler, #1066, 3 oz.	22.00
Stem, #1066, 7 oz., low sherbet	14.00	Tumbler, #1066, 5 oz., juice	14.00
Stem, #1066, 7 oz., tall sherbet	15.00	Tumbler, #1066, 9 oz., water	15.00
Stem, #1066, 11 oz., water	25.00	Tumbler, #1066, 12 oz., tea	22.00
Stem, #3122, 1 oz., cordial	55.00	Tumbler, #3106, 3 oz., ftd.	20.00
Stem, #3122, 2½ oz., wine	30.00	Tumbler, #3106, 5 oz., ftd., juice	18.00
Stem, #3122, 3 oz., cocktail	14.00	Tumbler, #3106, 9 oz., ftd., water	14.00
Stem, #3122, 4½ oz., claret	40.00	Tumbler, #3106, 12 oz., ftd., tea	22.00
Stem, #3122, 4½ oz., oyster/cocktail	16.00	Tumbler, #3122, 2½ oz.	30.00
Stem, #3122, 7 oz., low sherbet	14.00	Tumbler, #3122, 5 oz., juice	15.00
Stem, #3122, 7 oz., tall sherbet	18.00	Tumbler, #3122, 9 oz., water	17.00
Stem, #3122, 9 oz., water goblet	25.00	Tumbler, #3122, 12 oz., tea	20.00
Sugar, indiv., #3500 (pie crust edge)	13.00	Tumbler, #3135, 2½ oz., ftd., bar	35.00
Sugar, indiv., #3900, scalloped edge	13.00	Tumbler, #3135, 10 oz., ftd., tumbler	16.00
Sugar, scroll handle, #3400	14.00	Tumbler, #3135, 12 oz., ftd., tea	28.00
Tumbler, 2½ oz., sham bottom	42.00	Vase, 5", globe	35.00
Tumbler, 5 oz., ft., juice	30.00	Vase, 6", high ft., flower	40.00
Tumbler, 5 oz., sham bottom	32.50	Vase, 8", high ft., flower	55.00
Tumbler, 7 oz., old-fashioned, w/sham		Vase, 9", keyhole base	60.00
bottom	45.00	Vase, 10", bud	50.00
Tumbler, 8 oz., ft.	25.00	Vase, 11", flower	65.00
Tumbler, 10 oz., sham bottom	32.00	Vase, 11", ped. ft., flower	75.00
Tumbler, 12 oz., sham bottom	35.00	Vase, 12", keyhole base	85.00
Tumbler, 13 oz.	32.00	Vase, 13", flower	110.00
Tumbler, 14 oz., sham bottom	40.00		

Note: See Page 228 – 229 for stem identification.

ELAINE, Cambridge Glass Company, 1934 – 1950's

Colors: crystal

    I've just observed that even veteran dealers confuse Elaine with Chantilly! Chantilly has a thick scroll... with "C's" (for Chantilly) on both ends. Elaine's scroll is thin and **angled**... like the capital letter "*E*" (for Elaine) is angled as you write it. You may find additional pieces not listed here. I have used as much listing space as I possibly can. Many of the same pieces found in Rose Point are also etched Elaine. Remember the prices for Elaine will be less than those for Rose Point due to collector demand.

	Crystal
Basket, 6", 2 hdld. (upturned sides)	20.00
Bowl, #3104, finger, w/liner	32.00
Bowl, 3", indiv. nut, 4 ftd.	50.00
Bowl, 5¼", 2 hdld., bonbon	13.00
Bowl, 6", 2 hdld., ftd., bonbon	20.00
Bowl, 6", 2 pt., relish	20.00
Bowl, 6½", 3 pt., relish	20.00
Bowl, 7", 2 pt., pickle or relish	20.00
Bowl, 7", ftd., tab hdld. bonbon	30.00
Bowl, 7", pickle or relish	25.00
Bowl, 9", 3 pt., celery & relish	35.00
Bowl, 9½", pickle (like corn dish)	25.00
Bowl, 10", 4 ftd., flared	30.00
Bowl, 11", tab hdld.	40.00
Bowl, 11½", ftd., tab hdld.	40.00
Bowl, 12", 3 pt., celery & relish	35.00
Bowl, 12", 4 ftd., flared	40.00
Bowl, 12", 4 ftd., oval, "ear" hdld.	45.00
Bowl, 12", 5 pt. celery & relish	37.50
Candlestick, 5"	20.00
Candlestick, 6", 2-lite	32.50
Candlestick, 6", 3-lite	40.00
Candy box, w/cover, rnd.	85.00
Cocktail icer, 2 pc.	60.00
Comport, 5½"	30.00
Comport, 5⅜", #3500 stem	40.00
Comport, 5⅜", blown	42.00
Creamer (several styles)	12.00
Creamer, indiv.	15.00
Cup	20.00
Decanter, lg., ftd.	185.00
Hat, 9"	295.00
Hurricane lamp, candlestick base	125.00
Hurricane lamp, keyhole ft., w/prisms	210.00
Ice bucket, w/chrome handle	65.00
Mayonnaise (cupped "sherbet" w/ladle)	35.00
Mayonnaise (div. bowl, liner, 2 ladles)	45.00
Mayonnaise, w/liner & ladle	40.00
Oil, 6 oz., hdld., w/stopper	95.00
Pitcher, ball	150.00
Pitcher, Doulton	300.00
Pitcher, upright	185.00
Plate, 6", 2 hdld.	10.00
Plate, 6½", bread/butter	7.00
Plate, 8", 2 hdld., ftd.	18.00
Plate, 8", salad	15.00
Plate, 8", tab hdld., bonbon	18.00
Plate, 10½", dinner	65.00
Plate, 11½" 2 hdld., ringed "Tally Ho" sand.	30.00
Plate, 12", 4 ftd., service	30.00
Plate, 13", 4 ftd., torte	35.00
Plate, 13½", tab hdld., cake	35.00
Plate, 14", torte	35.00
Salt & pepper, flat, pr.	35.00

	Crystal
Salt & pepper, ftd., pr.	35.00
Salt & pepper, hdld., pr.	40.00
Saucer	3.00
Stem, #1402, 1 oz., cordial	60.00
Stem, #1402, 3 oz., wine	25.00
Stem, #1402, 3½ oz., cocktail	20.00
Stem, #1402, 5 oz., claret	27.50
Stem, #1402, low sherbet	14.00
Stem, #1402, tall sherbet	15.00
Stem, #1402, goblet	20.00
Stem, #3104, (very tall stems), ¾ oz., brandy	150.00
Stem, #3104, 1 oz., cordial	150.00
Stem, #3104, 1 oz., pousse-cafe	150.00
Stem, #3104, 2 oz., sherry	125.00
Stem, #3104, 2½ oz., creme de menthe	125.00
Stem, #3104, 3 oz., wine	100.00
Stem, #3104, 3½ oz., cocktail	65.00
Stem, #3104, 4½ oz., claret	85.00
Stem, #3104, 5 oz., roemer	85.00
Stem, #3104, 5 oz., tall hock	80.00
Stem, #3104, 7 oz., tall sherbet	70.00
Stem, #3104, 9 oz., goblet	125.00
Stem, #3121, 1 oz., cordial	60.00
Stem, #3121, 3 oz., cocktail	24.00
Stem, #3121, 3½ oz., wine	35.00
Stem, #3121, 4½ oz., claret	40.00
Stem, #3121, 4½ oz., oyster cocktail	18.00
Stem, #3121, 5 oz., parfait, low stem	30.00
Stem, #3121, 6 oz., low sherbet	16.00
Stem, #3121, 6 oz., tall sherbet	18.00
Stem, #3121, 10 oz., water	25.00
Stem, #3500, 1 oz., cordial	60.00
Stem, #3500, 2½ oz., wine	35.00
Stem, #3500, 3 oz., cocktail	24.00
Stem, #3500, 4½ oz., claret	40.00
Stem, #3500, 4½ oz., oyster cocktail	18.00
Stem, #3500, 5 oz., parfait, low stem	30.00
Stem, #3500, 7 oz., low sherbet	16.00
Stem, #3500, 7 oz., tall sherbet	18.00
Stem, #3500, 10 oz., water	25.00
Sugar (several styles)	10.00
Sugar, indiv.	12.00
Tumbler, #1402, 9 oz., ftd., water	18.00
Tumbler, #1402, 12 oz., tea	30.00
Tumbler, #1402, 12 oz., tall ftd., tea	30.00
Tumbler, #3121, 5 oz., ftd., juice	22.00
Tumbler, #3121, 10 oz., ftd., water	25.00
Tumbler, #3121, 12 oz., ftd., tea	30.00
Tumbler, #3500, 5 oz., ftd., juice	20.00
Tumbler, #3500, 10 oz., ftd., water	22.00
Tumbler, #3500, 12 oz., ftd., tea	30.00
Vase, 6", ftd.	40.00
Vase, 8", ftd.	55.00
Vase, 9", keyhole, ftd.	60.00

Note: see pages 228 – 229 for stem identification.

EMPRESS, Blank #1401, A.H. Heisey & Co.

Colors: "Flamingo" pink, "Sahara" yellow, "Moongleam" green, cobalt and "Alexandrite"; some Tangerine

I have included a shelf shot of Empress in Alexandrite. Notice that crystal is no longer priced here. You will find crystal prices listed under the name Queen Ann. When the colors were made this pattern was called Empress; but when crystal was added later, the name was changed to Queen Ann. Prices for the Alexandrite have been increasing in almost all pieces except the ever present plates.

Row 1: 9" vase, 7" candlestick (#135) , 6" square plate, 8" square plate
Row 2: Nut dish, 6" mint, 11" floral bowl, cup and saucer
Row 3: Ash tray, sugar, creamer, mayonnaise w/ladle
Row 4: 7" round plate, shaker, 10" celery tray, shaker, 7" 3-part relish

	Flam.	Sahara	Moon.	Cobalt	Alexan.
Ash tray.	85.00	60.00	375.00	300.00	210.00
Bonbon, 6"	20.00	25.00	30.00		
Bowl, cream soup	26.00	27.00	35.00		75.00
Bowl, cream soup, w/sq. liner	25.00	30.00	45.00		165.00
Bowl, frappe, w/center	45.00	60.00	75.00		
Bowl, nut, dolphin ftd., indiv.	22.00	26.00	32.00		160.00
Bowl, 4½", nappy	8.00	10.00	12.50		
Bowl, 5", preserve, 2 hdld.	18.00	22.00	27.50		
Bowl, 6", ftd., jelly, 2 hdld.	17.00	23.00	27.50		
Bowl, 6", dolp. ftd., mint	20.00	25.00	30.00		225.00
Bowl, 6", grapefruit, sq. top, grnd. bottom	12.50	15.00	22.50		
Bowl, 6½", oval, lemon, w/cover	65.00	75.00	90.00		
Bowl, 7", 3 pt., relish, triplex	40.00	30.00	45.00		300.00
Bowl, 7", 3 pt., relish, ctr. hand.	45.00	50.00	75.00		
Bowl, 7½", dolp. ftd., nappy	60.00	65.00	75.00	275.00	325.00
Bowl, 7½", dolp. ftd., nasturtium	120.00	120.00	130.00	325.00	400.00
Bowl, 8", nappy	30.00	35.00	40.00		
Bowl, 8½", ftd., floral, 2 hdld	40.00	50.00	65.00		
Bowl, 9", floral, rolled edge	32.00	38.00	42.00		
Bowl, 9", floral, flared	70.00	75.00	90.00		
Bowl, 10", 2 hdld., oval dessert	45.00	60.00	65.00		
Bowl, 10", lion head, floral	550.00	550.00	700.00		
Bowl, 10", oval, veg.	35.00	45.00	55.00		
Bowl, 10", square, salad, 2 hdld.	40.00	55.00	65.00		
Bowl, 10", triplex, relish	45.00	55.00	65.00		
Bowl, 11", dolphin ftd., floral	60.00	60.00	90.00	375.00	500.00
Bowl, 13", pickle/olive, 2 pt.	18.00	30.00	32.00		
Bowl, 15", dolp. ftd., punch	800.00	850.00	1,000.00		
Candlestick, low, 4 ftd., w/2 hdld.	35.00	40.00	45.00		
Candlestick, 6", dolphin ftd.	115.00	100.00	120.00	260.00	265.00
Candy, w/cover, 6", dolphin ftd.	120.00	150.00	200.00	425.00	
Comport, 6", ftd.	50.00	55.00	65.00		
Comport, 6", square	70.00	75.00	85.00		
Comport, 7", oval	60.00	66.00	75.00		
Compotier, 6", dolphin ftd.	250.00	200.00	250.00		
Creamer, dolphin ftd.	40.00	35.00	42.50		250.00
Creamer, indiv.	40.00	35.00	40.00		210.00
Cup	27.00	31.00	36.00		110.00
Cup, after dinner	50.00	50.00	60.00		
Cup, bouillon, 2 hdld.	25.00	25.00	30.00		
Cup, 4 oz., custard or punch	25.00	28.00	30.00		
Cup, #1401½, has rim as demi-cup	28.00	32.00	40.00		
Grapefruit, w/square liner	25.00	30.00	35.00		
Ice tub, w/metal handles	95.00	100.00	135.00		
Jug, 3 pint, ftd.	175.00	200.00	225.00		

EMPRESS

	Flam.	Sahara	Moon.	Cobalt	Alexan.
Jug, flat			165.00		
Marmalade, w/cover, dolphin ftd.	70.00	80.00	95.00		
Mayonnaise, 5½", ftd. with ladle....................	50.00	55.00	65.00		350.00
Mustard, w/cover...	75.00	70.00	85.00		
Oil bottle, 4 oz...	100.00	120.00	130.00		
Plate...	7.00	10.00	12.00		
Plate, bouillon liner......................................	9.00	13.00	15.00		20.00
Plate, 4½"..	6.00	6.00	8.00		
Plate, 6"...	11.00	14.00	16.00		35.00
Plate, 6", square...	10.00	13.00	15.00		30.00
Plate, 7"..	12.00	15.00	17.00		40.00
Plate, 7", square...	12.00	15.00	17.00	55.00	45.00
Plate, 8", square...	18.00	22.00	35.00	70.00	65.00
Plate, 8"..	16.00	20.00	24.00	70.00	65.00
Plate, 9"..	25.00	35.00	40.00		
Plate, 10½"...	100.00	100.00	125.00		300.00
Plate, 10½", square	100.00	100.00	125.00		300.00
Plate, 12"..	45.00	55.00	65.00		
Plate, 12", muffin, sides upturned.................	50.00	60.00	70.00		
Plate, 12", sandwich, 2 hdld..........................	35.00	40.00	50.00		165.00
Plate, 13", hors d'oeuvre, 2 hdld.	40.00	45.00	55.00		
Plate, 13", square, 2 hdld...............................	40.00	45.00	55.00		
Platter, 14"..	35.00	40.00	47.50		
Salt & pepper, pr..	100.00	110.00	135.00		450.00
Saucer, square	8.00	14.00	16.00		25.00
Saucer, after dinner......................................	7.00	10.00	10.00		
Saucer..	8.00	14.00	16.00		25.00
Stem, 2½ oz., oyster cocktail	20.00	25.00	30.00		
Stem, 4 oz., saucer champagne	35.00	40.00	60.00		
Stem, 4 oz., sherbet.......................................	22.00	28.00	35.00		
Stem, 9 oz., Empress stemware, unusual........	55.00	65.00	75.00		
Sugar, indiv.	40.00	35.00	40.00		210.00
Sugar, dolphin ftd., 3 hdld.	40.00	35.00	35.00		250.00
Tray, condiment & liner for indiv.					
sugar/creamer......................................	40.00	30.00	50.00		
Tray, 10", 3 pt., relish....................................	25.00	30.00	35.00		
Tray, 10", 7 pt., hors d'oeuvre........................	160.00	150.00	200.00		
Tray, 10", celery...	16.00	22.00	26.00		150.00
Tray, 12", ctr. hdld., sand..............................	48.00	57.00	65.00		
Tray, 12", sq. ctr. hdld., sand.	52.00	60.00	67.50		
Tray, 13", celery...	20.00	24.00	30.00		
Tray, 16", 4 pt., buffet relish	75.00	75.00	86.00		160.00
Tumbler, 8 oz., dolphin ftd., unusual	125.00	150.00	195.00		
Tumbler, 8 oz., grnd. bottom	40.00	35.00	39.50		
Tumbler, 12 oz., tea, grnd. bottom..................	45.00	40.00	50.00		
Vase, 8", flared..	80.00	90.00	105.00		
Vase, 9", dolp, ftd...	110.00	110.00	160.00		850.00

FAIRFAX NO. 2375, Fostoria Glass Company, 1927 – 1944

Colors: blue, Azure blue, Orchid, amber, Rose, green, Topaz; some Ruby, black, and Wisteria

Fairfax is the Fostoria blank on which many of the most popular Fostoria etchings are found, notably June, Versailles, and Trojan. Most collectors do not get as excited about this #2375 line without an etching. Azure blue (shown on page 92) and Orchid (illustrated on top of page 91) are the most collected Fairfax colors. For those who confuse pink and Orchid, I have placed them on the opposite page so you can see how much darker the Orchid really is! Those stems and tumblers shown in Orchid have the Spartan pattern etched on them, but you can find unetched pieces. I point that out to save a few letters over the next two years from readers with magnifiers looking for errors. (I kid you not!)

Fairfax collectors have a choice of stems. In the photo at the top of page 92 are stem and tumbler line #5299; this is more commonly found in yellow with Trojan etch. Some collectors call this stem a cascading "waterfall." The other stem line, #5298, is shown in the lower photo and it is usually used for Versailles and June etchings. Some collectors are mixing stem lines; but tumblers are more difficult to mix because they have distinctly different shapes. The #5299 tumblers are more cone-shaped than the #5298 that are rounded.

Due to confusion among collectors and dealers alike, I have shown the various configurations of Fostoria's stemware on page 93 so that all shapes can be seen. The claret and high sherbets are major concerns. Each is 6" high. Notice that the claret is shaped like the wine. Note, too, the parfait is taller than the juice! Knowing these differences can make or save you money!

	Rose, Blue, Orchid	Amber	Green, Topaz
Ash tray, 2½"	15.00	8.00	11.00
Ash tray, 4"	17.50	10.00	12.50
Ash tray, 5½"	20.00	13.00	17.50
Baker, 9", oval	30.00	16.00	22.00
Baker, 10½", oval	38.00	20.00	25.00
Bonbon	12.50	9.00	10.00
Bottle, salad dressing	175.00	75.00	90.00
Bouillon, ftd.	15.00	8.00	10.00
Bowl, 9", lemon, 2 hdld.	12.00	6.00	7.00
Bowl, sweetmeat	15.00	10.00	12.00
Bowl, 5", fruit	14.00	6.00	7.00
Bowl, 6", cereal	22.00	9.00	12.00
Bowl, 6⅞", 3 ftd.	15.00	10.00	13.00
Bowl, 7", soup	35.00	15.00	20.00
Bowl, 8", rnd., nappy	35.00	15.00	17.00
Bowl, lg., hdld., dessert	35.00	14.00	17.00
Bowl, 12"	35.00	17.00	22.00
Bowl, 12", centerpiece	30.00	17.50	22.00
Bowl, 13", oval, centerpiece	35.00	20.00	25.00
Bowl, 15", centerpiece	40.00	22.00	26.00
Butter dish, w/cover	135.00	80.00	90.00
Candlestick, flattened top	20.00	10.00	12.00
Candlestick, 3"	16.00	9.00	12.00
Candy w/cover, flat, 3 pt	60.00	40.00	50.00
Cancy w/cover, ftd.	70.00	45.00	60.00
Celery, 11½"	24.00	12.00	16.00
Cheese & cracker set (2 styles)	40.00	20.00	25.00
Cigarette box	30.00	18.00	22.00
Comport, 5"	25.00	12.00	18.00
Comport, 7"	30.00	14.00	20.00
Cream soup, ftd.	20.00	9.00	12.00
Creamer, flat		10.00	14.00
Creamer, ftd.	13.00	7.00	10.00
Creamer, tea	20.00	8.00	12.00
Cup, after dinner	25.00	10.00	15.00
Cup, flat		4.00	6.00
Cup, ftd.	10.00	6.00	7.00
Flower holder, oval, window box	75.00	22.00	35.00
Grapefruit	32.50	15.00	22.50
Grapefruit liner	27.50	12.00	17.50
Ice bucket	50.00	30.00	35.00
Ice bowl	20.00	12.00	14.00
Ice bowl liner	20.00	12.00	* 10.00
Mayonnaise	15.00	9.00	10.00
Mayonnaise ladle	35.00	20.00	25.00
Mayonnaise liner, 7"	8.00	4.00	5.00
Nut cup, blown	30.00	15.00	20.00
Oil, ftd.	135.00	85.00	100.00
Pickle, 8½"	25.00	8.00	12.00
Pitcher, #5000	210.00	110.00	135.00
Plate, canape	18.00	10.00	10.00
Plate, whipped cream	11.00	8.00	9.00
Plate, 6", bread/butter	4.00	2.00	2.50
Plate, 7½", salad	5.00	3.00	3.50
Plate, 7½", cream soup or mayonnaise liner	8.00	4.00	5.00
Plate, 8¾", salad	10.00	4.50	5.00
Plate, 9½", luncheon	15.00	6.00	7.00
Plate, 10¼", dinner	40.00	17.00	25.00
Plate, 10¼", grill	35.00	15.00	22.00
Plate, 10", cake	22.00	13.00	15.00
Plate, 12", bread, oval	40.00	25.00	27.50
Plate, 13", chop	25.00	14.00	16.00
Platter, 10½", oval	35.00	17.00	25.00
Platter, 12", oval	40.00	20.00	30.00
Platter, 15", oval	70.00	27.00	40.00
Relish, 3 part, 8½"	20.00	10.00	12.00
Relish, 11½"	22.00	11.00	13.00
Sauce boat	45.00	20.00	25.00
Sauce boat liner	17.50	9.00	10.00
Saucer, after dinner	8.00	4.00	5.00
Saucer	4.00	2.50	3.00
Shaker, ftd., pr	60.00	30.00	40.00
Shaker, indiv., ftd., pr.		20.00	25.00
Stem, 4", ¾ oz., cordial	65.00	25.00	40.00
Stem, 4¼", 6 oz., low sherbet	18.00	9.00	11.00
Stem, 5¼", 3 oz., cocktail	24.00	12.00	18.00
Stem, 5½", 3 oz., wine	30.00	18.00	22.50
Stem, 6", 4 oz., claret	40.00	25.00	30.00
Stem, 6", 6 oz., high sherbet	20.00	10.00	12.50
Stem, 8¼", 10 oz., water	30.00	16.00	20.00
Sugar, flat		10.00	12.00
Sugar, ftd.	10.00	6.00	8.00
Sugar cover	35.00	20.00	25.00
Sugar pail	55.00	25.00	35.00
Sugar, tea	20.00	8.00	12.00
Tray, 11", ctr. hdld.	25.00	14.00	18.00
Tumbler, 2½ oz., ftd.	30.00	12.00	16.00
Tumbler, 4½", 5 oz., ftd.	18.00	10.00	11.00
Tumbler, 5¼", 9 oz., ftd.	20.00	12.00	13.00
Tumbler, 6", 12 oz., ftd.	28.00	13.50	18.00
Vase, 8" (2 styles)	75.00	35.00	50.00
Whipped cream pail	55.00	25.00	35.00

* Green $20.00

See page 93 for stem identification.

FOSTORIA STEMS AND SHAPES

Top Row: Left to Right
1. Water, 10 oz., 8¼"
2. Claret, 4 oz., 6"
3. Wine, 3 oz., 5½"
4. Cordial, ¾ oz., 4"
5. Sherbet, low, 6 oz., 4¼"
6. Cocktail, 3 oz., 5¼"
7. Sherbet, high, 6 oz., 6"

Bottom Row: Left to Right
1. Grapefruit and liner
2. Ice tea tumbler, 12 oz., 6"
3. Water tumbler, 9 oz., 5¼"
4. Parfait, 6 oz., 5¼"
5. Juice tumbler, 5 oz., 4½"
6. Oyster cocktail, 5½ oz.
7. Bar tumbler, 2½ oz.

93

FIRST LOVE, Duncan & Miller Glass Company, 1937

Color: crystal

First Love by Duncan & Miller is their best known etching! There were several mould lines incorporated into making this extensive pattern. They include #30 (Pall Mall), #111 (Terrace), #115 (Canterbury), #117 (Three Feathers), #126 (Venetian), #5111½ (Terrace blown stemware). Terrace is a newly listed pattern in this book (pages 204 – 205). I have included four catalog pages (98 – 101) that should show you examples of each of these mould lines as well as one page showing the different stemware.

Thanks again to the First Love collectors and dealers in Washington, Pennsylvania, who helped me compile and price this list. Any additional pieces or pricing contributions that you have, please let me know!

	Crystal		Crystal
Ash tray, 3½" sq., #111	17.50	Candy jar, 5" x 7¼", w/lid, ftd., #25	75.00
Ash tray, 3½" x 2½", #30	16.50	Candy, 6½", w/5" lid, #115	65.00
Ash tray, 5" x 3", #12, club	35.00	Carafe, w/stopper, water, #5200	125.00
Ash tray, 5" x 3¼", #30	24.00	Cheese stand, 3" x 5¼", #111	25.00
Ash tray, 6½" x 4¼", #30	35.00	Cheese stand, 5¾" x 3½", #115	25.00
Basket, 9¼" x 10" x 7¼", #115	145.00	Cigarette box w/lid, 4" x 4¼"	32.00
Basket,10" x 4¼" x 7", oval hdld., #115	165.00	Cigarette box w/lid, 4½" x 3½", #30	35.00
Bottle, oil w/stopper, 8", #5200	60.00	Cigarette box w/lid, 4¾" x 3¾"	35.00
Bowl, 3" x 5", rose, #115	40.00	Cocktail shaker, 14 oz., #5200	115.00
Bowl, 4" x 1½" finger, #30	32.00	Cocktail shaker, 16 oz., #5200	115.00
Bowl, 4¼", finger, #5111½	35.00	Cocktail shaker, 32 oz., #5200	150.00
Bowl, 6" x 2½", oval, olive, #115	25.00	Comport w/lid, 8¾" x 5½", #111	125.00
Bowl, 6¾" x 4¼", ftd., flared rim, #111	30.00	Comport, 3½"x 4¾"W, #111	30.00
Bowl, 7½" x 3", 3 pt., ftd., #117	35.00	Comport, 5" x 5½", flared rim, #115	32.00
Bowl, 8" sq. x 2½", hdld., #111	55.00	Comport, 5¼" x 6¾", flat top, #115	32.00
Bowl, 8½" x 4", #115	37.50	Comport, 6" x 4¾", low #115	37.50
Bowl, 9" x 4½", ftd., #111	42.00	Creamer, 2½", individual, #115	18.00
Bowl, 9½" x 2½", hdld., #111	45.00	Creamer, 3", 10 oz., #111	18.00
Bowl, 10" x 3¾", ftd., flared rim, #111	55.00	Creamer, 3¾", 7 oz., #115	15.00
Bowl, 10" x 4½", #115	45.00	Creamer, sugar w/butter pat lid, breakfast set, #28	60.00
Bowl, 10½" x 5", crimped, #115	44.00	Cruet, #25	90.00
Bowl, 10½" x 7" x 7", #126	60.00	Cruet, #30	90.00
Bowl, 10¾" x 4¾" #115	42.50	Cup, #115	18.00
Bowl, 11" x 1 ¾", #30	55.00	Decanter w/stopper, 16 oz., #5200	125.00
Bowl, 11" x 3¼", flared rim, #111	62.50	Decanter w/stopper, 32 oz., #30	145.00
Bowl, 11" x 5¼", flared rim, #6	67.50	Decanter w/stopper, 32 oz., #5200	145.00
Bowl, 11½" x 8¼", oval, #115	45.00	Hat, 4½", #30	300.00
Bowl, 12" x 3½", #6	65.00	Hat, 5½" x 8½" x 6¼", #30	325.00
Bowl, 12" x 3¼", flared, #115	60.00	Honey dish, 5" x 3", #91	25.00
Bowl, 12" x 4" x 7½", oval, #117	65.00	Ice bucket, 6", #30	90.00
Bowl, 12½", flat, ftd., #126	70.00	Lamp, hurricane, w/prisms, 15", #115	145.00
Bowl, 13" x 3¼" x 8¾", oval, flared, #115	55.00	Lamp shade only, #115	100.00
Bowl, 13" x 7" x 9¼", #126	67.50	Lid for candy urn, #111	35.00
Bowl, 13" x 7", #117	62.50	Mayonnaise, 4¾" x 4½", div. w/7½" underplate	35.00
Bowl, 14" x 7½" x 6", oval, #126	65.00	Mayonnaise, 5¼" x 3", div. w/6½" plate, #115	35.00
Box, candy w/lid, 4¾" x 6¼"	60.00	Mayonnaise, 5½" x 2½", ftd., hdld., #111	35.00
Butter or cheese, 7" sq. x 1¼", #111	115.00	Mayonnaise, 5½" x 2¾", #115	35.00
Candelabra, 2-lite, #41	35.00	Mayonnaise, 5½" x 3½", crimped, #11	32.00
Candelabrum, 6", 2-lite w/prisms, #30	55.00	Mayonnaise, 5¾" x 3", w/dish hdld. tray, #111	35.00
Candle, 3", 1-lite, #111	25.00	Mayonnaise, w/7" tray hdld., #111	35.00
Candle, 3", low, #115	25.00	Mustard w/lid & underplate	57.50
Candle, 3½", #115	25.00	Nappy, 5" x 1", w/bottom star, #25	20.00
Candle, 4", cornucopia, #117	25.00	Nappy, 5" x 1¾", one hdld., #115	18.00
Candle, 4", low, #111	25.00	Nappy, 5½" x 2", div., hdld., #111	18.00
Candle, 5¼", 2-lite, globe, #30	35.00	Nappy, 5½" x 2", one hdld., heart, #115	28.00
Candle, 6", 2-lite, #30	35.00	Nappy, 6" x 1¾", hdld., #111	22.00
Candy box, 6" x 3½", 3 hdld., 3 pt., w/lid, #115	65.00		
Candy box, 6" x 3½", 3 pt., w/lid, crown finial, #106	75.00		

FIRST LOVE

	Crystal		Crystal
Perfume tray, 8" x 5", #5200	25.00	Stem, 5", 5 oz., saucer champagne,	
Perfume, 5", #5200	75.00	#5111½	18.00
Pitcher, #5200	145.00	Stem, 5¼", 3 oz., wine, #5111½	32.50
Pitcher, 9", 80 oz., ice lip, #5202	155.00	Stem, 5¼", 5 oz., ftd. juice, #5111½	24.00
Plate, 6", #111	12.00	Stem, 5¾", 10 oz., low luncheon	
Plate, 6", #115	12.00	goblet #5111½	17.50
Plate, 6", hdld. lemon, #111	14.00	Stem, 6", 4½ oz., claret, #5111½	45.00
Plate, 6", sq., #111	14.00	Stem, 6½", 12 oz., ftd. ice tea, #5111½	35.0
Plate, 7", #111	17.50	#5111½	24.00
Plate, 7½", #111	18.00	Stem, 6¾", 14 oz., ftd. ice tea, #5111½	35.00
Plate, 7½", #115	18.00	Stem, cordial, #111	17.50
Plate, 7½", mayonnaise liner, hdld.		Sugar, 2½", individual, #115	14.00
#115	15.00	Sugar, 3", 7 oz., #115	14.00
Plate, 7½", sq., #111	19.00	Sugar, 3", 10 oz., #111	15.00
Plate, 7½", 2 hdld., #115	19.00	Tray, 8" x 2", hdld. celery, #111	17.50
Plate, 8½", #30	20.00	Tray, 8" x 4¾", individual sug/cr. #115	17.50
Plate, 8½", #111	20.00	Tray, 8¾", celery, #91	30.00
Plate, 8½", #115	20.00	Tray, 11", celery, #91	40.00
Plate, 11", #111	47.50	Tumbler, 2", 1½ oz., whiskey, #5200	55.00
Plate, 11", 2 hdld., sandwich #115	30.00	Tumbler, 2½" x 3⅜", sham,	
Plate, 11", hdld., #111	40.00	Teardrop, ftd.	57.50
Plate, 11", hdld., cracker w/ring #115	40.00	Tumbler, 3", sham, #5200	32.50
Plate, 11", hdld., cracker w/ring, #111	40.00	Tumbler, 4¾", 10 oz., sham, #5200	37.50
Plate, 11", hdld., sandwich, #111	40.00	Tumbler, 5½", 12 oz., sham, #5200	37.50
Plate, 11¼", dinner, #115	55.00	Tumbler, 6", 14 oz., sham, #5200	37.50
Plate, 12", egg, #30	115.00	Tumbler, 8 oz., flat, #115	30.00
Plate, 12", torte, rolled edge, #111	40.00	Urn, 4½" x 4½", #111	27.50
Plate, 13", torte, flat edge, #111	50.00	Urn, 4½" x 4½", #115	27.50
Plate, 13", torte, rolled edge, #111	57.50	Urn, 4¾", rnd ft.	27.50
Plate, 13¼", torte, #111	57.50	Urn, 5", #525	37.50
Plate, 13½", cake, hdld., #115	50.00	Urn, 5½", ring hdld, sq. ft.	60.00
Plate, 14", #115	50.00	Urn, 5½", sq. ft.	37.50
Plate, 14", cake, #115	50.00	Urn, 6½", sq. hdld.	70.00
Plate, 14½", cake, lg. base, #30	55.00	Urn, 7", #529	37.50
Plate, 14½", cake, sm. base, #30	55.00	Vase, 4", flared rim, #115	25.00
Relish, 6" x 1¾", hdld., 2 pt., #111	20.00	Vase, 4½" x 4¾", #115	30.00
Relish, 6" x 1¾", hdld., 2 pt., #115	20.00	Vase, 5" x 5", crimped, #115	35.00
Relish, 8" x 4½", pickle, 2 pt., #115	25.00	Vase, 6", #507	55.00
Relish, 8", 3 pt., hdld., #115	25.00	Vase, 8" x 4¾", cornucopia, #117	65.00
Relish, 9" x 1½", 2 pt. pickle, #115	25.00	Vase, 8", ftd., #506	90.00
Relish, 9" x 1½", 3 hdld, 3 pt., #115	32.50	Vase, 8", ftd., #507	90.00
Relish, 9" x 1½", 3 hdld., flared, #115	32.50	Vase, 8½" x 2¾", #505	100.00
Relish, 10", 5 pt. tray, #30	65.00	Vase, 8½" x 6", #115	90.00
Relish, 10½" x 1½", hdld., 5 pt., #111	75.00	Vase, 9" x 4½", #505	95.00
Relish, 10½" x 1¼", 2 hdld, 3 pt., #115	57.50	Vase, 9", #509	90.00
Relish, 10½" x 7", #115	37.50	Vase, 9", bud, #506	80.00
Relish, 11¾", tray, #115	45.00	Vase, 9½" x 3½", #506	110.00
Relish, 12", 4 pt., hdld., #111	40.00	Vase, 10" x 4¾", #5200	90.00
Relish, 12", 5 pt., hdld., #111	50.00	Vase, 10", #507	95.00
Salt and pepper pr., #30	30.00	Vase, 10, ftd., #111	115.00
Salt and pepper pr., #115	40.00	Vase, 10", ftd., #505	115.00
Sandwich tray, 12" x 5¼", ctr. handle,		Vase, 10", ftd., #506	115.00
#115	80.00	Vase, 10½" x 12 x 9½", #126	145.00
Saucer, #115	8.50	Vase, 10½", #126	135.00
Stem, 3¾", 1 oz., cordial, #5111½	60.00	Vase, 11" x 5¼", #505	145.00
Stem, 3¾", 4½ oz., oyster cocktail,		Vase, 11½ x 4½", #506	140.00
#5111½	22.50	Vase, 12", flared #115	145.00
Stem, 4", 5 oz., ice cream, #5111½	14.00	Vase, 12", ftd., #506	145.00
Stem, 4¼", 3 oz., cocktail, #115	22.50	Vase, 12", ftd., #507	145.00
Stem, 4½", 3½ oz., cocktail, #5111½	22.50		

A PAIR OF

Duncan

HURRICANES

*. . . a gift that looks like
a million dollars*

HURRICANE CANDELABRA with hand-cut
and polished imported prisms are breath-
taking . . . but with the lacy First Love
etching on the hurricane shade they
are irresistible.

These Hurricane Candelabra are made
by the makers of "the loveliest glassware in America." Many pieces of
Duncan glass are now collector's items
and are in antique shows.

If your department store or jewelry
or gift shops do not have the Duncan
First Love Hurricane Candelabra, they
will be glad to order them for you.
There is also a full line of stemware
and flatware and decorative pieces with
the same etching. Write for the First
Love folder.

The loveliest glassware in America

THE DUNCAN & MILLER GLASS COMPANY

WASHINGTON, PA.

FIRST LOVE

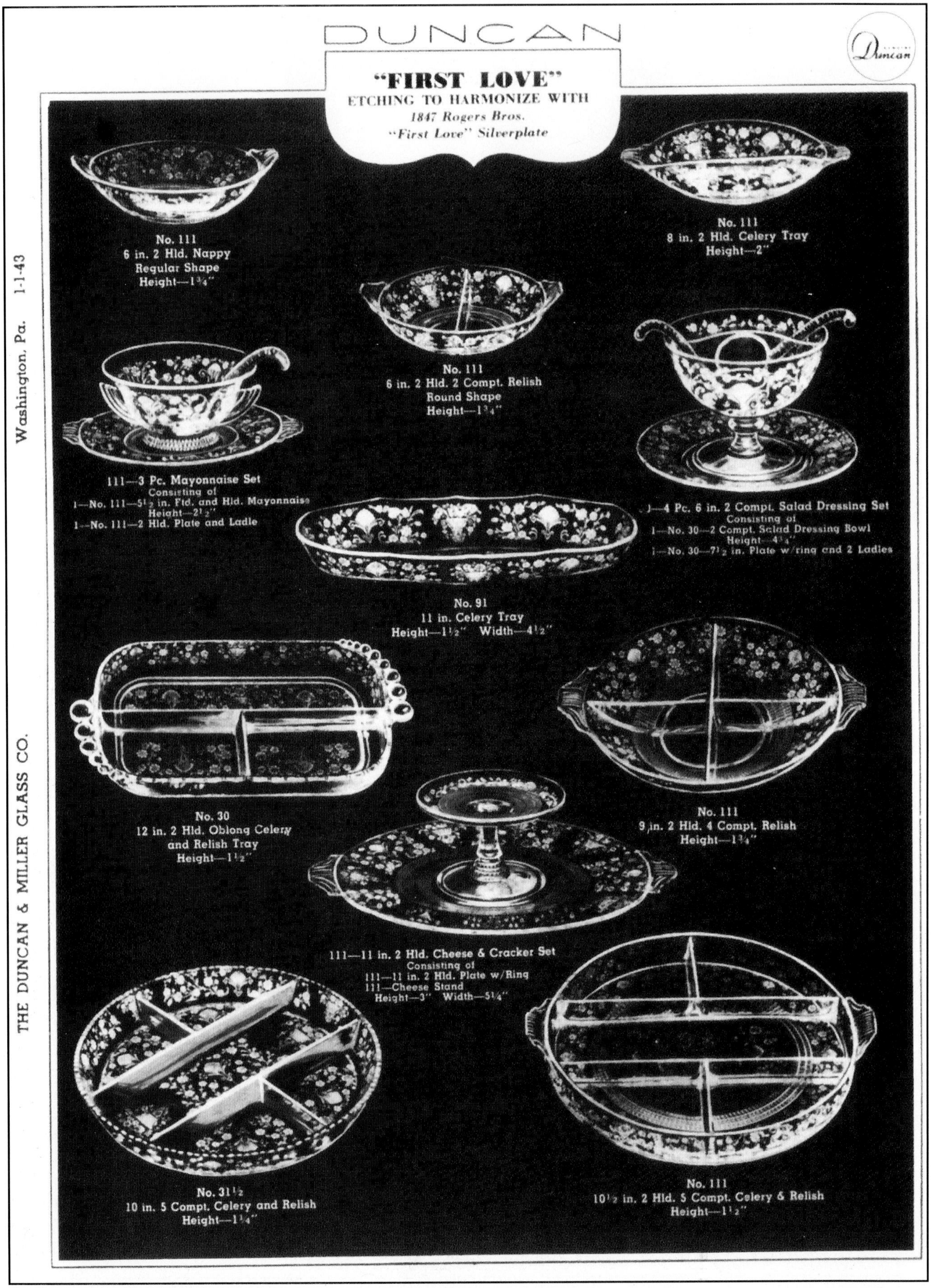

DUNCAN
Duncan
"FIRST LOVE"
ETCHING TO HARMONIZE WITH
1847 Rogers Bros.
"First Love" Silverplate
No. 111
6 in. 2 Hld. Nappy
Regular Shape
Height—1¾"
No. 111
8 in. 2 Hld. Celery Tray
Height—2"
No. 111
6 in. 2 Hld. 2 Compt. Relish
Round Shape
Height—1¾"
111—3 Pc. Mayonnaise Set
Consisting of
1—No. 111—5½ in. Ftd. and Hld. Mayonnaise
Height—2½"
1—No. 111—2 Hld. Plate and Ladle
—4 Pc. 6 in. 2 Compt. Salad Dressing Set
Consisting of
1—No. 30—2 Compt. Salad Dressing Bowl
Height—4¾"
No. 30—7½ in. Plate w/ring and 2 Ladles
No. 91
11 in. Celery Tray
Height—1½" Width—4½"
No. 30
12 in. 2 Hld. Oblong Celery
and Relish Tray
Height—1½"
No. 111
9 in. 2 Hld. 4 Compt. Relish
Height—1¾"
111—11 in. 2 Hld. Cheese & Cracker Set
Consisting of
111—11 in. 2 Hld. Plate w/Ring
111—Cheese Stand
Height—3" Width—5¼"
No. 31½
10 in. 5 Compt. Celery and Relish
Height—1¼"
No. 111
10½ in. 2 Hld. 5 Compt. Celery & Relish
Height—1½"
THE DUNCAN & MILLER GLASS CO.
Washington, Pa.
1-1-43

DUNCAN

"FIRST LOVE"
ETCHING TO HARMONIZE WITH
1847 Rogers Bros.
"First Love" Silverplate

Washington, Pa.   1-1-43

THE DUNCAN & MILLER GLASS CO.

No. 5111½
10 oz. Tall Goblet
Height—6¾"

No. 5111½
5 oz. Saucer Champagne
Height—5"

No. 5111½
3½ oz. Liquor Cocktail
Height—4½"

No. 5111½
3 oz. Wine
Height—5¼"

No. 5111½
4½ oz. Claret
Height—6"

No. 5111½
1 oz. Cordial
Height—3¾"

No. 5111½
12 oz. Ftd. Ice Tea
Height—6½"

No. 5111½
14 oz. Ftd. Ice Tea
Height—6¾"

No. 5111½
10 oz. Low Luncheon Goblet
Height—5¾"

No. 5111½
4½ oz. Oyster Cocktail
Height—3¾"

No. 5111½
5 oz. Ftd. Orange Juice
Height—5¼"

No. 5111½
5 oz. Ice Cream
Height—4"

No. 5200
1½ oz. Whiskey or Cordial
Tumbler, Sham
Height—2"

No. 5200
3½ oz. Cocktail Tumbler,
Sham
Height—3"

No. 5200
14 oz. Tumbler, Sham
Height—4¾"
Also made 12 oz. and 10 oz.

No. 5111½
Fingerbowl
Diameter—4¼"

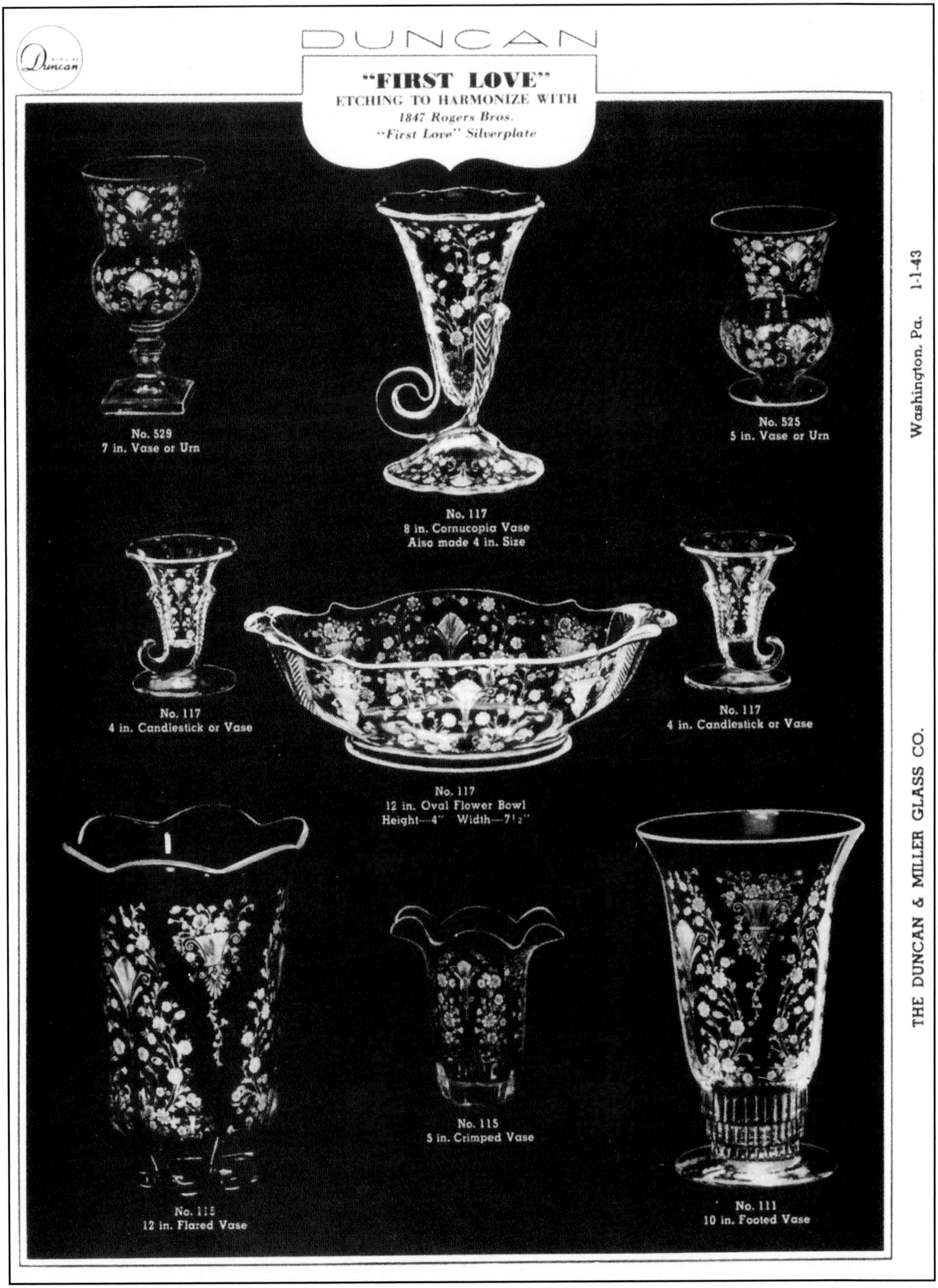

DUNCAN

"FIRST LOVE"
ETCHING TO HARMONIZE WITH
1847 Rogers Bros.
"First Love" Silverplate

No. 529
7 in. Vase or Urn

No. 117
8 in. Cornucopia Vase
Also made 4 in. Size

No. 525
5 in. Vase or Urn

No. 117
4 in. Candlestick or Vase

No. 117
4 in. Candlestick or Vase

No. 117
12 in. Oval Flower Bowl
Height—4" Width—7½"

No. 115
12 in. Flared Vase

No. 115
5 in. Crimped Vase

No. 111
10 in. Footed Vase

Washington, Pa. 1-1-43

THE DUNCAN & MILLER GLASS CO.

DUNCAN

"FIRST LOVE"
ETCHING TO HARMONIZE WITH
1847 Rogers Bros.
"First Love" Silverplate

No. 111
4 in. Low Candlestick

No. 111
4 in. Low Candlestick

No. 111
11 in. Flared Bowl
Height—3¾"   Width—11"

No. 30
2 Light Candlestick
Height—6"   Width—7"

No. 6
12 in. Flower Bowl, Flared
Height—3½"

No. 41
5 in. 2 Light Candlestick
Width—8½"

No. 126
14 in. Oval Bowl
Height—7½"   Width—6"

No. 30
2 Light Candelabrum
w prisms
Height—6"   Width—8"

No. 30
2 Light Candelabrum
w prisms
Height—6"   Width—8"

Washington, Pa. 1-1-43

THE DUNCAN & MILLER GLASS CO.

101

FLANDERS, Tiffin Glass Company, Mid 1910's – Mid 1930's

Colors: crystal, pink, yellow

Tiffin's Flanders is regularly confused with Cambridge's Gloria by collectors, particularly in yellow and crystal. Refer to Gloria to see the distinctive differences in the floral designs.

Stemware is normally found on Tiffin's #17024 blank. This line usually has a crystal foot and stem with tops of crystal, pink, or yellow. Other color combinations include green foot with pink stems, and pink tumblers as well as pitchers with crystal handle and foot. I have seen few pieces with green stems, but I would enjoy a set of that combination.

Shakers have remained the most elusive item in Flanders. I have only seen three pairs in pink, three single shakers in crystal, and none in yellow. I've had reports of yellow; I just have never seen them. New pieces continue to be found and the listings continue to grow! Collectors are quickly shelling out for each precious piece.

Round plates are line #8800 and each size plate has a different number. Scalloped plates are line #5831. Pitchers were sold both with and without a top. Remember that the pitcher cover is plain with no pattern etched on it. Do not buy a top without having your pitcher available to see if the top will fit. Many topless pitchers remain that way because a top was not originally designed to fit it.

Note the heavy foot on the console bowl in the top photo, while the rolled edge bowl at the bottom has little foot at all. A pink two-handled bouillon has been seen and a "Chinese type" hurricane lamp has been found in crystal. (See Fuchsia on page 105 for example.) You will also find these shades converted to electric lamps with three bulbs inside. Fuchsia and Flanders lamps will both be shown in my new *Very Rare Glassware of the Depression Years, Fifth Series.*

	Crystal	Pink	Yellow
Ash tray, 2¼x3¾" w/cigarette rest	40.00		
Bowl, 2 hdld., bouillon	40.00	125.00	75.00
Bowl, finger, w/liner	25.00	75.00	45.00
Bowl, 2 hdld., bonbon	20.00	50.00	35.00
Bowl, 11", ftd. console	35.00	85.00	60.00
Bowl, 12", flanged rim, console	35.00	85.00	60.00
Candlestick, 2 styles	30.00	65.00	40.00
Candy jar, w/cover, flat	125.00	325.00	225.00
Candy jar, w/cover, ftd.	90.00	225.00	165.00
Celery, 11"	25.00	65.00	45.00
Cheese & cracker	40.00	110.00	85.00
Comport, 3½"	25.00	65.00	35.00
Comport, 6"	50.00	125.00	85.00
Creamer, flat	40.00	125.00	80.00
Creamer, ftd.	35.00	110.00	65.00
Cup, 2 styles	48.00	85.00	55.00
Decanter	150.00	325.00	225.00
Electric lamp	300.00		

	Crystal	Pink	Yellow
Grapefruit, w/liner	50.00	125.00	75.00
Hurricane lamp, Chinese style	200.00		
Mayonnaise, w/liner	30.00	85.00	60.00
Nut cup, ftd., blown	30.00	65.00	55.00
Oil bottle & stopper	125.00	295.00	225.00
Parfait, 5⅜", hdld.	60.00	150.00	90.00
Pitcher & cover	200.00	350.00	275.00
Plate, 6"	4.00	12.00	9.00
Plate, 8"	9.00	15.00	12.50
Plate, 10¼", dinner	30.00	70.00	50.00
Relish, 3 pt.	25.00	65.00	45.00
Salt & pepper, pr.	150.00	300.00	250.00
Saucer	8.00	15.00	10.00
Stem, 4½", oyster cocktail	15.00	40.00	25.00
Stem, 4½", sherbet	10.00	28.00	17.50
Stem, 4¾", cocktail	15.00	40.00	30.00
Stem, 5", cordial	55.00	95.00	75.00
Stem, 5⅝", parfait	30.00	85.00	60.00
Stem, 6⅛", wine	28.00	70.00	40.00
Stem, 6¼", saucer champagne	15.00	35.00	20.00
Stem, claret	40.00	125.00	75.00
Stem, 8¼", water	15.00	45.00	27.50
Sugar, flat	40.00	120.00	75.00
Sugar, ftd.	35.00	110.00	60.00
Tumbler, 2¾", 2½ oz., ftd.	40.00	80.00	50.00
Tumbler, 4¾", 9 oz., ftd., water	14.00	40.00	22.00
Tumbler, 4¾", 10 oz., ftd.	17.00	45.00	28.00
Tumbler, 5⅞", 12 oz., ftd., tea	22.00	50.00	30.00
Vase, bud	30.00	75.00	45.00
Vase, ftd.	85.00	225.00	145.00
Vase, Dahlia style	125.00	250.00	185.00
Vase, fan	85.00	195.00	125.00

FUCHSIA, Tiffin Glass Company, Late 1937 – 1940

Colors: crystal

There are over twenty new listings for Fuchsia including a flat pitcher, lamp, and bitters bottle. The bitters bottle is in the top row and the pitcher on the bottom. That Chinese hurricane shade pictured on the bottom has been found surrounding three electric bulbs, making a lamp. It can be seen in *Very Rare Glassware of the Depression Years, Fifth Series*.

There are several serious collectors vying for the best Fuchsia set obtainable. Because of this, dealers will search every nook and cranny to keep supplying their collections. That may be the reason that so many new pieces are being discovered in Fuchsia.

There are now three known stemware lines for Fuchsia, but #15083 is the most often found. The first item in the middle row is a three-footed whipped cream bowl. Most companies listed this bowl style as a mayonnaise. The cup and saucer are pictured in the same row. I traded with a collector to obtain this set; and as with my Caribbean cordial, that collector is now trying to talk me out of it. Sometimes money can't buy what you want, but trades for items can oft times be worked out if you can find something that is needed by the other collector!

	Crystal		Crystal
Ash tray, 2¼" x 3¾" w/cigarette rest	30.00	Plate, 9½", dinner, #5902	55.00
Bell, 5", #15083	75.00	Plate, 10½", 2 hdld., cake, #5831	55.00
Bitters bottle	300.00	Plate, 10½", muffin tray, pearl edge	55.00
Bowl, 4", finger, ftd., #041	50.00	Plate, 13", lily roled and crimped edge	65.00
Bowl, 4½" finger, w/#8814 liner	65.00	Plate, 14¼", sandwich, #8833	45.00
Bowl, 5³⁄₁₆", 2 hdld., #5831	27.50	Relish, 6⅜", 3 pt., #5902	25.00
Bowl, 6¼", cream soup, ftd., #5831	50.00	Relish, 9¼", square, 3 pt.	40.00
Bowl, 7¼", salad, #5902	40.00	Relish, 10½" x 12½", hdld., 3 pt., #5902	60.00
Bowl, 8⅜", 2 hdld., #5831	55.00	Relish, 10½" x 12½", hdld., 5 pt.	70.00
Bowl, 9¾", deep salad	70.00	Salt and pepper, pr., #2	100.00
Bowl, 10", salad	65.00	Saucer, #5831	15.00
Bowl, 10½", console, fan shaped sides, #319	65.00	Stem, 4¹⁄₁₆", cordial, #15083	32.50
Bowl, 11⅞", console, flared, 5902	80.00	Stem, 4⅛", sherbet, #15083	12.00
Bowl, 12", flanged rim, console #5831	60.00	Stem, 4¼", cocktail, #15083	18.00
Bowl, 12⅝", console, flared, #5902	90.00	Stem, 4⅝", 3½ oz., cocktail, #17453	37.50
Bowl, 13", crimped #5902	75.00	Stem, 4⅞", saucer champagne, hollow stem	75.00
Candlestick, 2-lite, w/pointed center, #5831	75.00	Stem, 5¹⁄₁₆", wine, #15083	30.00
Candlestick, 2-lite, tapered center, #15306	75.00	Stem, 5¼", claret, #15083	35.00
Candlestick, 5", 2-lite, ball center	75.00	Stem, 5⅜", cocktail, "S" stem, #17457	45.00
Candlestick, 5⅝, 2-lite, w/fan center, #5902	75.00	Stem, 5⅜", cordial, "S" stem, #17457	100.00
Candlestick, single, #348	35.00	Stem, 5⅜", 7 oz., saucer champagne, #17453	30.00
Celery, 10", oval, #5831	35.00	Stem, 5⅜", saucer champagne, #15083	15.00
Celery, 10½", rectangular, #5902	37.50	Stem, 5⅝", saucer champagne, "S" stem, #17457	35.00
Cigarette box, w/lid, 4" x 2¾", #9305	100.00	Stem, 5¹⁵⁄₁₆", parfait, #15083	35.00
Cocktail shaker, 8", w/metal top	225.00	Stem, 6¼", low water, #15083	25.00
Comport, 6¼", #5831	30.00	Stem, 7⅜", 9 oz., water, #17453	40.00
Comport, 6½", w/beaded stem, #15082	35.00	Stem, 7½", water, high, #15083	25.00
Creamer, 2⅞", individual, #5831	40.00	Stem, 7⅝", water, "S" stem, #17457	55.00
Creamer, 3⅜", flat w/beaded handle, #5902	27.50	Sugar, 2⅞", individual, #5831	40.00
Creamer, 4½", ftd., #5831	22.50	Sugar, 3⅜", flat, w/beaded handle, #5902	27.50
Cup, #5831	75.00	Sugar, 4½", ftd., #5831	22.50
Electric lamp	300.00	Tray, sugar/creamer	45.00
Hurricane, 12", Chinese style	200.00	Tray, 9½", 2 hdld. for cream/sugar	45.00
Icer, with insert	135.00	Tumbler, 2⁷⁄₁₆", 2 oz., bar, flat, #506	60.00
Mayonnaise, flat, w/6¼" liner #5902 w/ladle	45.00	Tumbler, 3⁵⁄₁₆", oyster cocktail, #14196	14.00
Mayonnaise, ftd., w/ladle, #5831	45.00	Tumbler, 3⅜", old-fashioned, flat, #580	40.00
Nut dish, 6¼"	35.00	Tumbler, 4¹³⁄₁₆", flat, juice	25.00
Pickle, 7⅜", #5831	40.00	Tumbler, 4⁵⁄₁₆", 5 oz., ftd., juice, #15083	18.00
Pitcher & cover, #194	350.00	Tumbler, 5⅛", water, flat, #517	27.50
Plate, 6¼", bread and butter, #5902	8.00	Tumbler, 5⁵⁄₁₆", 9 oz., ftd., water, #15083	15.00
Plate, 6¼", sherbet, #8814	10.00	Tumbler, 6⁵⁄₁₆", 12 oz., ftd., tea, #15083	30.00
Plate, 6⅜", 2 hdld., #5831	12.50	Vase, 6½", bud, #14185	30.00
Plate, 7", marmalade, 3-ftd., #310½	25.00	Vase, 8³⁄₁₆", flared, crimped	85.00
Plate, 7⅞", clam soup or mayo liner, #5831	12.50	Vase, 8¼", bud, #14185	35.00
Plate, 7⅞", salad, #8814	15.00	Vase, 10½", bud, #14185	45.00
Plate, 7½", salad, #5831	15.00	Vase, 10¾", bulbous bottom, #5872	160.00
Plate, 8¼", luncheon, #5902	17.50	Vase, 10⅞", beaded stem, #15082	75.00
Plate, 8⅛", luncheon, #8833	22.50	Vase, 11¾", urn, 2 hdld., trophy	105.00
Plate, 8⅜", bonbon, pearl edge	25.00	Whipped cream, 3-ftd., #310	40.00

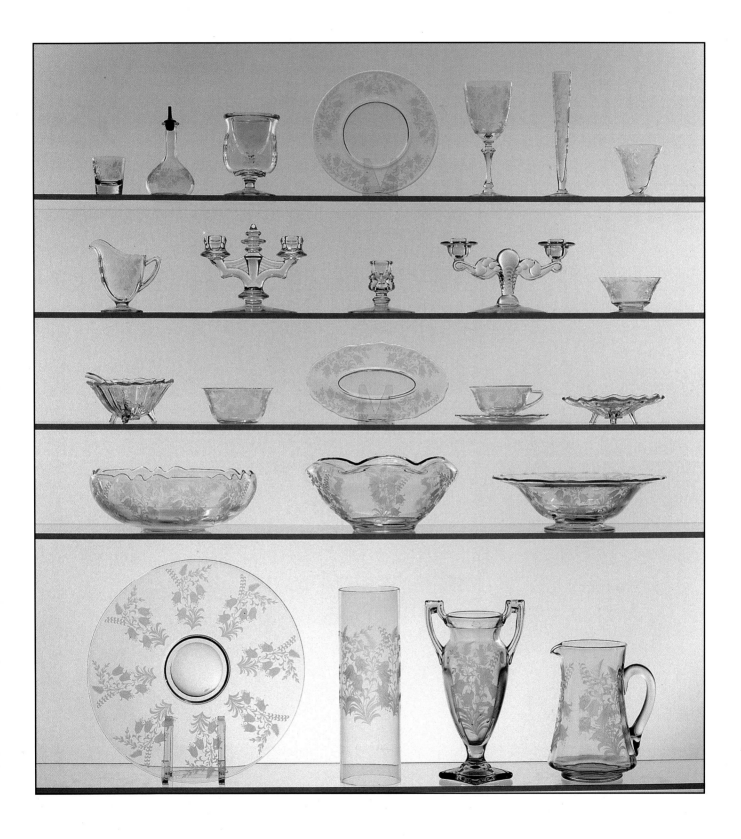

GAZEBO, Paden City Glass Company, 1930's

Colors: black, blue, crystal, yellow

Gazebo and another pattern, Utopia, are two very similar Paden City designs made about the same time. Collectors have rarely paid any attention to the differences; but I wish to point out that there are some minute variances. Utopia was the first pattern and Gazebo was its progeny. The etchings on Utopia are larger and fuller than Gazebo. Who cares? You probably will not find enough pieces to bother your sensibilities toward matching pieces.

Cathy started gathering a few pieces of this pattern years ago, and we have accumulated enough representative examples to now include it in this book. As with all Paden City patterns, there is never enough to satisfy collectors; but there is enough available to whet your appetite. In our travels, we found few people knew what the pattern was; but all the pieces were priced at least $45.00!

Several different blanks seem to have been used for this etching, but I have not found any catalog listings yet. All measurements are taken from actual pieces. Other pieces listed, but not shown, were found after photography. There may be a tidbit since the 13" plate has a hole drilled in the center.

The cheese dish we owned was blue, but was sold before Cathy decided to keep the pattern. All pieces may not be found in color! You are sure find other items; so please keep me informed.

	Crystal	All Colors		Crystal	All Colors
Bowl, 9", fan handles	45.00	65.00	Mayonnaise, bead handles	25.00	
Bowl, 9", bead handles	45.00	65.00	Plate, 10¾"	45.00	65.00
Bowl, 13", flat edge	55.00	75.00	Plate, 12½", bead handles	55.00	75.00
Bowl, 14", low flat	55.00	75.00	Plate, 13" fan handles	50.00	70.00
Candlestick, 5¼"	45.00	65.00	Plate, 16", beaded edge		85.00
Candy w/lid, 10¼", small	65.00	95.00	Relish, 9¾", three part	35.00	55.00
Candy w/lid, 11", large	85.00		Server, 10", swan handle	50.00	
Cheese dish and cover	85.00	145.00	Server, 11", center handle	40.00	65.00
Cocktail shaker, w/glass stopper	85.00		Sugar	22.50	
Creamer	22.50		Vase, 10¼"	75.00	125.00*
Mayonnaise liner	15.00				

*Black $150.00

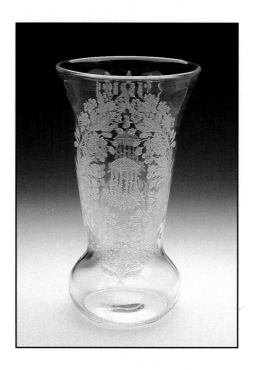

GLORIA, Etching 1746, Cambridge Glass 3400 Line Dinnerware, Introduced 1930

Colors: crystal, yellow, Peach-Blo, green, Emerald green, amber, blue, Heatherbloom

Gloria is most often confused with Tiffin's Flanders. Look closely at these two patterns and notice that the flower on Gloria bends the stem. They are easily distinguished once you see them side by side.

Yellow or crystal sets can be assembled with work and patience, but any other color will take more than patience. Actually, there is more yellow available than crystal; so if you like that color, this would be a set to consider. Gold decorated items fetch about 20% to 25% more than those without. However, worn gold pieces are difficult to sell at that premium price.

Note the amber footed stem in the top picture. There is a minute amount of this combination available. Personally, I like that combination better than just yellow or amber. For those who are wondering, Peach-Blo is a Cambridge term for pink!

The bottom photograph shows a few pieces of Heatherbloom and blue. These will cost up to 80% more than the prices listed for other colors. I have not been able to find a saucer for my blue or Heatherbloom cups pictured. I seem to have trouble with Heatherbloom saucers in other patterns, too. Additionally, I have shown the Heatherbloom creamer as a pattern shot on page 110. The single shot may show that color better than in a grouping. Color separations at the printers sometimes disguise color to some extent.

The pitchers shown atop page 111 are all rarely seen. The amber one is a Doulton style and is usually found in color without an etching! This pattern is attractive in the dark Emerald green; alas, very little of that color is found.

	Crystal	Green, Pink/Yellow		Crystal	Green, Pink/Yellow
Basket, 6", 2 hdld. (sides up)	20.00	35.00	Comport, 5", 4 ftd.	17.00	37.50
Bowl, 3", indiv. nut, 4 ftd.	50.00	70.00	Comport, 6", 4 ftd.	20.00	40.00
Bowl, 3½", cranberry	25.00	55.00	Comport, 7", low	30.00	55.00
Bowl, 5", ftd., crimped edge, bonbon	20.00	34.00	Comport, 7", tall	35.00	75.00
Bowl, 5", sq. fruit, "saucer"	15.00	25.00	Comport, 9½", tall, 2 hdld., ftd. bowl	65.00	140.00
Bowl, 5½", bonbon, 2 hdld.	20.00	32.00	Creamer, ftd.	12.00	20.00
Bowl, 5½", bonbon, ftd.	15.00	28.00	Creamer, tall, ftd.	13.00	22.00
Bowl, 5½", flattened, ftd., bonbon	15.00	28.00	Cup, rnd. or sq.	15.00	27.00
Bowl, 5½", fruit, "saucer"	15.00	25.00	Cup, 4 ftd., sq.	25.00	65.00
Bowl, 6", rnd., cereal	18.00	32.00	Cup, after dinner (demitasse), rnd.		
Bowl, 6", sq., cereal	16.00	30.00	or sq.	65.00	110.00
Bowl, 8", 2 pt., 2 hdld., relish	20.00	32.00	Fruit cocktail, 6 oz., ftd. (3 styles)	9.00	17.50
Bowl, 8", 3 pt., 3 hdld., relish	22.50	38.00	Ice pail, metal handle w/tongs	45.00	85.00
Bowl, 8¾", 2 hdld., figure "8" pickle	17.50	35.00	Icer, w/insert	60.00	90.00
Bowl, 8¾", 2 pt., 2 hdld., figure "8"			Mayonnaise, w/liner & ladle,		
relish	20.00	35.00	(4 ftd. bowl)	35.00	65.00
Bowl, 9", salad, tab hdld.	35.00	65.00	Oil, w/stopper; tall, ftd., hdld.	90.00	175.00
Bowl, 9½", 2 hdld., veg.	55.00	90.00	Oyster cocktail, #3035, 4½ oz.	12.00	20.00
Bowl, 10", oblong, tab hdld., "baker"	37.50	70.00	Oyster cocktail, 4½ oz., low stem	12.00	20.00
Bowl, 10", 2 hdld.	35.00	70.00	Pitcher, 67 oz., middle indent	150.00	275.00
Bowl, 11", 2 hdld., fruit	35.00	70.00	Pitcher, 80 oz., ball	160.00	260.00
Bowl, 12", 4 ftd., console	35.00	65.00	Pitcher, w/cover, 64 oz.	175.00	310.00
Bowl, 12", 4 ftd., flared rim	35.00	65.00	Plate, 6", 2 hdld.	9.00	15.00
Bowl, 12", 4 ftd., oval	35.00	75.00	Plate, 6", bread/butter	6.00	9.00
Bowl, 12", 5 pt., celery & relish	35.00	55.00	Plate, 7½", tea	8.00	12.00
Bowl, 13", flared rim	35.00	65.00	Plate, 8½"	9.00	15.00
Bowl, cream soup, w/rnd. liner	22.00	40.00	Plate, 9½", dinner	55.00	80.00
Bowl, cream soup, w/sq. saucer	22.00	40.00	Plate, 10", tab hdld. salad	18.00	35.00
Bowl, finger, flared edge, w/rnd. plate	27.00	38.00	Plate, 11", 2 hdld.	20.00	40.00
Bowl, finger, ftd.	20.00	30.00	Plate, 11", sq., ftd. cake	85.00	235.00
Bowl, finger, w/rnd. plate	27.00	38.00	Plate, 11½", tab hdld., sandwich	17.50	40.00
Butter, w/cover, 2 hdld.	125.00	295.00	Plate, 14", chop or salad	40.00	75.00
Candlestick, 6", ea.	20.00	35.00	Plate, sq., bread/butter	6.00	9.00
Candy box, w/cover, 4 ftd. w/tab hdld.	70.00	120.00	Plate, sq., dinner	60.00	85.00
Cheese compote w/11½" cracker plate,			Plate, sq., salad	7.00	12.00
tab hdld.	35.00	65.00	Plate, sq., service	22.00	45.00
Cocktail shaker, grnd. stopper, spout			Platter, 11½"	55.00	115.00
(like pitcher)	110.00	210.00	Salt & pepper, pr., short	40.00	75.00
Comport, 4", fruit cocktail	13.00	26.00	Salt & pepper, pr., w/glass top, tall	42.00	125.00

GLORIA

	Crystal	Green Pink/Yellow		Crystal	Green Pink/Yellow
Salt & pepper, ftd., metal tops..............	50.00	125.00	Tray, 4 pt., ctr. hdld., relish...................	30.00	45.00
Saucer, rnd...	2.00	4.00	Tray, 9", pickle, tab hdld.	16.00	35.00
Saucer, rnd. after dinner	8.00	15.00	Tumbler, #3035, 5 oz., high ftd.	11.00	20.00
Saucer, sq., after dinner (demitasse)....	10.00	17.00	Tumbler, #3035, 10 oz., high ftd.	12.00	22.00
Saucer, sq...	2.00	3.00	Tumbler, #3035, 12 oz., high ftd.	17.00	30.00
Stem, #3035, 2½ oz., wine	20.00	40.00	Tumbler, #3115, 5 oz., ftd., juice	12.00	20.00
Stem, #3035, 3 oz., cocktail	17.50	28.00	Tumbler, #3115, 8 oz., ftd.	12.00	20.00
Stem, #3035, 3½ oz., cocktail..............	17.00	27.00	Tumbler, #3115, 10 oz., ftd.	13.00	21.00
Stem, #3035, 4½ oz., claret	30.00	55.00	Tumbler, #3115, 12 oz., ftd.	17.00	30.00
Stem, #3035, 6 oz., low sherbet	11.00	16.00	Tumbler, #3120, 2½ oz., ftd. (used		
Stem, #3035, 6 oz., tall sherbet	12.50	18.00	w/cocktail shaker)	25.00	45.00
Stem, #3035, 9 oz., water	15.00	30.00	Tumbler, #3120, 5 oz., ftd.	12.00	20.00
Stem, #3035, 3½ oz., cocktail..............	17.00	30.00	Tumbler, #3120, 10 oz., ftd.	12.00	20.00
Stem, #3115, 9 oz., goblet	15.00	30.00	Tumbler, #3120, 12 oz., ftd.	17.00	30.00
Stem, #3120, 1 oz., cordial..................	60.00	135.00	Tumbler, #3120, 2½ oz., ftd. (used		
Stem, #3120, 4½ oz., claret	30.00	55.00	w/shaker)	25.00	45.00
Stem, #3120, 6 oz., low sherbet	10.00	15.00	Tumbler, #3130, 5 oz., ftd.	12.00	20.00
Stem, #3120, 6 oz., tall sherbet............	11.00	16.00	Tumbler, #3130, 10 oz., ftd.	13.00	20.00
Stem, #3120, 9 oz., water	15.00	25.00	Tumbler, #3130, 12 oz., ftd.	15.00	25.00
Stem, #3130, 2½ oz., wine	20.00	42.50	Tumbler, #3135, 5 oz., juice	12.00	20.00
Stem, #3130, 6 oz., low sherbet	10.00	15.00	Tumbler, #3135, 10 oz., water..............	12.00	20.00
Stem, #3130, 6 oz., tall sherbet............	11.00	16.00	Tumbler, #3135, 12 oz., tea	17.00	30.00
Stem, #3130, 8 oz., water	18.00	30.00	Tumbler, 12 oz., flat, (2 styles), one		
Stem, #3135, 1 oz., cordial..................	65.00	145.00	indent side to match 67 oz. pitcher.	18.00	35.00
Stem, #3135, 6 oz., low sherbet	11.00	15.00	Vase, 9", oval, 4 indent.........................	85.00	165.00
Stem, #3135, 6 oz., tall sherbet............	12.00	16.00	Vase, 10", keyhole base	60.00	120.00
Stem, #3135, 8 oz., water	18.00	30.00	Vase, 10", squarish top	75.00	165.00
Sugar, ftd...	11.00	18.00	Vase, 11"...	55.00	110.00
Sugar, tall, ftd.	11.00	20.00	Vase, 11", neck indent	75.00	135.00
Sugar shaker, w/glass top.....................	165.00	295.00	Vase, 12", keyhole base, flared rim	60.00	125.00
Syrup, tall, ftd..	65.00	115.00	Vase, 12", squarish top	60.00	130.00
Tray, 11", ctr. hdld., sandwich	20.00	37.50	Vase, 14", keyhole base, flared rim	75.00	165.00
Tray, 2 pt., ctr. hdld., relish.................	25.00	37.50			

Note: See Pages 228-229 for stem identification.

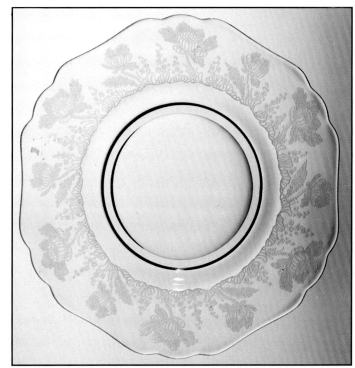

GREEK KEY, A.H. Heisey & Co.

Colors: crystal; "Flamingo" pink punch bowl and cups only

Note the many price increases in Greek Key due to heavy collector demand!

	Crystal		Crystal
Bowl, finger	20.00	Pitcher, 1 pint (jug)	90.00
Bowl, jelly, w/cover, 2 hdld. ftd	145.00	Pitcher, 1 quart (jug)	150.00
Bowl, indiv., ftd., almond	30.00	Pitcher, 3 pint (jug)	180.00
Bowl, 4", nappy	20.00	Pitcher, ½ gal. (tankard)	220.00
Bowl, 4", shallow, low ft., jelly	25.00	Oil bottle, 2 oz., squat, w/#8 stopper	100.00
Bowl, 4½", nappy	20.00	Oil bottle, 2 oz., w/#6 stopper	110.00
Bowl, 4½", scalloped, nappy	20.00	Oil bottle, 4 oz., squat, w/#8 stopper	80.00
Bowl, 4½", shallow, low ft., jelly	25.00	Oil bottle, 4 oz., w/#6 stopper	80.00
Bowl, 5", ftd., almond	35.00	Oil bottle, 6 oz., w/#6 stopper	100.00
Bowl, 5", ftd., almond, w/cover	90.00	Oil bottle, 6 oz., squat, w/#8 stopper	100.00
Bowl, 5", hdld., jelly	75.00	Plate, 4½"	20.00
Bowl, 5", low ft., jelly, w/cover	100.00	Plate, 5"	25.00
Bowl, 5", nappy	24.00	Plate, 5½"	25.00
Bowl, 5½", nappy	35.00	Plate, 6"	30.00
Bowl, 5½", shallow nappy, ftd.	60.00	Plate, 6½"	30.00
Bowl, 6", nappy	25.00	Plate, 7"	45.00
Bowl, 6", shallow nappy	27.50	Plate, 8"	60.00
Bowl, 6½", nappy	30.00	Plate, 9"	70.00
Bowl, 7", low ft., straight side	90.00	Plate, 10"	80.00
Bowl, 7", nappy	80.00	Plate, 16", orange bowl liner	140.00
Bowl, 8", low ft., straight side	70.00	Puff box, #1, w/cover	85.00
Bowl, 8", nappy	70.00	Puff box, #3, w/cover	95.00
Bowl, 8", scalloped nappy	65.00	Salt & pepper, pr.	75.00
Bowl, 8", shallow, low ft.	75.00	Sherbet, 4½ oz., ftd., straight rim	20.00
Bowl, 8½", shallow nappy	75.00	Sherbet, 4½ oz., ftd., flared rim	20.00
Bowl, 9", flat banana split	30.00	Sherbet, 4½ oz., high ft., shallow	20.00
Bowl, 9", ftd. banana split	40.00	Sherbet, 4½ oz., ftd., shallow	20.00
Bowl, 9", low ft., straight side	65.00	Sherbet, 4½ oz., ftd., cupped rim	20.00
Bowl, 9", nappy	60.00	Sherbet, 6 oz., low ft.	15.00
Bowl, 9", shallow, low ft.	60.00	Spooner, lg.	75.00
Bowl, 9½", shallow nappy	60.00	Spooner, 4½", (or straw jar)	75.00
Bowl, 10", shallow, low ft.	85.00	Stem, ¾ oz., cordial	250.00
Bowl, 11", shallow nappy	60.00	Stem, 2 oz., wine	110.00
Bowl, 12", orange bowl	150.00	Stem, 2 oz., sherry	200.00
Bowl, 12", punch, ftd.	200.00	Stem, 3 oz., cocktail	50.00
(Flamingo)	750.00	Stem, 3½ oz., burgundy	125.00
Bowl, 12", orange, flared rim	115.00	Stem, 4½ oz., saucer champagne	40.00
Bowl, 14½", orange, flared rim	220.00	Stem, 4½ oz., claret	170.00
Bowl, 15", punch, ftd.	225.00	Stem, 7 oz.	95.00
Bowl, 18", punch, shallow	225.00	Stem, 9 oz.	125.00
Butter, indiv. (plate)	35.00	Stem, 9 oz., low ft.	110.00
Butter/jelly, 2 hdld., w/cover	180.00	Straw jar, w/cover	300.00
Candy, w/cover, ½ lb.	135.00	Sugar	40.00
Candy, w/cover, 1 lb.	140.00	Sugar, oval, hotel	45.00
Candy, w/cover, 2 lb.	195.00	Sugar, rnd., hotel	40.00
Cheese & cracker set, 10"	100.00	Sugar & creamer, oval, individual	90.00
Compote, 5"	60.00	Tray, 9", oval celery	45.00
Compote, 5", w/cover	90.00	Tray, 12", oval celery	50.00
Creamer	40.00	Tray, 12½", French roll	120.00
Creamer, oval, hotel	45.00	Tray, 13", oblong	200.00
Creamer, rnd., hotel	40.00	Tray, 15", oblong	160.00
Cup, 4½ oz., punch	20.00	Tumbler, 2½ oz., (or toothpick)	300.00
Cup, punch, (Flamingo)	45.00	Tumbler, 5 oz., flared rim	40.00
Coaster	12.00	Tumbler, 5 oz., straight side	40.00
Egg cup, 5 oz.	70.00	Tumbler, 5½ oz., water	40.00
Hair receiver	125.00	Tumbler, 7 oz., flared rim	55.00
Ice tub, lg., tab hdld.	140.00	Tumbler, 7 oz., straight side	50.00
Ice tub, sm., tab hdld.	120.00	Tumbler, 8 oz., w/straight, flared, cupped,	
Ice tub, w/cover, hotel	190.00	shallow	50.00
Ice tub, w/cover, 5", individual w/5" plate	120.00	Tumbler, 10 oz., flared rim	80.00
Jar, 1 qt., crushed fruit, w/cover	300.00	Tumbler, 10 oz., straight wide	80.00
Jar, 2 qt., crushed fruit, w/cover	325.00	Tumbler, 12 oz., flared rim	90.00
Jar, lg. cover, horseradish	120.00	Tumbler, 12 oz., straight side	90.00
Jar, sm. cover, horseradish	110.00	Tumbler, 13 oz., straight side	95.00
Jar, tall celery	80.00	Tumbler, 13 oz., flared rim	95.00
Jar, w/knob cover, pickle	140.00	Water bottle	185.00

HERMITAGE, #2449, Fostoria Glass Company, 1932 – 1945

Colors: Amber, Azure (blue), crystal, Ebony, green, Topaz, Wisteria

My listings are from a Fostoria catalog that had January 1, 1933, entered on the front page in pencil. If you find a piece in a color not listed, please let me know. Not all pieces were made in all colors according to this catalog. If there is no price listed, it means that no piece is supposed to have been made. If you have such an item, please let me know!

	Crystal	amber/green/Topaz	Azure/Wisteria
Ash tray holder, #2449	5.00	8.00	12.00
*Ash tray, #2449	3.00	5.00	8.00
Bottle, 3 oz., oil, #2449	17.50	35.00	
Bottle, 27 oz., bar w/stopper, #2449	45.00		
Bowl, 4½", finger, #2449½	4.00	6.00	10.00
Bowl, 5", fruit, #2449½	5.00	8.00	12.00
Bowl, 6", cereal, #2449½	6.00	10.00	16.00
Bowl, 6½", salad, #2449½	6.00	9.00	14.00
Bowl, 7", soup, #2449½	8.00	12.00	20.00
Bowl, 7½", salad, #2449½	8.00	12.00	20.00
Bowl, 8", deep, ped., ft., #2449	17.50	32.00	50.00
Bowl, 10", ftd., #2449	20.00	35.00	
Bowl, grapefruit w/crystal liner #2449	20.00	35.00	
Candle, 6", #2449	12.50	22.00	35.00
Coaster, 5⅝", #2449	5.00	7.50	11.00
Comport, 6", #2449	12.00	17.50	27.50
Creamer, ftd., #2449	4.00	6.00	10.00
Cup, ftd.,#2449	6.00	10.00	15.00
Decanter, 28 oz., w/stopper, #2449	35.00	50.00	75.00
Fruit cocktail, 2⅜", 5 oz., ftd., #2449	5.00	7.50	12.00
Ice tub, 6", #2449	17.50	35.00	50.00
Icer, #2449	10.00	18.00	30.00
Mayonnaise, 5⅝" w/7" plate, #2449	20.00	35.00	
Mug, 9 oz., ftd., #2449	12.50		
Mug, 12 oz., ftd., #2449	15.00		
Mustard w/cover & spoon, #2449	17.50	35.00	
Pitcher, pint, #2449	22.50	40.00	60.00
Pitcher, 3 pint, #2449	30.00	60.00	110.00
Plate, 6", #2449½	3.00	5.00	8.00
Plate, 7" ice dish liner	4.00	6.00	10.00
Plate, 7", #2449½	4.00	6.00	10.00
Plate, 7⅜", crescent salad, #2449	10.00	17.50	30.00
Plate, 8", #2449½	6.00	10.00	15.00
Plate, 9", #2449½	12.50	20.00	30.00
Plate, 12", sandwich, #2449		12.50	20.00
Relish, 6", 2 pt., #2449	6.00	10.00	15.00
Relish, 7¼", 3 pt., #2449	8.00	11.00	17.50
Relish, 8", pickle, #2449	8.00	11.00	17.50
Relish, 11", celery, #2449	10.00	15.00	25.00
Salt & pepper, 3⅜", #2449	20.00	35.00	60.00
Salt, indiv., #2449	4.00	6.00	10.00
Saucer, #2449	2.00	3.50	5.00
Sherbet, 3", 7 oz., low, ftd., #2449	6.00	8.00	12.50
Stem, 3¼", 5½ oz., high sherbet, #2449	8.00	11.00	17.50
Stem, 4⅝", 4 oz., claret, #2449	10.00	15.00	
Stem, 5¼", 9 oz., water goblet, #2449	10.00	15.00	25.00
Sugar, ftd., #2449	4.00	6.00	10.00
Tray, 6½", condiment, #2449	6.00	12.00	20.00
Tumbler, 2½", 2 oz., #2449½	4.00	6.00	12.00
Tumbler, 2½", 2 oz., ftd., #2449	5.00	8.00	
Tumbler, 3", 4 oz., cocktail, ftd., #2449	5.00	7.50	12.00
Tumbler, 3¼", 6 oz. old-fashioned, #2449½	6.00	10.00	17.00
Tumbler, 3⅞", 5 oz., #2449½	5.00	8.00	12.00
Tumbler, 4", 5 oz., ftd., #2449	5.00	8.00	12.00
Tumbler, 4⅛", 9 oz., ftd., #2449	6.00	10.00	15.00
Tumbler, 4¾", 9 oz., #2449½	6.00	10.00	15.00
Tumbler, 5¼", 12 oz., ftd., iced tea, #2449	10.00	16.00	28.00
Tumbler, 5⅞", 13 oz., #2449½	10.00	16.00	28.00
Vase, 6", ftd.	22.00	32.50	

* Ebony - $10.00

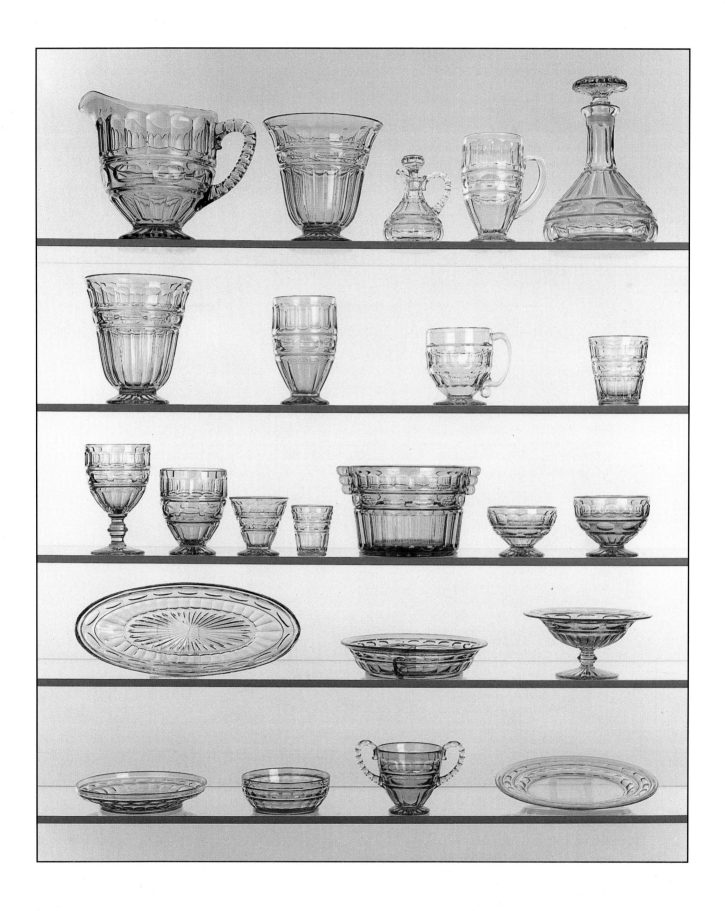

IMPERIAL HUNT SCENE, #718, Cambridge Glass Company, Late 1920's – 1930's

Colors: amber, black, crystal, Emerald green, green, pink, Willow blue

A pink Imperial Hunt Scene luncheon set turned up in an antique mall in Ohio. Since cups, saucers, creamers, sugars, and shakers are not easily found, this made the set even more interesting. Hunt Scene, as it is usually referred to, reminds me of most Tiffin patterns because stems are abundant. Serving pieces are rare. You will find bi-colored Hunt Scene stemware. Pink bowl with a green stem is the norm. This is another Cambridge pattern that is found with gold decorated ware. Be wary of worn gold; it is not very desirable!

I have asked for years if anyone has ever seen an Imperial Hunt Scene cup and have always received the answer that they are pictured in the catalog, so they must exist. A crystal #1402 Tally-Ho cup is now pictured; has anyone seen some crystal Tally-Ho saucers with Imperial Hunt Scene etching? You can also see a pink cup and saucer in my *Very Rare Glassware of the Depression Years, Fifth Series.*

Black and dark Emerald green sells 25% to 50% higher than prices listed.

	Crystal	Colors
Bowl, 6", cereal	15.00	28.00
Bowl, 8"	35.00	70.00
Bowl, 8½", 3 pt.	25.00	65.00
Candlestick, 2-lite, keyhole.	17.50	37.50
Candlestick, 3-lite, keyhole.	27.50	65.00
Comport, 5½", #3085		40.00
Creamer, flat	12.00	30.00
Creamer, ftd.	15.00	30.00
Cup	45.00	55.00
Decanter		235.00
Finger bowl, w/plate, #3085		40.00
Humidor, tobacco		375.00
Ice bucket	50.00	85.00
Ice tub.	40.00	75.00
Mayonnaise, w/liner.	30.00	50.00
Pitcher, w/cover, 63 oz., #3085.		295.00
Pitcher, w/cover, 76 oz., #711.	150.00	275.00
Plate, 8".	12.00	22.00
Salt & pepper, pr.	50.00	150.00
Saucer	10.00	15.00
Stem, 1 oz., cordial, #1402	60.00	
Stem, 2½ oz., wine, #1402.	45.00	
Stem, 3 oz., cocktail, #1402.	40.00	
Stem, 6 oz., tomato, #1402.	40.00	
Stem, 6½ oz., sherbet, #1402.	35.00	
Stem, 7½ oz., sherbet, #1402.	40.00	
Stem, 10 oz., water, #1402.	40.00	
Stem, 14 oz., #1402.	50.00	
Stem, 18 oz., #1402.	60.00	
Stem, 1 oz., cordial, #3085		175.00
Stem, 2½ oz., cocktail, #3085.		40.00
Stem, 2½ oz., wine, #3085		55.00
Stem, 4½ oz., claret, #3085		67.50
Stem, 5½ oz., parfait, #3085		60.00
Stem, 6 oz., low sherbet, #3085.		22.50
Stem, 6 oz., high sherbet, #3085.		27.50
Stem, 9 oz., water, #3085.		45.00
Sugar, flat w/ lid	40.00	75.00
Sugar, ftd.	15.00	30.00
Tumbler, 2½ oz., 2⅞", flat, #1402.	25.00	
Tumbler, 5 oz., flat, #1402.	20.00	
Tumbler, 7 oz., flat, #1402.	20.00	
Tumbler, 10 oz., flat, #1402.	23.00	
Tumbler, 10 oz., flat, tall, #1402.	25.00	
Tumbler, 15 oz., flat, #1402.	35.00	
Tumbler, 2½ oz., ftd., #3085.		45.00
Tumbler, 5 oz., 3⅞", ftd., #3085.		30.00
Tumbler, 8 oz., ftd., #3085.		30.00
Tumbler, 10 oz., ftd., #3085.		35.00
Tumbler, 12 oz., 5⅜", ftd., #3085.		40.00

IPSWICH, Blank #1405, A.H. Heisey & Co.

Colors: crystal, "Flamingo" pink, "Sahara" yellow, "Moongleam" green, cobalt, and "Alexandrite"

To save answering about fifty letters, I repeat, "If you find any colored piece of Ipswich, other than those listed below, it was made at Imperial and not Heisey. Even if it is marked Heisey, it was still manufactured at Imperial. Mostly, I get letters on (Alexandrite) candy jars that are actually Imperial's Heather color."

Most of the price adjustments (higher, of course), have been in Moongleam color. There seems to be a scarcity of tumblers in all sizes; therefore, you will have to pay more when, and if, you see them.

Only the Ipswich goblet was made in Alexandrite. If you have any problems in determining whether a piece you have is Alexandrite or not, look in the back of this book on page 230. We have been able to show this color more consistently than any other book ever has. You can also take an Alexandrite piece outside in natural light where it will look pink, and then near a fluorescent bulb where it will change to a blue hue. Many collectors have been fooled by artificial lights when looking for Alexandrite Heisey.

Notice the candle vase in green (between the creamer and sugar) that goes atop the candlestick centerpiece. This is the most difficult piece of the candlestick centerpiece to find in crystal. The bottom arrived after we had photographed the large set-up; so it is included as a pattern shot. No matter how many times you photograph glassware for books, some item you can not leave out shows up when it is nearly impossible to include it!

	Crystal	Pink	Sahara	Green	Cobalt	Alexandrite
Bowl, finger w/underplate	20.00	55.00	60.00	70.00		
Bowl, 11", ftd., floral	70.00		250.00		350.00	
Candlestick, 6", 1-lite	75.00	205.00	150.00	200.00	350.00	
Candlestick centerpiece, ftd., vase, "A" prisms, complete	120.00	300.00	350.00	450.00	500.00	
Candy jar, ¼ lb., w/cover	150.00					
Candy jar, ½ lb., w/cover	150.00	225.00	250.00	300.00		
Cocktail shaker, 1 quart, strainer #86 stopper	225.00	600.00	700.00	800.00		
Creamer	30.00	50.00	50.00	100.00		
Stem, 4 oz., oyster cocktail, ftd	22.00	37.50	35.00	40.00		
Stem, 5 oz., saucer champagne, (knob in stem)	22.00	37.50	35.00	40.00		
Stem, 10 oz., goblet, (knob in stem)	30.00	50.00	45.00	55.00		750.00
Stem, 12 oz., schoppen, flat bottom	30.00					
Pitcher, ½ gal.	150.00	250.00	350.00	750.00		
Oil bottle, 2 oz., ftd., #86 stopper	80.00	185.00	175.00	200.00		
Plate, 7", square	20.00	40.00	25.00	40.00		
Plate, 8", square	20.00	45.00	30.00	45.00		
Sherbet, 4 oz., ftd., (knob in stem)	10.00	30.00	25.00	35.00		
Sugar	30.00	50.00	50.00	100.00		
Tumbler, 5 oz., ftd., (soda)	30.00	40.00	40.00	70.00		
Tumbler, 8 oz., ftd., (soda)	30.00	40.00	40.00	80.00		
Tumbler, 10 oz., cupped rim, flat bottom	40.00	60.00	50.00	80.00		
Tumbler, 10 oz., straight rim, flat bottom	40.00	60.00	50.00	80.00		
Tumbler, 12 oz., ftd., (soda)	35.00	65.00	55.00	85.00		

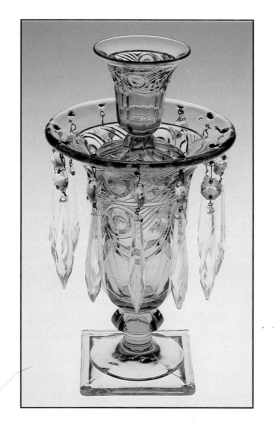

JANICE, LINE 4500, New Martinsville Glass Company, 1926 – 1944; Viking Glass Company, 1944 – 1970

Colors: crystal, Cobalt, Ruby, Light Blue, Emerald, Amethyst

Janice is another newly listed pattern that I have had many requests to include in this book. I haven't had great success in finding it to photograph and I have only scratched the surface of listings as there is a separate line of swan handled items that I have not included here. I also had very little luck in finding someone knowledgeable enough to help in pricing swan handled items. In the bottom photo is a crystal plate that I paid $25.00 for to have a representative example.

I might point out that the blue flat tumbler is a Duncan & Miller piece and not New Martinsville's Janice. Collectors sometimes use this tumbler for lack of a flat one in Janice since they are of similar design and color.

There are actual swans in several colors in Janice, so be aware of that. If you are an advanced collector of Janice, let me know what additional pieces you have found and be sure to suggest any pricing ideas you may have when you write!

	Crystal	Blue/Red		Crystal	Blue/Red
Basket, 6½", 9" high	65.00	125.00	Ice tub, 6", ftd.	85.00	225.00
Basket, 11"	75.00	150.00	Jam jar w/cover, 6"	20.00	45.00
Basket, 12", oval, 10" high	85.00	165.00	Mayonnaise liner, 7", 2-hdl.	9.00	14.00
Bon bon, 5½", 2-hdl., 4½" high	18.00	30.00	Mayonnaise plate, 6"	7.50	12.50
Bon bon, 6", 2-hdl., 4" high	20.00	33.00	Mayonnaise, 6", 2-hdl.	18.00	30.00
Bon bon, 7", 2-hdl., 4¾" high	25.00	40.00	Mayonnaise, round	15.00	27.50
Bowl, 5½", flower w/eight crimps	22.00	35.00	Oil, 5 oz., w/stopper	35.00	85.00
Bowl, 6", 2-hdl., crimped	20.00	33.00	Pitcher, 15 oz., berry cream	37.50	110.00
Bowl, 9½", cupped	35.00	55.00	Plate, 7", 2-hdl.	9.00	14.00
Bowl, 9½", flared	35.00	55.00	Plate, 8½", salad	10.00	17.50
Bowl, 9", 2-hdl.	37.50	60.00	Plate, 11", cheese	22.50	40.00
Bowl, 10"	37.50	65.00	Plate, 11", ftd., rolled edge	27.50	50.00
Bowl, 10½", cupped, 3-toed	45.00	75.00	Plate, 12", 2-hdl.	25.00	45.00
Bowl, 10½", flared, 3-toed	45.00	75.00	Plate, 13"	30.00	60.00
Bowl, 11" oval	40.00	65.00	Plate, 13", 2-hdl.	32.50	65.00
Bowl, 11", cupped, ftd.	45.00	75.00	Plate, 14", ftd., rolled edge	37.50	75.00
Bowl, 11", flared	40.00	65.00	Plate, 15"	40.00	
Bowl, 12", flared	42.50	67.50	Plate, 15", rolled edge torte	45.00	
Bowl, 12", fruit, ruffled top	50.00	85.00	Platter, 13", oval	32.50	70.00
Bowl, 12", oval	42.50	70.00	Relish, 6", 2-part, 2-hdl.	15.00	37.50
Bowl, 12", salad, scalloped top	50.00	85.00	Salt and pepper, pr.	35.00	70.00
Bowl, 12", six crimps	52.50	85.00	Saucer	2.00	4.50
Bowl, 13", flared	50.00	75.00	Sherbet	12.00	25.00
Canape set: tray w/ftd. juice	30.00		Sugar, 6 oz.	12.00	20.00
Candelbra, 5", 2-lt., 5" wide	40.00		Sugar, individual, flat	10.00	20.00
Candlestick, 5½", 1-lt., 5" wide	35.00		Sugar, individual, ftd.	12.50	22.50
Candlestick, 6", 1-lt., 4½" wide	37.50		Sugar, tall	15.00	25.00
Candy box w/cover, 5½"	45.00	85.00	Syrup, w/dripcut top	55.00	
Celery, 11"	20.00	45.00	Tray, oval, 2-hdl., ind. sug/cr	12.00	20.00
Comport, cracker for cheese plate	12.20	22.50	Tumbler	12.00	25.00
Condiment set: tray and 2 cov. jars	55.00	100.00	Vase, 4", ivy, 3½" high	22.00	40.00
Creamer, 6 oz.	12.00	20.00	Vase, 4", ivy, 4½" high w/base peg	25.00	50.00
Creamer, individual, flat	12.00	20.00	Vase, 7", ftd.	35.00	65.00
Creamer, individual, ftd.	12.50	22.50	Vase, 8", ball, 7½" high	45.00	95.00
Creamer, tall	15.00	25.00	Vase, 8", cupped, 3-toed	50.00	100.00
Cup	8.00	22.00	Vase, 8", flared, 3-toed	50.00	100.00
Guest set: bottle w/tumbler	65.00		Vase, 9", ball	55.00	110.00
Ice pail, 10", hld.	65.00	145.00			

JUNE, Fostoria Glass Company, 1928 – 1944

Colors: crystal, "Azure" blue, "Topaz" yellow, "Rose" pink

Prices for blue and pink June continue to spiral upward. While there have been a few increases in crystal and yellow items, demand for those colors does not compare to the frenzied buying of the other colors. Both pink and blue are selling as fast as dealers can find it for their customers.

I never heard any more about the pink set of June that ran through an Atlanta estate sale. The pink decanter has now been sold at least four times, and each time the seller has made money.

There is not enough room in this book to list all the line numbers for the items in June! If you will refer to Versailles, I have listed all the Fostoria line numbers for each piece. Since these are virtually the same listings, you can use the item number listings from Versailles if you need such information. There is other Fostoria information under Versailles you need to read if you collect June! Be sure to see the stemware representatives on page 93. You wouldn't want to buy a high sherbet as a claret!

	Crystal	Rose, Blue	Topaz		Crystal	Rose, Blue	Topaz
Ash tray	25.00	50.00	35.00	Ice dish liner (tomato, crab, fruit)	5.00	20.00	10.00
Bottle, salad dressing, #2083 or #2375	175.00	795.00	350.00	Mayonnaise, w/liner	25.00	65.00	40.00
Bowl, baker, 9", oval	35.00	125.00	65.00	Oil, ftd.	200.00	595.00	325.00
Bowl, baker, 10", oval	40.00	135.00	75.00	Oyster cocktail, 5½ oz.	16.00	35.00	25.00
Bowl, bonbon	12.50	30.00	23.00	Parfait, 5¼"	30.00	110.00	60.00
Bowl, bouillon, ftd.	12.00	38.00	23.00	Pitcher	225.00	550.00	310.00
Bowl, finger, w/liner	32.50	58.00	30.00	Plate, canape	15.00	40.00	25.00
Bowl, mint, 3-ftd., 4½"	10.00	42.00	28.00	Plate, lemon	14.00	25.00	20.00
Bowl, 6", nappy, 3-ftd., jelly	12.00	40.00	23.00	Plate, 6", bread/butter	4.50	12.00	6.00
Bowl, 6½", cereal	20.00	55.00	35.00	Plate, 6", finger bowl liner	4.50	12.00	8.00
Bowl, 7", soup	50.00	150.00	150.00	Plate, 7½", salad	5.00	9.00	8.00
Bowl, lg., dessert, hdld.	30.00	115.00	65.00	Plate, 7½, cream soup	4.00	12.00	7.50
Bowl, 10"	30.00	110.00	65.00	Plate, 8¾", luncheon	6.00	18.00	12.00
Bowl, 10", Grecian	40.00	100.00	60.00	Plate, 9½", sm. dinner	10.00	38.00	24.00
Bowl, 11", centerpiece	30.00	75.00	50.00	Plate, 10", grill	35.00	100.00	70.00
Bowl, 12", centerpiece, three types	35.00	95.00	55.00	Plate, 10", cake, hdld (no indent)	20.00	60.00	40.00
Bowl, 13", oval centerpiece, w/flower frog	65.00	195.00	95.00	Plate, 10", cheese with indent, hdld.	20.00	60.00	40.00
Candlestick, 2"	14.00	30.00	22.00	Plate, 10¼", dinner	35.00	100.00	65.00
Candlestick, 3"	12.00	35.00	22.00	Plate, 13", chop	22.00	75.00	50.00
Candlestick, 3", Grecian	20.00	50.00	30.00	Plate, 14", torte		95.00	65.00
Candlestick, 5", Grecian	25.00	60.00	35.00	Platter, 12"	30.00	110.00	70.00
Candy, w/cover, 3 pt.		285.00		Platter, 15"	45.00	195.00	110.00
Candy, w/cover, ½ lb., ¼ lb.			175.00	Relish, 8½", 3-part	20.00		35.00
Celery, 11½"	25.00	95.00	45.00	Sauce boat	40.00	275.00	100.00
Cheese & cracker set, #2368 or #2375	40.00	110.00	65.00	Sauce boat liner	15.00	75.00	35.00
Comport, 5", #2400	20.00	60.00	35.00	Saucer, after dinner	6.00	20.00	10.00
Comport, 6", #5298 or #5299	22.00	85.00	45.00	Saucer	4.00	7.50	5.00
Comport, 7", #2375	25.00	110.00	50.00	Shaker, ftd., pr	60.00	175.00	110.00
Comport, 8", #2400	40.00	140.00	60.00	Sherbet, high, 6", 6 oz.	17.50	35.00	25.00
Cream soup, ftd.	18.00	45.00	32.50	Sherbet, low, 4¼", 6 oz.	15.00	30.00	20.00
Creamer, ftd.	12.00	25.00	17.50	Sugar, ftd., straight or scalloped top	12.00	25.00	20.00
Creamer, tea	25.00	60.00	45.00	Sugar cover	50.00	210.00	130.00
Cup, after dinner	25.00	80.00	45.00	Sugar pail	65.00	225.00	135.00
Cup, ftd.	15.00	30.00	22.00	Sugar, tea	25.00	60.00	45.00
Decanter	400.00	2,000.00	575.00	Sweetmeat	15.00	35.00	20.00
Goblet, claret, 6", 4 oz.	40.00	135.00	75.00	Tray, service and lemon		325.00	275.00
Goblet, cocktail, 5¼", 3 oz.	20.00	45.00	32.50	Tray, 11", ctr. hdld.	20.00	45.00	35.00
Goblet, cordial, 4", ¾ oz.	50.00	135.00	70.00	Tumbler, 2½ oz., ftd.	20.00	65.00	40.00
Goblet, water, 8¼", 10 oz.	25.00	55.00	35.00	Tumbler, 5 oz., 4½", ftd.	15.00	42.00	28.00
Goblet, wine, 5½", 3 oz.	25.00	95.00	50.00	Tumbler, 9 oz., 5¼", ftd.	15.00	42.00	25.00
Grapefruit	30.00	100.00	60.00	Tumbler, 12 oz., 6", ftd.	20.00	58.00	35.00
Grapefruit liner	25.00	75.00	40.00	Vase, 8", 2 styles	75.00	250.00	175.00
Ice bucket	50.00	150.00	80.00	Vase, 8½", fan, ftd.	75.00	210.00	135.00
Ice dish	25.00	55.00	42.00	Whipped cream bowl	10.00	20.00	14.00
				Whipped cream pail	75.00	210.00	135.00

Note: See stemware identification on page 93.

JUNE NIGHT, Tiffin Glass Company, 1940's – 1950's

Colors: crystal

     June Night is a Tiffin Glass Company pattern that is beginning to be noticed by the collecting world. You will note many similarities to the pieces in Cherokee Rose. The pitcher and shakers seem to be the most difficult items to acquire. A few years ago, an editorial staff member at Collector books, told me she was collecting this pattern and to watch out for any pieces I could find. I have been helping add to her collection. The pieces pictured here belong to her. (She has long since left Collector Books, but has consented to come back and arrange the glass set-ups for photography sessions. Without her help and ability to see what the photographer wants, we would be lost.)

     June Night can be found on several different stemware lines, but the most often seen is Tiffin's 17392. The pattern shot on the next page illustrates this line. You will find line numbers 17378, 17441, and 17471. The later line has a bow tie looking stem, but I, personally, have never seen June Night on it. This pattern with gold trim was called Cherry Laurel. Name changing within same patterns is another idiosyncrasy of Tiffin!

	Crystal		Crystal
Bowl, 5", finger.	15.00	Shaker, pr.	175.00
Bowl, 6", fruit or nut	20.00	Stem, 1 oz., cordial	40.00
Bowl, 7", salad	30.00	Stem, 2 oz., sherry	35.00
Bowl, 10", deep salad	60.00	Stem, 3½ oz., cocktail	18.00
Bowl, 12", crimped	65.00	Stem, 3½ oz., wine	27.50
Bowl, 12½" centerpiece, flared	60.00	Stem, 4 oz., claret	35.00
Bowl, 13", centerpiece	75.00	Stem, 4½ oz., parfait	30.00
Candlesticks, pr., double branch	85.00	Stem, 5½ oz., sherbet/champagne	16.00
Celery, 10½", oblong	35.00	Stem, 9 oz., water	22.00
Creamer	15.00	Sugar	15.00
Mayonnaise, liner and ladle	45.00	Table bell	75.00
Pitcher	255.00	Tumbler, 4½ oz., oyster cocktail	18.00
Plate, 6", sherbet	5.00	Tumbler, 5 oz., ftd., juice	16.00
Plate, 8", luncheon	10.00	Tumbler, 8 oz., ftd., water	17.50
Plate, 13½", turned-up edge, lily	40.00	Tumbler, 10½ oz., ftd., ice tea	22.50
Plate, 14", sandwich	40.00	Vase, 6", bud	20.00
Relish, 6½", 3 pt.	35.00	Vase, 8", bud	30.00
Relish, 12½", 3 pt.	65.00	Vase, 10", bud	35.00

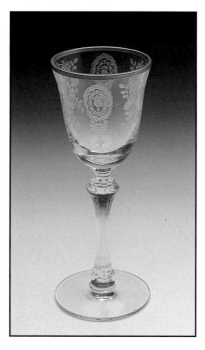

KASHMIR, Fostoria Glass Company, 1930 – 1934

Colors: "Topaz" yellow, green; some blue

Kashmir isn't exactly plentiful, but more seems to be showing up in the Midwest. Still, it is not immediately vanishing as do some of the other Fostoria patterns. If you are looking for a Fostoria set to collect, this may be it. While everyone else is acquiring June and Versailles, you could sneak up on a beautiful set without as much competition. I see groups of yellow pieces for sale; yet, there are few buyers! You could put a set of yellow Kashmir together cheaper than any other etched yellow Fostoria pattern.

The stemware and tumbler line are #5099 which is the same line on which Trojan is found. This is the cascading waterfall stem!

Both styles of after dinner cups are shown in the picture of blue. The square saucer set is more difficult to find than the round. Notice that I have found very little green in my travels. Those two cup and saucer sets are all I have ever been able to buy!

	Yellow, Green	Blue		Yellow, Green	Blue
Ash tray	25.00	30.00	Pitcher, ftd.	275.00	395.00
Bowl, cream soup	22.00	25.00	Plate, 6", bread & butter	5.00	6.00
Bowl, finger	15.00	20.00	Plate, 7", salad, rnd.	6.00	7.00
Bowl, 5", fruit	13.00	15.00	Plate, 7", salad, sq.	6.00	7.00
Bowl, 6", cereal	30.00	35.00	Plate, 8", salad	8.00	10.00
Bowl, 7", soup	30.00	55.00	Plate, 9" luncheon	9.00	12.00
Bowl, 8½", pickle	20.00	30.00	Plate, 10", dinner	40.00	55.00
Bowl, 9", baker	37.50	45.00	Plate, 10", grill	35.00	50.00
Bowl, 10"	40.00	45.00	Plate, cake, 10"	35.00	
Bowl, 12", centerpiece	40.00	50.00	Salt & pepper, pr.	100.00	150.00
Candlestick, 2"	15.00	17.50	Sandwich, center hdld.	35.00	40.00
Candlestick, 3"	20.00	25.00	Sauce boat, w/liner	75.00	115.00
Candlestick, 5"	22.50	27.50	Saucer, rnd.	5.00	10.00
Candlestick, 9½"	40.00	60.00	Saucer, after dinner, sq.	8.00	
Candy, w/cover	75.00	95.00	Saucer, after dinner, rnd.	8.00	15.00
Cheese and cracker set	65.00	85.00	Stem, ¾ oz., cordial	85.00	110.00
Comport, 6"	35.00	45.00	Stem, 2½ oz., ftd.	30.00	45.00
Creamer, ftd.	17.50	20.00	Stem, 2 oz., ftd., whiskey	30.00	45.00
Cup	15.00	20.00	Stem, 2½ oz., wine	32.00	40.00
Cup, after dinner, flat	38.00		Stem, 3 oz., cocktail	22.00	25.00
Cup, after dinner, ftd.	38.00	55.00	Stem, 3½ oz., ftd., cocktail	22.00	25.00
Grapefruit	50.00		Stem, 4 oz., claret	35.00	50.00
Grapefruit liner	40.00		Stem, 4½ oz., oyster cocktail	16.00	18.00
Ice bucket	65.00	90.00	Stem, 5½ oz., parfait	30.00	40.00
Oil, ftd.	275.00	450.00	Stem, 5 oz., ftd., juice	15.00	25.00
			Stem, 5 oz., low sherbet	13.00	20.00
			Stem, 6 oz., high sherbet	17.50	22.50
			Stem, 9 oz., water	20.00	35.00
			Stem, 10 oz., ftd., water	22.00	30.00
			Stem, 11 oz.	22.50	
			Stem, 12 oz., ftd.	25.00	35.00
			Stem, 13 oz., ftd., tea	25.00	
			Stem, 16 oz., ftd., tea	35.00	
			Sugar, ftd.	15.00	20.00
			Sugar lid	50.00	85.00
			Vase, 8"	90.00	125.00

Note: See stemware identification on page 93.

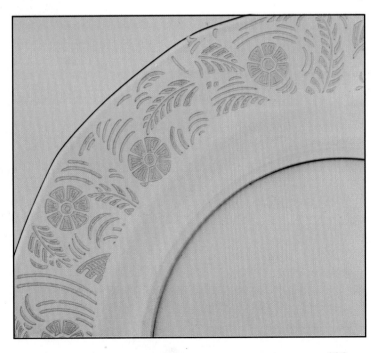

LARIAT, Blank #1540, A.H. Heisey & Co.

Colors: crystal; rare in black and amber

If you owned a set of Lariat in the last two years your net worth has increased considerably. Prices for Lariat have made some hefty leaps. The cutting most often found on Lariat is Moonglo. We have tried to blow your mind with the number of pieces this time. Enjoy! The ad shown on page 130 is from an October 1948 issue of *Better Homes and Gardens*.

	Crystal
Ash tray, 4"	15.00
Basket, 7½", bonbon	100.00
Basket, 8½", ftd.	165.00
Basket, 10", ftd.	195.00
Bowl, 2-hdld., cream soup	45.00
Bowl, 7 quart, punch	130.00
Bowl, 4", nut, individual	24.00
Bowl, 7", 2 pt., mayo	24.00
Bowl, 7", nappy	20.00
Bowl, 8", flat, nougat	20.00
Bowl, 9½", camellia	28.00
Bowl, 10", hdld., celery	35.00
Bowl, 10½", 2 hdld., salad	38.00
Bowl, 10½", salad	40.00
Bowl, 11", 2 hdld., oblong, relish	30.00
Bowl, 12", floral or fruit	30.00
Bowl, 13", celery	40.00
Bowl, 13", gardenia	35.00
Bowl, 13", oval, floral	35.00
Candlestick, 1-lite, individual	20.00
Candlestick, 2-lite	35.00
Candlestick, 3-lite	40.00
Candy box, w/cover, caramel	75.00
Candy, w/cover, 7"	90.00
Candy, w/cover, 8", w/horsehead finial (rare)	1,500.00
Cheese, 5", ftd., w/cover	50.00
Cheese dish, w/cover, 8"	60.00
Cigarette box	45.00
Coaster, 4"	10.00
Cologne	75.00

	Crystal
Compote, 10", w/cover	100.00
Creamer	20.00
Creamer & sugar, w/tray, indiv.	45.00
Cup	15.00
Cup, punch	8.00
Ice tub	75.00
Jar, w/cover, 12", urn	175.00
Lamp & globe, 7", black-out	120.00
Lamp & globe, 8", candle, handled	95.00
Mayonnaise, 5" bowl, 7" plate w/ladle set	60.00
Oil bottle, 4 oz., hdld., w/#133 stopper	130.00
Oil bottle, 6 oz., oval	75.00
Plate, 6", finger bowl liner	7.00
Plate, 7", salad	12.00
Plate, 8", salad	16.00
Plate, 10½", dinner	115.00
Plate, 11", cookie	25.00
Plate, 12", demi-torte, rolled edge	30.00
Plate, 13", deviled egg, round	170.00
Plate, 14", 2 hdld., sandwich	50.00
Plate, 15", deviled egg, oval	185.00
Plate, 21", buffet	70.00
Platter, 15", oval	60.00
Salt & pepper, pr.	200.00
Saucer	5.00
Stem, 1 oz., cordial, double loop	250.00
Stem, 1 oz., cordial blown, single loop	150.00
Stem, 2½ oz., wine, blown	25.00
Stem, 3½ oz., cocktail, pressed	20.00
Stem, 3½ oz., cocktail, blown	20.00
Stem, 3½ oz., wine, pressed	24.00
Stem, 4 oz., claret, blown	28.00
Stem, 4¼ oz., oyster cocktail or fruit	18.00
Stem, 4½ oz., oyster cocktail, blown	18.00
Stem, 5½ oz., sherbet/saucer champagne blown	17.00
Stem, 6 oz., low sherbet	10.00
Stem, 6 oz., sherbet/saucer champagne, pressed	15.00
Stem, 9 oz., pressed	22.00
Stem, 10 oz., blown	22.00
Sugar	20.00
Tray, rnd., center hdld., w/ball finial	165.00
Tray for sugar & creamer, 8" 2-handled	22.00
Tumbler, 5 oz., ftd., juice	20.00
Tumbler, 5 oz., ftd., juice, blown	20.00
Tumbler, 12 oz., ftd., ice tea	24.00
Tumbler, 12 oz., ftd., ice tea, blown	24.00
Vase, 7", ftd., fan	25.00
Vase, swung	125.00

CORDIAL, YET CAREFREE··· *that's Heisey* Lariat

Lariat carries an air of matchless charm, expressed in its lighthearted loop design. Cordial, yet carefree, it will be esteemed by you as highly as any of your treasures. Rare as the western air, this hand-cast crystal gaily blends your own good taste with the trend that is today. Your Heisey dealer will be pleased to show you the complete selection of LARIAT stemware and table accessories.

Lariat is one of several patterns pictured in "CHOOSING YOUR CRYSTAL PATTERN," an informal, streamlined guide to proper crystal, china and silver. Send 10c to Department H8, A. H. HEISEY & CO., NEWARK, OHIO

THE FINEST IN GLASSWARE, MADE IN AMERICA BY HAND

LODESTAR, Pattern #1632, A.H. Heisey & Co.

Color: Dawn

Only this Heisey pattern in the Dawn color is named Lodestar. Crystal pieces in the pattern are called Satellite and the prices drop dramatically! Note the star-like shape on each base design. As with most Heisey patterns, there are higher prices being asked and obtained.

	Dawn
Ash tray	90.00
Bowl, 4½", sauce dish, #1626	40.00
Bowl, 5", mayonnaise	75.00
Bowl, 6¾", #1565	55.00
Bowl, 8"	60.00
Bowl, 11", crimped	95.00
Bowl, 12", deep floral	80.00
Bowl, 14", shallow	100.00
Candleblock, 2¾" tall, 1-lite star, #1543, pr., (Satellite)	275.00
Candlestick, 2" tall, 1-lite centerpiece, pr	100.00
Candlestick, 5¾" tall, 2-lite, pr	600.00
Candy jar, w/cover, 5"	135.00
Celery, 10"	60.00
Creamer	60.00
Creamer, w/handle	90.00
Jar, w/cover, 8", #1626	140.00
Pitcher, 1 qt., #1626	170.00
Plate, 8½"	65.00
Plate, 14"	90.00
Relish, 7½", 3 pt.	55.00
Salt and pepper, pr., #1485	250.00
Sugar	60.00
Sugar, w/handles	90.00
Tumbler, 6 oz., juice	45.00
Vase, 8", #1626	140.00
Vase, 8", crimped, #1626	175.00

MINUET, Etching #1530 on QUEEN ANN Blank, #1509; TOUJOURS Blank, #1511; SYMPHONE Blank, #5010, et. al.; A.H. Heisey & Co., 1939 – 1950's

Colors: crystal

Minuet is one Heisey pattern where prices have remained rather steady. There have been a few price jumps such as in the individual sugar and creamer as well as dinner plates. Conversely, an over supply of wines has precipitated a $20.00 drop in their prices. Prices do not always go up! Demand and availability determine price. Now might be a good time to stock a few Minuet wines.

Stemware is rather abundant, but tumblers are not easily found. Serving pieces are troublesome to attain. That cocktail icer pictured on the bottom of the next page only sat on our table about fifteen minutes when we put it out for sale. You will have competition if you collect this pattern!

	Crystal
Bell, dinner, #3408	75.00
Bowl, finger, #3309	50.00
Bowl, 6", ftd., mint	17.50
Bowl, 6", ftd., 2 hdld., jelly	20.00
Bowl, 6½", salad dressings	25.00
Bowl, 7", salad dressings	30.00
Bowl, 7", triplex, relish	35.00
Bowl, 7½", sauce, ftd.	60.00
Bowl, 9½", 3 pt., "5 o'clock" relish	60.00
Bowl, 10", salad, #1511 TOUJOURS	60.00
Bowl, 11", 3 pt., "5 o'clock" relish	70.00
Bowl, 11", ftd., floral	95.00
Bowl, 12", oval, floral, #1511 TOUJOURS	60.00
Bowl, 12", oval, #1514	60.00
Bowl, 13", floral, #1511 TOUJOURS	55.00
Bowl, 13", pickle & olive	35.00
Bowl, 13½", shallow salad	75.00
Candelabrum, 1-lite w/prisms	95.00
Candelabrum, 2-lite, bobeche & prisms	165.00
Candlestick, 1-lite, #112	30.00
Candlestick, 2-lite, #1511 TOUJOURS	145.00
Candlestick, 3-lite, #142 CASCADE	65.00
Candlestick, 5", 2-lite, #134 TRIDENT	42.50
Centerpiece vase & prisms #1511 TOUJOURS	185.00
Cocktail icer, w/liner #3304 UNIVERSAL	195.00
Comport, 5½", #5010	35.00
Comport, 7½", #1511 TOUJOURS	50.00
Creamer, #1511 TOUJOURS	50.00
Creamer, dolphin ft.	42.50
Creamer, indiv., #1509 QUEEN ANN	37.50
Creamer, indiv., #1511 TOUJOURS	70.00
Cup	30.00
Ice bucket, dolphin ft.	150.00
Marmalade, w/cover, #1511 TOUJOURS (apple shape)	95.00
Mayonnaise, 5½", dolphin ft.	45.00
Mayonnaise, ftd., #1511 TOUJOURS	70.00
Pitcher, 73 oz., #4164	285.00
Plate, 7", mayonnaise liner	10.00

	Crystal
Plate, 7", salad	12.00
Plate, 7", salad, #1511 TOUJOURS	12.00
Plate, 8", luncheon	20.00
Plate, 8", luncheon, #1511 TOUJOURS	22.50
Plate, 10½", service	160.00
Plate, 12", rnd., 2 hdld., sandwich	50.00
Plate, 13", floral, salver, #1511 TOUJOURS	50.00
Plate, 14", torte, #1511 TOUJOURS	50.00
Plate, 15", sand., #1511 TOUJOURS	55.00
Plate, 16", snack rack, w/#1477 center	80.00
Salt & pepper, pr. (#10)	65.00
Saucer	10.00
Stem, #5010, SYMPHONE, 1 oz., cordial	135.00
Stem, #5010, 2½ oz., wine	50.00
Stem, #5010, 3½ oz., cocktail	35.00
Stem, #5010, 4 oz., claret	37.50
Stem, #5010, 4½ oz., oyster cocktail	20.00
Stem, #5010, 6 oz., saucer champagne	17.50
Stem, #5010, 6 oz., sherbet	15.00
Stem, #5010, 9 oz., water	30.00
Sugar, indiv., #1511 TOUJOURS	70.00
Sugar, indiv., #1509 QUEEN ANN	37.50
Sugar dolphin ft., #1509 QUEEN ANN	40.00
Sugar, #1511 TOUJOURS	50.00
Tray, 12", celery, #1511 TOUJOURS	32.50
Tray, 15", social hour	75.00
Tray for indiv. sugar & creamer	25.00
Tumbler, #5010, 5 oz., fruit juice	34.00
Tumbler, #5010, 9 oz., low ftd., water	35.00
Tumbler, #5010, 12 oz., tea	60.00
Tumbler, #2351, 12 oz., tea	60.00
Vase, 5", #5013	45.00
Vase, 5½", ftd., #1511 TOUJOURS	55.00
Vase, 6", urn, #5012	70.00
Vase, 7½", urn, #5012	85.00
Vase, 8", #4196	85.00
Vase, 9", urn, #5012	95.00
Vase, 10", #4192	95.00
Vase, 10", #4192, SATURN optic	110.00

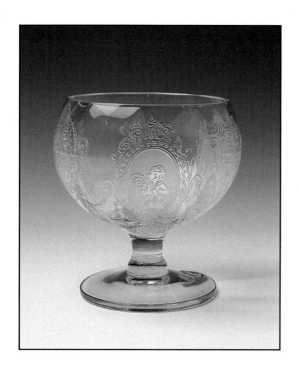

MORGAN, Central Glass Works, 1920's – 1930's

Colors: amethyst, black, blue, crystal, green, pink, lilac, crystal stems w/color bowls

At the Chicago 20-30-40's Society Depression Glass show in March of '96, a set of Morgan was displayed! Morgan is the first Central Glass Works pattern I have included in my books. I have little information about this company. A glass dealer who knew Cathy was buying Morgan sent me the material I have on the Morgan pattern. Also, special thanks belongs to collector Tim Schmidt who went out of his way to provide me with additional listings that I did not have.

Morgan was designed in 1920 by Joseph O. Baldo, who was better known for his Heisey designs. The pattern reputedly was adopted for use in the governor's mansion by a West Virginia governing family named Morgan. Thus, the very masculine pattern name attached to such a fey design.

My favorite piece of Morgan is the gold decorated bud vase shown as a pattern shot below. I've seen two of these. This one was bought at the National Heisey Convention a few years ago. The whiskey set pictured on the ribbed square tray was found in West Virginia on our way to the Morgantown convention. I saw another one in an antique mall in central Florida a couple of months ago. I was startled to see it properly identified; the price was a firm $325.00 with only four whiskeys. The owner told me that a lady working on a book on Central Glass products told her what it was. The set was on the same unetched tray; so evidently that is the proper one.

Stemware seems to be available. To date, cups and saucers appear to be scarce as are any pieces of blue. I had a call a few years ago about a large lilac set. This set supposedly had a pitcher and serving pieces. The price seemed rather high at the time, but the dealer that called did not buy it after I passed for $3,500.00. If you have knowledge of additional pieces, please let us know so we can expand the listings.

	*All Colors		*All Colors
Bonbon, 6", two handled	35.00	Mayonnaise liner	12.50
Bowl, 4¼" ftd. fruit	30.00	Oil bottle	55.00
Bowl, 10", console	50.00	Pitcher	150.00
Bowl, 13", console	65.00	Plate, 6½", fruit bowl liner	8.00
Candlestick, pr.	65.00	Plate, 7¼", salad	12.00
Candy w/lid, diamond shaped, 4 ftd.	125.00	Plate, 8½", luncheon	20.00
Comport, 6½" tall, 5" wide		Plate, 9¼", dinner	27.50
Comport, 6½" tall, 6" wide		Saucer	10.00
Creamer, ftd.	37.50	Server, 9½", octagonal, center handle	65.00
Cup	50.00	Server, 10⅜", round, center handle	65.00
Decanter w/stopper	150.00	Server, 11", octagonal, flat, center handle	65.00
Ice bucket, 4¾" x7½", 2 hdld.	95.00	Stem, 3¼", sherbet	15.00
Mayonnaise	40.00	Stem, 4⅜", sherbet, beaded stem	25.00
		Stem, 5⅛", cocktail, beaded stem	30.00
		Stem, 5⅜", high, sherbet, beaded stem	35.00
		Stem, 5⅞", high sherbet, straight stem	35.00
		Stem, 5⅞", wine	40.00
		Stem, 7¼", 10 oz., water	40.00
		Stem, 8¼", water	40.00
		Sugar, ftd.	37.50
		Tumbler, oyster cocktail	15.00
		Tumbler, 2⅛", whiskey	30.00
		Tumbler, 10 oz., flat water	25.00
		Tumbler, 4⅜", ftd. juice	25.00
		Tumbler, 5⅜", ftd., 10 oz., water	25.00
		Tumbler, 5¾", ftd., water	25.00
		Tumbler, 5⅞", ftd., 12 oz., tea	30.00
		Vase, 8", drape optic	75.00
		Vase, 9⅞", straight w/flared top	125.00
		**Vase, 10", bud	100.00

*Crystal 10% to 20% lower
 Blue, lilac 10% to 20% higher
** Gold decorated $250.00

MT. VERNON, Cambridge Glass Company, late 1920's – 1940's

Colors: amber, crystal, Carmen, Royal Blue, Heatherbloom, Emerald green (light and dark); rare in Violet

The expanse of colors in Mt. Vernon gives collectors a wide selection, but you can only complete a large set in amber or crystal. You can find luncheon sets in red, cobalt blue, and Heatherbloom; but only a few accessory pieces are available in those colors. Most prices for those three colors will double prices listed for amber and crystal. Many collectors accent their crystal Mt. Vernon sets with a splash of some of the colored pieces. Give it a try!

	Amber/ Crystal		Amber/ Crystal
Ash tray, 3½", #63	8.00	Honey jar, w/cover (marmalade), #74	32.00
Ash tray, 4", #68	12.00	Ice bucket, w/tongs, #92	35.00
Ash tray, 6" x 4½", oval, #71	12.00	Lamp, 9" hurricane, #1607	70.00
Bonbon, 7", ftd., #10	12.50	Mayonnaise, divided, 2 spoons, #107	25.00
Bottle, bitters, 2½ oz., #62	55.00	Mug, 14 oz., stein, #84	30.00
Bottle, 7 oz., sq., toilet, #18	65.00	Mustard, w/cover, 2½ oz., #28	25.00
Bowl, finger, #23	10.00	Pickle, 6", 1 hdld., #78	12.00
Bowl, 4½", ivy ball or rose, ftd., #12	27.50	Pitcher, 50 oz., #90	80.00
Bowl, 5¼", fruit, #6	10.00	Pitcher, 66 oz., #13	85.00
Bowl, 6", cereal, #32	12.50	Pitcher, 80 oz., ball, #95	95.00
Bowl, 6", preserve, #76	12.00	Pitcher, 86 oz., #91	115.00
Bowl, 6½", rose, #106	18.00	Plate, finger bowl liner, #23	4.00
Bowl, 8", pickle, #65	17.50	Plate, 6", bread & butter, #4	3.00
Bowl, 8½", 4 pt., 2 hdld., sweetmeat, #105	32.00	Plate, 6⅜", bread & butter, #19	4.00
Bowl, 10", 2 hdld., #39	20.00	Plate, 8½", salad, #5	7.00
Bowl, 10½", deep, #43	30.00	Plate, 10½", dinner, #40	30.00
Bowl, 10½", salad, #120	25.00	Plate, 11½", hdld., #37	20.00
Bowl, 11", oval, 4 ftd., #136	27.50	Relish, 6", 2 pt., 2 hdld., #106	12.00
Bowl, 11", oval, #135	25.00	Relish, 8", 2 pt., hdld., #101	17.50
Bowl, 11½", belled, #128	30.00	Relish, 8", 3 pt., 3 hdld., #103	20.00
Bowl, 11½", shallow, #126	30.00	Relish, 11", 3 part, #200	25.00
Bowl, 11½", shallow cupped, #61	30.00	Relish, 12", 2 part, #80	30.00
Bowl, 12", flanged, rolled edge, #129	32.50	Relish, 12", 5 part, #104	30.00
Bowl, 12", oblong, crimped, #118	32.50	Salt, indiv., #24	7.00
Bowl, 12", rolled edge, crimped, #117	32.50	Salt, oval, 2 hdld., #102	12.00
Bowl, 12½", flanged, rolled edge, #45	35.00	Salt & pepper, pr., #28	22.50
Bowl, 12½", flared, #121	35.00	Salt & pepper, pr., short, #88	20.00
Bowl, 12½", flared, #44	35.00	Salt & pepper, tall, #89	25.00
Bowl, 13", shallow, crimped, #116	35.00	Salt dip, #24	9.00
Box, 3", w/cover, round, #16	27.50	Sauce boat & ladle, tab hdld., #30-445	60.00
Box, 4", w/cover, sq., #17	30.00	Saucer, #7	7.50
Box, 4½", w/cover, ftd., round, #15	37.50	Stem, 3 oz., wine, #27	13.50
Butter tub, w/cover, #73	65.00	Stem, 3½ oz., cocktail, #26	9.00
Cake stand, 10½" ftd., #150	35.00	Stem, 4 oz., oyster cocktail, #41	9.00
Candelabrum, 13½", #38	125.00	Stem, 4½ oz., claret, #25	13.50
Candlestick, 4", #130	10.00	Stem, 4½ oz., low sherbet, #42	7.50
Candlestick, 5", 2-lite, #110	20.00	Stem, 6½ oz., tall sherbet, #2	10.00
Candlestick, 8", #35	25.00	Stem, 10 oz., water, #1	15.00
Candy, w/cover, 1 lb., ftd., #9	65.00	Sugar, ftd., #8	10.00
Celery, 10½", #79	15.00	Sugar, indiv., #4	12.00
Celery, 11", #98	17.50	Sugar, #86	10.00
Celery, 12", #79	20.00	Tray, for indiv., sugar & creamer, #4	10.00
Cigarette box, 6", w/cover, oval, #69	30.00	Tumbler, 1 oz., ftd., cordial, #87	22.00
Cigarette holder, #66	15.00	Tumbler, 2 oz., whiskey, #55	10.00
Coaster, 3", plain, #60	5.00	Tumbler, 3 oz., ftd., juice, #22	9.00
Coaster, 3", ribbed, #70	5.00	Tumbler, 5 oz., #56	12.00
Cocktail icer, 2 pc., #85	25.00	Tumbler, 5 oz., ftd., #21	12.00
Cologne, 2½ oz., w/stopper, #1340	35.00	Tumbler, 7 oz., old-fashioned, #57	15.00
Comport, 4½", #33	12.00	Tumbler, 10 oz., ftd., water, #3	15.00
Comport, 5½", 2 hdld., #77	15.00	Tumbler, 10 oz., table, #51	12.00
Comport, 6", #34	15.00	Tumbler, 10 oz., tall, #58	12.00
Comport, 6½", #97	17.50	Tumbler, 12 oz., barrel shape, #13	15.00
Comport, 6½", belled, #96	22.50	Tumbler, 12 oz., ftd., tea, #20	17.00
Comport, 7½" #11	25.00	Tumbler, 14 oz., barrel shape, #14	20.00
Comport, 8", #81	25.00	Tumbler, 14 oz., tall, #59	22.00
Comport, 9", oval, 2 hdld., #100	30.00	Urn, w/cover (same as candy), #9	65.00
Comport, 9½", #99	27.50	Vase, 5", #42	15.00
Creamer, ftd., #8	10.00	Vase, 6", crimped, #119	20.00
Creamer, indiv., #4	10.00	Vase, 6", ftd., #50	25.00
Creamer, #86	10.00	Vase, 6½", squat, #107	27.50
Cup, #7	6.50	Vase, 7", #58	30.00
Decanter, 11 oz., #47	50.00	Vase, 7", ftd., #54	35.00
Decanter, 40 oz., w/stopper, #52	70.00	Vase, 10", ftd., #46	50.00

NAVARRE, Plate Etching #327, Fostoria Glass Company, 1937 – 1980

Colors: crystal; all other colors found made very late

Fostoria's Navarre is fast becoming the most collected crystal pattern made by that company. It has edged out Chintz in the last few years for that distinction. Because of this popularity, prices continue to escalate. Harder to find pieces increase in price faster. It is better to buy them when you see them or take the chance they will cost even more later. Remember, a highly desirable pattern is easier to sell when the time comes.

Note the footed shakers in the bottom photo. They came with both glass and metal lids. Metal lids are prevalent.

Older crystal pieces of Navarre are priced in this Elegant book. Colors of pink, blue, and green were all made in the 1970's as were additional crystal pieces not originally made in the late 1930's and 1940's. These later pieces include carafes, roemer wines, continental champagnes, and brandies. You can find all of these later pieces in my *Collectible Glassware from the 40's, 50's & 60's....* Most of these pieces were signed "Fostoria" although some carried only a sticker. I am telling you this to make you aware of the colors made in Navarre. A few Depression era glass shows do not allow these pieces or colors to be sold since they were so recently manufactured.

	Crystal
Bell, dinner	50.00
Bowl, #2496, 4", square, hdld.	14.00
Bowl, #2496, 4⅜", hdld.	14.00
Bowl, #869, 4½", finger	45.00
Bowl, #2496, 4⅝", tri-cornered	15.00
Bowl, #2496, 5", hdld., ftd.	18.50
Bowl, #2496, 6", square, sweetmeat	17.50
Bowl, #2496, 6¼", 3 ftd., nut	20.00
Bowl, #2496, 7⅜", ftd., bonbon	27.50
Bowl, #2496, 10", oval, floating garden	55.00
Bowl, #2496, 10½", hdld., ftd.	70.00
Bowl, #2470½, 10½", ftd.	60.00
Bowl, #2496, 12", flared	62.50
Bowl, #2545, 12½", oval, "Flame"	60.00
Candlestick, #2496, 4"	22.00
Candlestick, #2496, 4½", double	37.50
Candlestick, #2472, 5", double	45.00
Candlestick, #2496, 5½"	30.00
Candlestick, #2496, 6", triple	47.50
Candlestick, #2545, 6¾", double, "Flame"	65.00
Candlestick, #2482, 6¾", triple	55.00
Candy, w/cover, #2496, 3 part	125.00
Celery, #2440, 9"	32.50
Celery, #2496, 11"	42.50
Comport, #2496, 3¼", cheese	27.50
Comport, #2400, 4½"	30.00
Comport, #2496, 4¾"	32.50
Cracker, #2496, 11" plate	42.50
Creamer, #2440, 4¼", ftd.	20.00
Creamer, #2496, individual	17.50
Cup, #2440	19.00
Ice bucket, #2496, 4⅜" high	120.00
Ice bucket, #2375, 6" high	150.00
Mayonnaise, #2375, 3 piece	67.50
Mayonnaise, #2496½, 3 piece	67.50
Pickle, #2496, 8"	27.50
Pickle, #2440, 8½"	30.00
Pitcher, #5000, 48 oz., ftd.	350.00
Plate, #2440, 6", bread/butter	11.00

	Crystal
Plate, #2440, 7½", salad	15.00
Plate, #2440, 8½", luncheon	22.00
Plate, #2440, 9½", dinner	45.00
Plate, #2496, 10", hdld., cake	50.00
Plate, #2440, 10½" oval cake	50.00
Plate, #2496, 14", torte	65.00
Plate, #2464, 16", torte	110.00
Relish, #2496, 6", 2 part, square	32.50
Relish, #2496, 10" x 7½", 3 part	47.50
Relish, #2496, 10", 4 part	52.50
Relish, #2419, 13¼", 5 part	87.50
Salt & pepper, #2364, 3¼", flat, pr.	60.00
Salt & pepper, #2375, 3½", ftd., pr.	105.00
Salad dressing bottle, #2083, 6½"	395.00
Sauce dish, #2496, div. mayo., 6½"	40.00
Sauce dish, #2496, 6½" x 5¼"	125.00
Sauce dish liner, #2496, 8" oval	30.00
Saucer, #2440	5.00
Stem, #6106, 1 oz., cordial, 3⅞"	50.00
Stem, #6106, 3¼ oz., wine, 5½"	35.00
Stem, #6106, 3½ oz., cocktail, 6"	25.00
Stem, #6106, 4 oz., oyster cocktail, 3⅝"	27.50
Stem, #6106, 4½ oz., claret, 6½"	42.50
Stem, #6106, 6 oz., low sherbet, 4⅜"	24.00
Stem, #6106, 6 oz., saucer champagne, 5⅝"	24.00
Stem, #6106, 10 oz., water, 7⅝"	30.00
Sugar, #2440, 3⅝", ftd.	18.00
Sugar, #2496, individual	16.00
Syrup, #2586, metal cut-off top, 5½"	395.00
Tid bit, #2496, 8¼", 3 ftd., turned up edge	22.00
Tray, #2496½, for ind. sugar/creamer	22.00
Tumbler, #6106, 5 oz., ftd., juice, 4⅝"	25.00
Tumbler, #6106, 10 oz., ftd., water, 5⅜"	25.00
Tumbler, #6106, 13 oz., ftd., tea, 5⅞"	32.00
Vase, #4108, 5"	95.00
Vase, #4121, 5"	95.00
Vase, #4128, 5"	95.00
Vase, #2470, 10", ftd.	165.00

NEW ERA, #4044, A.H. Heisey Co., 1934 – 1941; 1944 – 1957 (stems, celery tray, and candlesticks)

Colors: crystal, frosted crystal, some cobalt with crystal stem and foot.

New Era double branched candelabra with bobeches are probably the most recognized Heisey candles. These were made during both productions of this pattern. They are also sought by "Art Deco" collectors which keeps the price gradually rising even though these are rather plentiful. Desirability can make an abundant supply look scarce.

Cobalt stems and tumblers pictured in row 3 are truly difficult to find with prices averaging $125.00 to $150.00 each. The after dinner cup and saucer are rarely seen. Perfect plates without scratches in the centers are not easily found.

Many pieces in this pattern were monogrammed. Today, those pieces are very difficult to sell at any price unless you can find someone with the same three initials. That happens rarely, although I once found a Candlewick tray with my father-in-law's initials!

	Crystal		Crystal
Ash tray or indiv. nut	35.00	Stem, 1 oz. cordial	45.00
Bottle, rye w/stopper	120.00	Stem, 3 oz. wine	30.00
Bowl, 11" floral	60.00	Stem, 3½ oz., high, cocktail	12.00
Candelabra, 2-lite w/2 #4044 bobeche		Stem, 3½ oz. oyster cocktail	12.00
& prisms	80.00	Stem, 4 oz. claret	18.00
Creamer	35.00	Stem, 6 oz. champagne	12.50
Cup	12.00	Stem, 10 oz. goblet	18.00
Cup, after dinner	60.00	Stem, low, 6 oz. sherbet	10.00
Pilsner, 8 oz.	25.00	Sugar	35.00
Pilsner, 12 oz.	30.00	Tray, 13" celery	35.00
Plate, 5½" x 4½" bread & butter	15.00	Tumbler, 5 oz. ftd. soda	12.00
Plate, 9"x 7"	25.00	Tumbler, 8 oz. ftd. soda	10.00
Plate, 10" x 8"	40.00	Tumbler, 12 oz. ftd. soda	12.50
Relish, 13" 3-part	25.00	Tumbler, 14 oz. ftd. soda	15.00
Saucer	5.00	Tumbler, low, footed 10 oz.	10.00
Saucer, after dinner	10.00		

OCTAGON, Blank #1231 Ribbed, Blank #500, and Blank #1229, A.H. Heisey & Co.

Colors: crystal, "Flamingo" pink, "Sahara" yellow, "Moongleam" green, "Hawthorne" orchid, "Marigold," a deep, amber/yellow, and "Dawn"

Considering Octagon was regularly marked, it is one of those Heisey patterns that everyone recognizes, yet few collectors buy. True, it is one of the plainer patterns, but it does come in a multitude of colors! In the prices below the piece that jumps out at you is the 12", 4-part tray. Otherwise, Octagon is reasonably priced and is frequently just sitting around waiting for a new home.

Two Marigold Octagon pieces are pictured here. It is the only place that rare Heisey color is illustrated in this book. Be careful in buying Marigold since the color peels and cracks very easily. Then, it becomes wanted by no one!

	Crystal	Flam.	Sahara	Moon.	Hawth.	Marigold
Basket, 5", #500.	85.00	250.00	260.00	300.00	450.00	
Bonbon, 6", sides up, #1229	5.00	15.00	15.00	20.00	33.00	
Bowl, cream soup, 2 hdld.	10.00	20.00	25.00	30.00	40.00	
Bowl, 2-hdld, ind. nut bowl	10.00	17.50	25.00	20.00	60.00	65.00
Bowl, 5½", jelly, #1229	10.00	15.00	15.00	17.00	25.00	
Bowl, 6", mint, #1229	10.00	15.00	15.00	17.00	30.00	30.00
Bowl, 6", #500	14.00	20.00	22.00	25.00	35.00	
Bowl, 6½", grapefruit	10.00	20.00	22.00	25.00	35.00	
Bowl, 8", ftd., #1229 comport	15.00	25.00	35.00	45.00	55.00	
Bowl, 9", flat soup	10.00	15.00	20.00	27.50	30.00	
Bowl, 9", vegetable	15.00	20.00	25.00	30.00	50.00	
Candlestick, 3", 1-lite	15.00	25.00	27.00	30.00	40.00	
Cheese dish, 6", 2 hdld., #1229	7.00	10.00	10.00	12.00	15.00	
Creamer #500	7.00	20.00	30.00	35.00	40.00	
Creamer, hotel	10.00	15.00	15.00	20.00	30.00	
Cup, after dinner	5.00	15.00	15.00	20.00	42.00	
Cup #1231	5.00	15.00	20.00	20.00	35.00	
Dish, frozen dessert, #500	10.00	20.00	20.00	30.00	35.00	50.00
Ice tub, #500	30.00	70.00	75.00	80.00	115.00	150.00
Mayonnaise, 5½", ftd., #1229	10.00	25.00	30.00	35.00	45.00	
Nut, two hndld.	10.00	18.00	18.00	25.00	60.00	70.00
Plate, cream soup liner	3.00	5.00	7.00	9.00	12.00	
Plate, 6"	4.00	8.00	8.00	10.00	15.00	
Plate, 7", bread	5.00	10.00	10.00	15.00	20.00	
Plate, 8", luncheon	7.00	10.00	10.00	15.00	25.00	
Plate, 10", sand., #1229	15.00	20.00	25.00	30.00	35.00	
Plate, 10", muffin, #1229 sides up	15.00	25.00	30.00	35.00	40.00	
Plate, 10½"	17.00	25.00	30.00	35.00	45.00	
Plate, 10½", ctr. hdld., sandwich	25.00	40.00	40.00	45.00	70.00	
Plate, 12", muffin, #1229 sides up	20.00	27.00	30.00	35.00	45.00	
Plate, 13", hors d'oeuvre, #1229	20.00	30.00	30.00	40.00	55.00	
Plate, 14"	22.00	25.00	30.00	35.00	50.00	
Platter, 12¾" oval	20.00	25.00	30.00	40.00	50.00	
Saucer, after dinner	2.00	5.00	6.00	6.00	12.00	
Saucer, #1231	2.00	5.00	6.00	7.00	9.00	
Sugar #500	7.00	20.00	30.00	35.00	40.00	
Sugar, hotel	10.00	15.00	15.00	20.00	30.00	
Tray, 6", oblong, #500	5.00	10.00	12.00	12.00	20.00	
Tray, 9", celery	5.00	10.00	15.00	15.00	25.00	
Tray, 12", celery	7.00	15.00	17.00	17.00	35.00	**(Dawn)**
Tray, 12", 4 pt., #500 variety	40.00	100.00	125.00	140.00	250.00	350.00

OLD COLONY, Empress Blank #1401, Caracassone Blank #3390, and Old Dominion Blank #3380,
A.H. Heisey & Co., 1930 – 1939

Colors: crystal, "Flamingo" pink, "Sahara" yellow, "Moongleam" green, "Marigold," and deep, amber/yellow

	Crystal	Flam.	Sahara	Moon.	Marigold
Bouillon cup, 2 hdld., ftd.	12.50	18.00	20.00	24.00	
Bowl, finger, #4075	5.50	10.00	11.00	14.00	18.00
Bowl, ftd., finger, #3390	5.50	16.00	21.00	27.50	
Bowl, 4½", nappy	7.00	10.00	12.50	15.00	
Bowl, 5", ftd., 2 hdld.	12.50	17.50	22.50	27.50	
Bowl, 6", ftd., 2 hdld., jelly	15.00	20.00	25.00	32.50	
Bowl, 6", dolp. ftd., mint	16.00	22.00	27.50	35.00	
Bowl, 7", triplex, dish	15.00	22.00	25.00	28.00	
Bowl, 7½", dolphin ftd., nappy	22.00	60.00	65.00	75.00	
Bowl, 8", nappy	25.00	35.00	40.00	42.50	
Bowl, 8½", ftd., floral, 2 hdld.	32.00	47.00	57.50	67.50	
Bowl, 9", 3 hdld.	36.00	75.00	90.00	95.00	
Bowl, 10", rnd., 2 hdld., salad	32.00	47.50	57.50	65.00	
Bowl, 10", sq., salad, 2 hdld.	30.00	45.00	55.00	65.00	
Bowl, 10", oval, dessert, 2 hdld.	30.00	40.00	50.00	62.50	
Bowl, 10", oval, veg.	30.00	34.00	42.00	50.00	
Bowl, 11", floral, dolphin ft.	32.00	70.00	80.00	95.00	
Bowl, 13", ftd., flared	30.00	35.00	40.00	45.00	
Bowl, 13", 2 pt., pickle & olive	12.50	20.00	22.50	27.50	
Cigarette holder, #3390	16.00	47.50	42.50	55.00	
Comport, 7", oval, ftd.	40.00	75.00	80.00	85.00	
Comport, 7", ftd., #3368	30.00	57.50	62.50	85.00	95.00
Cream soup, 2 hdld.	12.00	20.00	22.00	27.00	
Creamer, dolphin ft.	20.00	32.00	45.00	50.00	
Creamer, indiv.	15.00	30.00	40.00	37.50	
Cup, after dinner	12.00	25.00	35.00	50.00	
Cup	10.00	26.00	32.00	38.00	
Decanter, 1 pt.	150.00	300.00	275.00	525.00	
Flagon, 12 oz., #3390	25.00	55.00	55.00	85.00	
Grapefruit, 6"	15.00	23.00	30.00	35.00	
Grapefruit, ftd., #3380	10.00	16.00	18.00	20.00	30.00
Ice tub, dolphin ft.	42.50	110.00	115.00	135.00	
Mayonnaise, 5½", dolp. ft.	36.00	55.00	70.00	80.00	
Oil, 4 oz., ftd.	42.50	70.00	105.00	120.00	
Pitcher, 3 pt., #3390	90.00	245.00	210.00	400.00	
Pitcher, 3 pt., dolphin ft.	125.00	195.00	200.00	210.00	
Plate, bouillon	5.00	8.00	12.00	15.00	
Plate, cream soup	5.00	8.00	12.00	15.00	
Plate, 4½", rnd.	3.00	6.00	7.00	8.00	
Plate, 6", rnd.	6.00	12.00	15.00	18.00	
Plate, 6", sq.	6.00	12.00	15.00	18.00	
Plate, 7", rnd.	8.00	14.00	18.00	20.00	
Plate, 7", sq.	8.00	14.00	18.00	20.00	
Plate, 8", rnd.	10.00	17.00	22.00	27.00	
Plate, 8", sq.	10.00	17.00	22.00	27.00	
Plate, 9", rnd.	15.00	22.00	25.00	28.00	
Plate, 10½", rnd.	28.50	60.00	70.00	75.00	
Plate, 10½", sq.	27.50	50.00	65.00	70.00	
Plate, 12", rnd.	31.00	57.50	70.00	75.00	
Plate, 12", 2 hdld., rnd., muffin	31.00	57.50	70.00	75.00	
Plate, 12", 2 hdld., rnd., sand.	31.00	57.50	70.00	75.00	
Plate, 13", 2 hdld., sq., sand.	35.00	40.00	45.00	50.00	
Plate, 13", 2 hdld., sq., muffin	35.00	40.00	45.00	50.00	
Platter, 14", oval	25.00	35.00	40.00	45.00	
Salt & pepper, pr.	52.50	80.00	110.00	130.00	
Saucer, sq.	4.00	8.00	10.00	10.00	
Saucer, rnd.	4.00	8.00	10.00	10.00	
Stem, #3380, 1 oz., cordial	75.00	135.00	135.00	155.00	375.00
Stem, #3380, 2½ oz., wine	18.00	40.00	35.00	50.00	75.00
Stem, #3380, 3 oz., cocktail	13.00	34.00	25.00	40.00	60.00
Stem, #3380, 4 oz., oyster/cocktail	8.00	13.00	15.00	17.00	25.00
Stem, #3380, 4 oz., claret	20.00	50.00	40.00	55.00	65.00

	Crystal	Flam.	Sahara	Moon.	Marigold
Stem, #3380, 5 oz., parfait	10.00	15.00	15.00	17.00	40.00
Stem, #3380, 6 oz., champagne	8.00	13.00	15.00	17.00	25.00
Stem, #3380, 6 oz., sherbet	6.00	11.00	13.00	15.00	25.00
Stem, #3380, 10 oz., short soda	7.00	18.00	15.00	22.00	30.00
Stem, #3380, 10 oz., tall soda		21.00	18.00	25.00	32.50
Stem, #3390, 1 oz., cordial	50.00	130.00	125.00	165.00	
Stem, #3390, 2½ oz., wine	12.00	20.00	27.50	35.00	
Stem, #3390, 3 oz., cocktail	7.00	15.00	20.00	25.00	
Stem, #3390, 3 oz., oyster/cocktail	7.00	15.00	20.00	25.00	
Stem, #3390, 4 oz., claret	12.00	22.50	27.50	32.50	
Stem, #3390, 6 oz., champagne	10.00	20.00	25.00	30.00	
Stem, #3390, 6 oz., sherbet	10.00	20.00	25.00	30.00	
Stem, #3390, 11 oz., low water	17.00	20.00	25.00	30.00	
Stem, #3390, 11 oz., tall water	10.00	22.00	27.00	32.00	
Sugar, dolphin ft.	17.50	30.00	45.00	50.00	
Sugar, indiv.	12.50	27.50	32.50	35.00	
Tray, 10", celery	14.00	20.00	25.00	30.00	
Tray, 12", ctr. hdld., sand.	35.00	65.00	75.00	85.00	
Tray, 12", ctr. hdld., sq.	35.00	65.00	75.00	85.00	
Tray, 13", celery	17.00	20.00	26.00	30.00	
Tray, 13", 2 hdld., hors d'oeuvre	30.00	36.00	45.00	55.00	
Tumbler, dolp. ft.	90.00	135.00	165.00	195.00	
Tumbler, #3380, 1 oz., ftd., bar	22.00	37.50	42.50	52.50	55.00
Tumbler, #3380, 2 oz., ftd., bar	12.00	20.00	20.00	25.00	35.00
Tumbler, #3380, 5 oz., ftd., bar	7.00	12.00	12.00	17.00	25.00
Tumbler, #3380, 8 oz., ftd., soda	10.00	21.00	18.00	25.00	32.50
Tumbler, #3380, 10 oz., ftd., soda	12.00	23.00	20.00	25.00	32.50
Tumbler, #3380, 12 oz., ftd., tea	13.00	25.00	22.00	27.00	35.00
Tumbler, #3390, 2 oz., ftd.	7.00	18.00	22.50	28.00	
Tumbler, #3390, 5 oz., ftd., juice	7.00	15.00	20.00	25.00	
Tumbler, #3390, 8 oz., ftd., soda	10.00	22.00	25.00	30.00	
Tumbler, #3390, 12 oz., ftd., tea	12.00	24.00	27.00	30.00	
Vase, 9", ftd.	75.00	130.00	150.00	175.00	

OLD SANDWICH, Blank #1404, A.H. Heisey & Co.

Colors: crystal, "Flamingo" pink, "Sahara" yellow, "Moongleam" green, cobalt, amber

Moongleam is the most desirable color in which a set of Old Sandwich can be accumulated. That Moongleam cup and saucer in the top photo is one of the few ever seen in Old Sandwich. For those who asked, the cupped in bowl in the center of the bottom photo is a popcorn bowl.

Cobalt blue pieces are expensive, but only a few items were made in that color.

	Crystal	Flam.	Sahara	Moon.	Cobalt
Ash tray, individual	9.00	45.00	35.00	55.00	45.00
Beer mug, 12 oz.	35.00	300.00	210.00	400.00	240.00
Beer mug, 14 oz.	45.00	325.00	225.00	425.00	250.00
* Beer mug, 18 oz.	50.00	400.00	270.00	475.00	300.00
Bottle, catsup, w/#3 stopper (like lg. cruet)	60.00	200.00	175.00	225.00	
Bowl, finger	12.00	50.00	60.00	60.00	
Bowl, ftd., popcorn, cupped	45.00	90.00	75.00	125.00	
Bowl, 11", rnd., ftd., floral	50.00	85.00	65.00	100.00	
Bowl, 12", oval, ftd., floral	35.00	80.00	70.00	80.00	
Candlestick, 6"	45.00	100.00	90.00	150.00	235.00
Cigarette holder	50.00	65.00	60.00	65.00	
Comport, 6"	40.00	95.00	90.00	100.00	
Creamer, oval	15.00	22.00	25.00	30.00	
Creamer, 12 oz.	32.00	165.00	170.00	175.00	300.00
Creamer, 14 oz.	35.00	175.00	180.00	185.00	
Creamer, 18 oz.	40.00	185.00	190.00	195.00	
Cup	40.00	65.00	65.00	125.00	
Decanter, 1 pint, w/#98 stopper	75.00	185.00	200.00	225.00	425.00
Floral block, #22	15.00	25.00	30.00	35.00	
Oil bottle, 2½ oz., #85 stopper	65.00	100.00	95.00	140.00	
Parfait, 4½ oz.	15.00	50.00	50.00	60.00	
Pilsner, 8 oz.	14.00	28.00	32.00	38.00	
Pilsner, 10 oz.	16.00	32.00	37.00	42.00	
Pitcher, ½ gallon, ice lip	85.00	175.00	165.00	185.00	
Pitcher, ½ gallon, reg.	85.00	175.00	165.00	185.00	
Plate, 6", sq., grnd. bottom	10.00	20.00	17.00	22.00	
Plate, 7", sq.	10.00	27.00	25.00	30.00	
Plate, 8", sq.	15.00	30.00	27.00	32.00	
Salt & pepper, pr.	40.00	65.00	75.00	85.00	
Saucer	10.00	15.00	15.00	25.00	
Stem, 2½ oz., wine	18.00	45.00	45.00	55.00	
Stem, 3 oz., cocktail	15.00	30.00	32.00	40.00	
Stem, 4 oz., claret	17.00	35.00	35.00	50.00	150.00
Stem, 4 oz., oyster cocktail	12.00	27.00	27.00	32.00	
Stem, 4 oz., sherbet	7.00	17.00	17.00	20.00	
Stem, 5 oz., saucer champagne	12.00	32.00	32.00	35.00	
Stem, 10 oz., low ft.	20.00	30.00	35.00	40.00	
Sugar, oval	15.00	22.00	25.00	30.00	
Sundae, 6 oz.	18.00	30.00	30.00	35.00	
Tumbler, 1½ oz., bar, grnd. bottom	20.00	130.00	120.00	135.00	100.00
Tumbler, 5 oz., juice	7.00	15.00	15.00	25.00	
Tumbler, 6½ oz., toddy	10.00	22.00	22.00	25.00	
Tumbler, 8 oz., grnd. bottom, cupped & straight rim	12.00	35.00	35.00	40.00	
Tumbler, 10 oz.	15.00	40.00	40.00	45.00	
Tumbler, 10 oz., low ft.	15.00	40.00	42.00	45.00	
Tumbler, 12 oz., ftd., iced tea	20.00	45.00	45.00	55.00	
Tumbler, 12 oz., iced tea	20.00	45.00	45.00	55.00	

*Amber; 300.00; Round creamer & sugar, $30.00 ea. piece, (unusual).
Whimsey Basket made from footed soda, $725.00.

ORCHID, Etching #1507 on WAVERLY Blank #1519 and QUEEN ANN Blank #1509,
A.H. Heisey & Co. 1940 – 1957

Colors: crystal

A 6¼" Cabochon candy has been found in Orchid. You will be able to see it in *Very Rare Glassware of the Depression Years, Fifth Series*. It amazes me how so few unusual pieces can turn up in a pattern as widely promoted as Orchid!

Orchid serving pieces and flatware have continued a slow rise in price, but prices in the ever present stemware have been slowly retreating! Most noticeably, water goblets and high sherbets have softened due to an over supply at present. Remember, I am reporting what is going on at the present and not trying to predict what will happen if everyone suddenly decides to collect Orchid and the supply dwindles overnight. It could happen!

Recently, everyone has been searching for the Waverly ice bucket, while the Queen Ann sits on the shelf gathering dust. I wish I understood collectors' whims!

	Crystal		Crystal
Ash tray, 3".	30.00	Bowl, 11", ftd., floral	110.00
Basket, 8½", LARIAT	950.00	Bowl, 12", crimped, floral, WAVERLY	80.00
Bell, dinner, #5022 or #5025	125.00	Bowl, 13", floral	110.00
Bottle, 8 oz., French dressings	175.00	Bowl, 13", crimped, floral, WAVERLY	90.00
Bowl, finger, #3309 or #5025	85.00	Bowl, 13", gardenia	70.00
Bowl, 4½", nappy, QUEEN ANN	37.50	Butter, w/cover, ¼ lb., CABOCHON	315.00
Bowl, 5½", ftd., mint, QUEEN ANN	35.00	Butter, w/cover, 6", WAVERLY	170.00
Bowl, 6", jelly, 2 hdld, QUEEN ANN	35.00	Candleholder, 6", deep epernette, WAVERLY	350.00
Bowl, 6½" oval, lemon, w/cover, QUEEN ANN	285.00	Candlestick, 1-lite, MERCURY	40.00
Bowl, 6", oval, lemon, w/cover, WAVERLY	850.00	Candlestick, 1-lite, QUEEN ANN w/prisms	125.00
Bowl, 6½", ftd., honey; cheese, QUEEN ANN	35.00	Candlestick, 2-lite, FLAME	155.00
Bowl, 6½", ftd., jelly, WAVERLY	60.00	Candlestick, 5", 2-lite, TRIDENT	50.00
Bowl, 6½", 2 pt., oval, dressings, WAVERLY	47.50	Candlestick, 2-lite, WAVERLY	60.00
Bowl, 7", lily, QUEEN ANN	120.00	Candlestick, 3-lite, CASCADE	75.00
Bowl, 7", salad	45.00	Candlestick, 3-lite, WAVERLY	90.00
Bowl, 7", 3 pt., rnd., relish	55.00	Candy box, w/cover, 6", low ft.	170.00
Bowl, 7", ftd., honey; cheese, WAVERLY	50.00	Candy, w/cover, 5", high ft., WAVERLY	240.00
Bowl, 7", ftd., jelly	40.00	Candy, w/cover, 6", bow knot finial	170.00
Bowl, 7", ftd., oval, nut, WAVERLY	85.00	Cheese (comport) & cracker (11½") plate	125.00
Bowl, 8", mint, ftd., QUEEN ANN	60.00	Cheese & cracker, 14" plate	145.00
Bowl, 8", nappy, QUEEN ANN	65.00	Chocolate, w/cover, 5", WAVERLY	185.00
Bowl, 8", 2 pt., oval, dressings, ladle	52.50	Cigarette box, w/cover, 4", PURITAN	135.00
Bowl, 8", pt., rnd., relish	57.50	Cigarette holder, #4035	80.00
Bowl, 8½", flared, QUEEN ANN	65.00	Cigarette holder, w/cover	160.00
Bowl, 8½", floral, 2 hdld., ftd., QUEEN ANN	57.50	Cocktail icer, w/liner, UNIVERSAL, #3304	225.00
Bowl, 9", 4 pt., rnd., relish	70.00	Cocktail shaker, pt., #4225	275.00
Bowl, 9", ftd., fruit or salad	125.00	Cocktail shaker, qt., #4036 or #4225	225.00
Bowl, 9", gardenia, QUEEN ANN	60.00	Comport, 5½", blown	87.50
Bowl, 9", salad, WAVERLY	160.00	Comport, 6", low ft., WAVERLY	50.00
Bowl, 9½", crimped floral, QUEEN ANN	65.00	Comport, 6½", low ft., WAVERLY	55.00
Bowl, 9½" epergne	500.00	Comport, 7", ftd., oval	135.00
Bowl, 10", crimped	70.00	Creamer, individual	35.00
Bowl, 10", deep salad	120.00	Creamer, ftd.	35.00
Bowl, 10", gardenia	70.00	Cup, WAVERLY or QUEEN ANN	40.00
Bowl, 10½", ftd., floral	110.00	Decanter, oval, sherry, pt.	225.00
Bowl, 11", shallow, rolled edge	70.00	Decanter, pt., ftd. #4036	325.00
Bowl, 11", 3 ftd., floral, seahorse ft.	145.00	Decanter, pt., #4036½	245.00
Bowl, 11", 3 pt., oblong, relish	67.50	Ice bucket, ftd., QUEEN ANN	225.00
Bowl, 11", 4 ftd., oval	85.00	Ice bucket, 2 hdld., WAVERLY	400.00
Bowl, 11", flared	130.00	Marmalade, w/cover	225.00
Bowl, 11", floral	65.00	Mayonnaise and liner, #1495, FERN	245.00

ORCHID

	Crystal
Mayonnaise, 5½", 1 hdl.	55.00
Mayonnaise, 5½", ftd.	55.00
Mayonnaise, 5½", 1 hdl., div.	50.00
Mayonnaise, 6½", 1 hdl.	65.00
Mayonnaise, 6½", 1 hdl., div.	65.00
Mustard, w/cover, QUEEN ANN	135.00
Oil, 3 oz., ftd.	175.00
Pitcher, 73 oz.	500.00
Pitcher, 64 oz., ice tankard	525.00
Plate, 6"	13.00
Plate, 7", mayonnaise	20.00
Plate, 7", salad	22.00
Plate, 8", salad, WAVERLY	24.00
Plate, 10½", dinner	140.00
Plate, 11", demi-torte	60.00
Plate, 11", sandwich	75.00
Plate, 12", ftd., salver, WAVERLY	225.00
Plate, 12", rnd sandwich, hdld.	70.00
Plate, 14", ftd., cake or salver	275.00
Plate, 14", torte, rolled edge	65.00
Plate, 14", torte, WAVERLY	90.00
Plate, 14", sandwich, WAVERLY	80.00
Plate, 15", sandwich, WAVERLY	65.00
Plate, 15½", QUEEN ANN	95.00
Salt & pepper, pr.	85.00
Salt & pepper, ftd., pr., WAVERLY	80.00
Saucer, WAVERLY or QUEEN ANN	12.50
Stem, #5022 or #5025, 1 oz., cordial	125.00

	Crystal
Stem, #5022 or #5025, 2 oz., sherry	120.00
Stem, #5022 or #5025, 3 oz., wine	75.00
Stem, #5022 or #5025, 4 oz., oyster cocktail	57.50
Stem, #5025, 4 oz., cocktail	40.00
Stem, #5022 or #5025, 4½ oz., claret	135.00
Stem, #5022 or #5025, 6 oz., saucer champagne	30.00
Stem, #5022 or #5025, 6 oz., sherbet	25.00
Stem, #5022 or #5025, 10 oz., low water goblet	37.50
Stem, #5022 or #5025, 10 oz., water goblet	40.00
Sugar, individual	35.00
Sugar, ftd.	35.00
Tray, indiv., creamer/sugar, QUEEN ANN	85.00
Tray, 12", celery	50.00
Tray, 13", celery	55.00
Tumbler, #5022 or #5025, 5 oz., fruit	55.00
Tumbler, #5022 or #5025, 12 oz., iced tea	65.00
Vase, 4", ftd., violet, WAVERLY	120.00
Vase, 6", crimped top	115.00
Vase, 7", ftd., fan	90.00
Vase, 7", ftd.	120.00
Vase, 7", crimped top, LARIAT	120.00
Vase, 8", ftd., bud	195.00
Vase, 8", sq., ftd., bud	215.00
Vase, 10", sq., ftd., bud	275.00
Vase, 12"	350.00
Vase, 14"	650.00

PLANTATION, Blank #1567, A.H. Heisey & Co.

Colors: crystal; rare in amber

Plantation prices have gone wild! This pattern has taken over the spotlight from Rose and Orchid. Dealers cannot get enough stock to satisfy collectors looking for Plantation!

I had two different people tell me that with a lot of practice you can grasp a goblet the way the model did in the ad on page 153. One collector said he broke two of his wife's wine glasses before he got it right!

	Crystal		Crystal
Ash tray, 3½"	35.00	Cup, punch	30.00
Bowl, 9 qt., Dr. Johnson, punch	600.00	Marmalade, w/cover	140.00
Bowl, 5", nappy	20.00	Mayonnaise, 4½", rolled ft.	55.00
Bowl, 5½", nappy	30.00	Mayonnaise, 5¼", w/liner	50.00
Bowl, 6½", 2 hdld., jelly	45.00	Oil bottle, 3 oz., w/#125 stopper	110.00
Bowl, 6½", flared, jelly	60.00	Pitcher, ½ gallon, ice lip, blown	400.00
Bowl, 6½", ftd., honey, cupped	75.00	Plate, coupe (rare)	400.00
Bowl, 8", 4 pt., rnd., relish	70.00	Plate, 7", salad	22.00
Bowl, 8½", 2 pt., dressing	70.00	Plate, 8", salad	32.00
Bowl, 9", salad	135.00	Plate, 10½", demi-torte	70.00
Bowl, 9½", crimped, fruit or flower	85.00	Plate, 13", ftd., cake salver	160.00
Bowl, 9½", gardenia	85.00	Plate, 14", sandwich	75.00
Bowl, 11", 3 part, relish	60.00	Plate, 18", buffet	110.00
Bowl, 11½", ftd., gardenia	140.00	Plate, 18", punch bowl liner	120.00
Bowl, 12", crimped, fruit or flower	90.00	Salt & pepper, pr.	70.00
Bowl, 13", celery	50.00	Saucer	7.00
Bowl, 13", 2 part, celery	50.00	Stem, 1 oz., cordial	125.00
Bowl, 13", 5 part, oval relish	90.00	Stem, 3 oz., wine, blown	75.00
Bowl, 13", gardenia	80.00	Stem, 3½ oz., cocktail, pressed	35.00
Butter, ¼ lb., oblong, w/cover	110.00	Stem, 4 oz., fruit/oyster cocktail	35.00
Butter, 5", rnd., (or cov. candy)	120.00	Stem, 4½ oz., claret, blown	65.00
Candelabrum, w/two #1503 bobeche & 10		Stem, 4½ oz., claret, pressed	65.00
"A" prisms	160.00	Stem, 4½ oz., oyster cocktail, blown	40.00
Candle block, hurricane type w/globe	160.00	Stem, 6½ oz., sherbet/saucer champagne,	
Candle block, 1-lite	90.00	blown	40.00
Candle holder, 5", ftd., epergne	110.00	Stem, 10 oz., pressed	50.00
Candlestick, 1-lite	90.00	Stem, 10 oz., blown	50.00
Candlestick, 2-lite	70.00	Sugar, ftd.	35.00
Candlestick, 3-lite	90.00	Syrup bottle, w/drip, cut top	100.00
Candy box, w/cover, 7" length, flat bottom	150.00	Tray, 8½", condiment/sugar & creamer	65.00
Candy, w/cover, 5", tall, ftd.	180.00	Tumbler, 5 oz., ftd., juice, pressed	50.00
Cheese, w/cover, 5", ftd.	90.00	Tumbler, 5 oz., ftd., juice, blown	40.00
Cigarette box, w/cover	180.00	Tumbler, 8 oz., water, pressed	125.00
Coaster, 4"	60.00	Tumbler, 10 oz., pressed	90.00
Comport, 5"	50.00	Tumbler, 12 oz., ftd., iced tea, pressed	80.00
Comport, 5", w/cover, deep	100.00	Tumbler, 12 oz., ftd., iced tea, blown	75.00
Creamer, ftd.	35.00	Vase, 5", ftd., flared	90.00
Cup	30.00	Vase, 9", ftd., flared	140.00

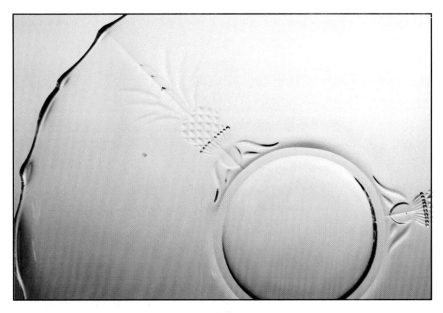

tradition in crystal...

Plantation Ivy...
hospitality's
traditional warmth
captured in
boldly etched
hand blown crystal

the finest in glassware, made in America by hand

Heisey
HAND-WROUGHT CRYSTAL

PLEAT & PANEL, Blank #1170, A.H. Heisey & Co.

Colors: crystal, "Flamingo" pink, "Moongleam" green

Pleat and Panel is a Heisey pattern that many exclusive Heisey dealers avoid because it looks too much like Depression glass! Heisey did make some patterns that are not exactly "elegant" looking, even though Heisey connoisseurs will not admit it. Most Pleat and Panel pieces carry the familiar H in diamond mark. Stems are marked on the stem itself and not the foot; so look there if you cannot find a mark.

Pleat and Panel makes an excellent starting pattern for elementary collectors. Some prices are beginning to rise due to demand, one of the first indications that new collectors are starting to buy a pattern!

Notice there are color variations in the pink and green pictured. Only Depression glass is supposed to have color variances. Yes, even Heisey had trouble holding color!

	Crystal	Flam.	Moongleam
Bowl, 4", chow chow	5.00	10.00	12.00
Bowl, 4½", nappy	5.00	10.00	12.00
Bowl, 5", 2 hdld., bouillon	7.00	12.00	15.00
Bowl, 5", 2 hdld., jelly	9.00	12.00	15.00
Bowl, 5", lemon, w/cover	20.00	40.00	50.00
Bowl, 6½", grapefruit/cereal	5.00	13.00	16.00
Bowl, 8", nappy	10.00	30.00	35.00
Bowl, 9", oval, vegetable	12.50	30.00	35.00
Cheese & cracker set, 10½", tray, w/compote	25.00	75.00	80.00
Compotier, w/cover, 5", hi. ftd.	35.00	60.00	80.00
Creamer, hotel	10.00	25.00	30.00
Cup	7.00	15.00	17.50
Marmalade, 4¾"	10.00	25.00	27.50
Oil bottle, 3 oz., w/pressed stopper	30.00	70.00	110.00
Pitcher, 3 pint, ice lip	45.00	130.00	145.00
Pitcher, 3 pint	45.00	130.00	145.00
Plate, 6"	4.00	8.00	8.00
Plate, 6¾", bouillon underliner	4.00	8.00	8.00
Plate, 7", bread	4.00	8.00	10.00
Plate, 8", luncheon	5.00	12.50	15.00
Plate, 10¾", dinner	15.00	42.50	47.50
Plate, 14", sandwich	15.00	30.00	35.00
Platter, 12", oval	15.00	40.00	45.00
Saucer	3.00	5.00	5.00
Sherbet, 5 oz., footed	4.00	10.00	12.00
Stem, 5 oz., saucer champagne	5.00	14.00	18.00
Stem, 7½ oz., low foot	12.00	30.00	35.00
Stem, 8 oz.	15.00	35.00	40.00
Sugar w/lid, hotel	10.00	25.00	30.00
Tray, 10", compartmented spice	10.00	25.00	30.00
Tumbler, 8 oz., ground bottom	5.00	15.00	20.00
Tumbler, 12 oz., tea, ground bottom	7.00	20.00	25.00
Vase, 8"	30.00	60.00	80.00

PORTIA, Cambridge Glass Company, 1932 – Early 1950's

Colors: crystal, yellow, Heatherbloom, green, amber

	Crystal		Crystal
Basket, 2 hdld. (upturned sides)	20.00	Saucer, sq. or rnd.	3.00
Basket, 7", 1 hdld.	225.00	Set: 3 pc. frappe (bowl, 2 plain inserts)	50.00
Bowl, 3", indiv. nut, 4 ftd.	50.00	Stem, #3121, 1 oz., cordial	60.00
Bowl, 3½", cranberry	25.00	Stem, #3121, 1 oz., low ftd., brandy	55.00
Bowl, 3½" sq., cranberry	25.00	Stem, #3121, 2½ oz., wine	35.00
Bowl, 5¼", 2 hdld., bonbon	20.00	Stem, #3121, 3 oz., cocktail	20.00
Bowl, 6", 2 pt., relish	18.00	Stem, #3121, 4½ oz., claret	40.00
Bowl, 6", ftd., 2 hdld., bonbon	20.00	Stem, #3121, 4½ oz., oyster cocktail	15.00
Bowl, 6", grapefruit or oyster	20.00	Stem, #3121, 5 oz., parfait	38.00
Bowl, 6½", 3 pt., relish	20.00	Stem, #3121, 6 oz., low sherbet	13.50
Bowl, 7", 2 pt., relish	22.00	Stem, #3121, 6 oz., tall sherbet	15.00
Bowl, 7", ftd., bonbon, tab hdld.	25.00	Stem, #3121, 10 oz., goblet	22.50
Bowl, 7", pickle or relish	25.00	Stem, #3124, 3 oz., cocktail	15.00
Bowl, 9", 3 pt., celery & relish, tab hdld.	35.00	Stem, #3124, 3 oz., wine	30.00
Bowl, 9½", ftd., pickle (like corn bowl)	25.00	Stem, #3124, 4½ oz., claret	40.00
Bowl, 10", flared, 4 ftd.	40.00	Stem, #3124, 7 oz., low sherbet	14.00
Bowl, 11", 2 pt., 2 hdld., "figure 8" relish	30.00	Stem, #3124, 7 oz., tall sherbet	15.00
Bowl, 11", 2 hdld.	37.50	Stem, #3124, 10 oz., goblet	18.00
Bowl, 12", 3 pt., celery & relish, tab hdld.	35.00	Stem, #3126, 1 oz., cordial	60.00
Bowl, 12", 5 pt., celery & relish	37.50	Stem, #3126, 1 oz., low ft., brandy	55.00
Bowl, 12", flared, 4 ftd.	45.00	Stem, #3126, 2½ oz., wine	35.00
Bowl, 12", oval, 4 ftd., "ears" handles	45.00	Stem, #3126, 3 oz., cocktail	17.50
Bowl, finger, w/liner #3124	35.00	Stem, #3126, 4½ oz., claret	40.00
Bowl, seafood (fruit cocktail w/liner)	65.00	Stem, #3126, 4½ oz., low ft., oyster cocktail	12.50
Candlestick, 5"	22.00	Stem, #3126, 7 oz., low sherbet	14.00
Candlestick, 6", 2-lite, "fleur-de-lis"	37.50	Stem, #3126, 7 oz., tall sherbet	15.00
Candlestick, 6", 3-lite	45.00	Stem, #3126, 9 oz., goblet	20.00
Candy box, w/cover, rnd.	70.00	Stem, #3130, 1 oz., cordial	60.00
Cigarette holder, urn shape	60.00	Stem, #3130, 2½ oz., wine	35.00
Cocktail icer, 2 pt.	65.00	Stem, #3130, 3 oz., cocktail	17.50
Cocktail shaker, w/stopper	95.00	Stem, #3130, 4½ oz., claret	40.00
Cocktail shaker, 80 oz., hdld. ball		Stem, #3130, 4½ oz., fruit/oyster cocktail	15.00
w/chrome top	185.00	Stem, #3130, 7 oz., low sherbet	14.00
Cologne, 2 oz., hdld. ball w/stopper	95.00	Stem, #3130, 7 oz., tall sherbet	15.00
Comport, 5½"	27.50	Stem, #3130, 9 oz., goblet	22.50
Comport, 5⅜", blown	35.00	Sugar, ftd., hdld. ball	30.00
Creamer, ftd.	12.00	Sugar, ftd.	12.00
Creamer, hdld. ball	30.00	Sugar, indiv.	11.50
Creamer, indiv.	12.50	Tray, 11", celery	35.00
Cup, ftd. sq.	18.00	Tumbler, #3121, 2½ oz., bar	35.00
Cup, rd.	15.00	Tumbler, #3121, 5 oz., ftd., juice	18.00
Decanter, 29 oz. ftd., sherry, w/stopper	195.00	Tumbler, #3121, 10 oz., ftd., water	16.50
Hurricane lamp, candlestick base	145.00	Tumbler, #3121, 12 oz., ftd., tea	25.00
Hurricane lamp, keyhole base, w/prisms	165.00	Tumbler, #3124, 3 oz.	15.00
Ice bucket, w/chrome handle	75.00	Tumbler, #3124, 5 oz., juice	15.00
Ivy ball, 5¼"	45.00	Tumbler, #3124, 10 oz., water	15.00
Mayonnaise, div. bowl, w/liner & 2 ladles	45.00	Tumbler, #3124, 12 oz., tea	22.00
Mayonnaise, w/liner & ladle	40.00	Tumbler, #3126, 2½ oz.	35.00
Oil, 6 oz., loop hdld., w/stopper	75.00	Tumbler, #3126, 5 oz., juice	14.00
Oil, 6 oz., hdld. ball, w/stopper	85.00	Tumbler, #3126, 10 oz., water	15.00
Pitcher, ball	155.00	Tumbler, #3126, 12 oz., tea	22.00
Pitcher, Doulton	310.00	Tumbler, #3130, 5 oz., juice	16.00
Plate, 6", 2 hdld.	15.00	Tumbler, #3130, 10 oz., water	15.00
Plate, 6½", bread/butter	7.50	Tumbler, #3130, 12 oz., tea	22.00
Plate, 8", salad	12.50	Tumbler, 12 oz., "roly-poly"	28.00
Plate, 8", ftd., 2 hdld.	17.50	Vase, 5", globe	45.00
Plate, 8", ftd., bonbon, tab hdld.	20.00	Vase, 6", ftd.	50.00
Plate, 8½", sq.	15.00	Vase, 8", ftd.	65.00
Plate, 10½", dinner	65.00	Vase, 9", keyhole ft.	75.00
Plate, 13", 4 ftd., torte	40.00	Vase, 10", bud	55.00
Plate, 13½", 2 hdld., cake	40.00	Vase, 11", flower	65.00
Plate, 14", torte	55.00	Vase, 11", pedestal ft.	75.00
Puff box, 3½", ball shape, w/lid	155.00	Vase, 12", keyhole ft.	95.00
Salt & pepper, pr., flat	25.00	Vase, 13", flower	110.00

PROVINCIAL, Blank #1506, A.H. Heisey & Co.

Colors: crystal, "Limelight" green

	Crystal	Limelight Green
Ash tray, 3" square	12.50	
Bonbon dish, 7", 2 hdld., upturned sides	12.00	37.50
Bowl, 5 quart, punch	120.00	
Bowl, individual, nut/jelly	20.00	35.00
Bowl, 4½", nappy	12.00	70.00
Bowl, 5", 2 hdld., nut/jelly	15.00	
Bowl, 5½", nappy	15.00	40.00
Bowl, 5½", round, hdld., nappy	15.00	
Bowl, 5½", tri-corner, hdld., nappy	20.00	55.00
Bowl, 10", 4 part, relish	40.00	195.00
Bowl, 12", floral	35.00	
Bowl, 13", gardenia	40.00	
Box, 5½", footed, candy, w/cover	75.00	550.00
Butter dish, w/cover	85.00	
Candle, 1-lite, block	25.00	
Candle, 2-lite	80.00	
Candle, 3-lite, #4233, 5", vase	95.00	
Cigarette box w/cover	50.00	
Cigarette lighter	30.00	
Coaster, 4"	12.00	
Creamer, footed	20.00	95.00
Creamer & sugar, w/tray, individual	65.00	
Cup, punch	10.00	
Mayonnaise, 7" (plate, ladle, bowl)	40.00	150.00
Mustard	110.00	
Oil bottle, 4 oz., #1 stopper	45.00	
Oil & vinegar bottle, (french dressing)	60.00	
Plate, 5", footed, cheese	18.00	
Plate, 7", 2 hdld., snack	12.00	
Plate, 7", bread	10.00	
Plate, 8", luncheon	15.00	50.00
Plate, 14", torte	35.00	
Plate, 18", buffet	60.00	175.00
Salt & pepper, pr.	40.00	
Stem, 3½ oz., oyster cocktail	15.00	
Stem, 3½ oz., wine	15.00	
Stem, 5 oz., sherbet/champagne	7.00	
Stem, 10 oz.	15.00	
Sugar, footed	20.00	95.00
Tray, 13", oval, celery	22.00	
Tumbler, 5 oz., footed, juice	12.00	60.00
Tumbler, 8 oz.	15.00	
Tumbler, 9 oz., footed	15.00	65.00
Tumbler, 12 oz., footed, iced tea	17.00	75.00
Tumbler, 13", flat, ice tea	20.00	
Vase, 3½", violet	30.00	95.00
Vase, 4", pansy	35.00	
Vase, 6", sweet pea	45.00	

QUEEN ANN, Blank #1401, A.H. Heisey & Co.

Queen Ann is the pattern name given to Empress when it was made in crystal (c.1938). There are few collectors for this crystal pattern, but it is not as easily gathered as one might assume by the inexpensive prices! An ice bucket is pictured to help you see the typical dolphin on the footed pieces.

	Crystal
Ash tray	30.00
Bonbon, 6"	10.00
Bowl, cream soup	15.00
Bowl, cream soup, w/sq. liner	20.00
Bowl, frappe, w/center	20.00
Bowl, nut, dolphin ftd., indiv.	17.00
Bowl, 4½", nappy	5.00
Bowl, 5", preserve, 2 hdld.	12.00
Bowl, 6", ftd., jelly, 2 hdld.	12.00
Bowl, 6", dolp. ftd., mint	14.00
Bowl, 6", grapefruit, sq. top, grnd. bottom	9.00
Bowl, 6½", oval, lemon, w/cover	40.00
Bowl, 7", 3 pt., relish, triplex	15.00
Bowl, 7", 3 pt., relish, ctr. hand.	20.00
Bowl, 7½", dolp. ftd., nappy	25.00
Bowl, 7½", dolp. ftd., nasturtium	30.00
Bowl, 8", nappy	22.00
Bowl, 8½", ftd., floral, 2 hdld	30.00
Bowl, 9", floral, rolled edge	22.00
Bowl, 9", floral, flared	30.00
Bowl, 10", 2 hdld., oval dessert	30.00
Bowl, 10", lion head, floral	250.00
Bowl, 10", oval, veg.	27.00
Bowl, 10", square, salad, 2 hdld.	30.00
Bowl, 10", triplex, relish	20.00
Bowl, 11", dolphin ftd., floral	32.00
Bowl, 13", pickle/olive, 2 pt.	15.00
Bowl, 15", dolp. ftd., punch	400.00
Candlestick, 3", 3 ftd	45.00
Candlestick, low, 4 ftd., w/2 hdld.	15.00
Candlestick, 6", dolphin ftd.	50.00
Candy, w/cover, 6", dolphin ftd.	40.00
Comport, 6", ftd.	25.00
Comport, 6", square	40.00
Comport, 7", oval	35.00
Compotier, 6", dolphin ftd.	70.00
Creamer, dolphin ftd.	20.00
Creamer, indiv.	15.00
Cup	12.00
Cup, after dinner	15.00
Cup, bouillon, 2 hdld.	16.00
Cup, 4 oz., custard or punch	12.00
Cup, #1401½, has rim as demi-cup	20.00
Grapefruit, w/square liner	15.00
Ice tub, w/metal handles	40.00
Jug, 3 pint, ftd.	70.00

	Crystal
Marmalade, w/cover, dolp. ftd.	50.00
Mayonnaise, 5½", ftd., w/ladle	25.00
Mustard, w/cover	30.00
Oil bottle, 4 oz.	40.00
Plate, bouillon liner	4.00
Plate, cream soup liner	5.00
Plate, 4½"	5.00
Plate, 6"	5.00
Plate, 6", square	5.00
Plate, 7"	8.00
Plate, 7", square	7.00
Plate, 8", square	10.00
Plate, 8"	9.00
Plate, 9"	12.00
Plate, 10½"	40.00
Plate, 10½", square	40.00
Plate, 12"	25.00
Plate, 12", muffin, sides upturned	30.00
Plate, 12", sandwich, 2 hdld.	25.00
Plate, 13", hors d'oeuvre, 2 hdld.	28.00
Plate, 13", square, 2 hdld.	28.00
Platter, 14"	25.00
Salt & pepper, pr.	50.00
Saucer, square	3.00
Saucer, after dinner	2.00
Saucer	3.00
Stem, 2½ oz., oyster cocktail	15.00
Stem, 4 oz., saucer champagne	20.00
Stem, 4 oz., sherbet	15.00
Stem, 9 oz., Empress stemware, unusual	30.00
Sugar, indiv.	15.00
Sugar, dolphin ftd., 3 hdld.	20.00
Tray, condiment & liner for indiv. sugar/creamer	15.00
Tray, 10", 3 pt., relish	18.00
Tray, 10", 7 pt., hors d'oeuvre	50.00
Tray, 10", celery	12.00
Tray, 12", ctr. hdld., sand.	30.00
Tray, 12", sq. ctr. hdld., sand.	32.50
Tray, 13", celery	16.00
Tray, 16", 4 pt., buffet relish	30.00
Tumbler, 8 oz., dolp. ftd., unusual	75.00
Tumbler, 8 oz., grnd. bottom	15.00
Tumbler, 12 oz., tea, grnd. bottom	18.00
Vase, 8", flared	45.00

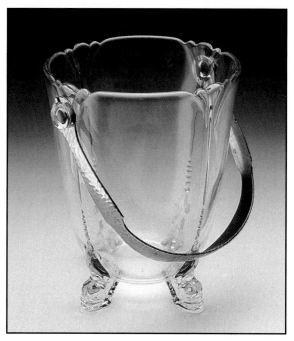

RIDGELEIGH, Blank #1469, A.H. Heisey & Co.

Colors: crystal, "Sahara," "Zircon," rare

	Crystal
Ash tray, round..	14.00
Ash tray, square	10.00
Ash tray, 4", round	22.00
Ash tray, 6", square......................................	35.00
Ash trays, bridge set (heart, diamond, spade, club)	40.00
Basket, bonbon	15.00
Bottle, rock & rye, w/#104 stopper	140.00
Bottle, 4 oz., cologne	100.00
Bottle, 5 oz., bitters, w/tube	100.00
Bowl, indiv., nut...	10.00
Bowl, oval, indiv., jelly	14.00
Bowl, indiv., nut, 2 part	14.00
Bowl, 4½", nappy, bell or cupped	12.00
Bowl, 4½", nappy, scalloped........................	12.00
Bowl, 5", lemon, w/cover	65.00
Bowl, 5", nappy, straight	10.00
Bowl, 5", nappy, square	22.00
Bowl, 6", 2 hdld., divided, jelly....................	14.00
Bowl, 6", 2 hdld., jelly................................	16.00
Bowl, 7", 2 part, oval, relish........................	16.00
Bowl, 8", centerpiece...................................	38.00
Bowl, 8", nappy, square...............................	45.00
Bowl, 9", nappy, square	65.00
Bowl, 9", salad...	37.00
Bowl, 10", flared, fruit................................	45.00
Bowl, 10", floral...	45.00
Bowl, 11", centerpiece.................................	45.00
Bowl, 11", punch..	200.00
Bowl, 11½", floral	50.00
Bowl, 12", oval, floral.................................	55.00
Bowl, 12", flared, fruit	50.00
Bowl, 13", cone, floral.................................	50.00
Bowl, 14", oblong, floral..............................	60.00
Bowl, 14", oblong, swan hdld., floral	280.00
Box, 8", floral	40.00
Candle block, 3", #1469½............................	20.00
Candle vase, 6"	30.00
Candlestick, 2", 1-lite	30.00
Candlestick, 2-lite, bobeche & "A" prisms...........	70.00
Candlestick, 7", w/bobeche & "A" prisms............	110.00
Cheese, 6", 2 hdld.......................................	14.00
Cigarette box, w/cover, oval..........................	75.00
Cigarette box, w/cover, 6"	35.00
Cigarette holder, oval, w/2 comp. ashtrays	60.00
Cigarette holder, round	14.00
Cigarette holder, square	14.00
Cigarette holder, w/cover.............................	30.00
Coaster or cocktail rest................................	5.00
Cocktail shaker, 1 qt., w/#1 strainer & #86 stopper	225.00
Comport, 6", low ft., flared..........................	20.00
Comport, 6", low ft., w/cover........................	35.00
Creamer...	20.00
Creamer, indiv.	15.00
Cup...	15.00
Cup, beverage	12.00
Cup, punch	10.00
Decanter, 1 pint, w/#95 stopper	175.00
Ice tub, 2 hdld.	85.00
Marmalade, w/cover, (scarce)........................	75.00
Mayonnaise	35.00

	Crystal
Mustard, w/cover	50.00
Oil bottle, 3 oz., w/#103 stopper	50.00
Pitcher, ½ gallon, ball shape	300.00
Pitcher, ½ gallon, ice lip, ball shape	300.00
Plate, oval, hors d'oeuvres	90.00
Plate, 2 hdld., ice tub liner	50.00
Plate, 6", round	10.00
Plate, 6", scalloped	10.00
Plate, 6", square	14.00
Plate, 7", square	15.00
Plate, 8", round	17.50
Plate, 8", square	25.00
Plate, 13½", sandwich	45.00
Plate, 13½", ftd., torte	45.00
Plate, 14", salver	50.00
Plate, 20", punch bowl underplate	140.00
Salt & pepper, pr.	45.00
Salt dip, indiv.	13.00
Saucer	5.00
Soda, 12 oz., ftd., no knob in stem, (rare)	50.00
Stem, cocktail, pressed	22.00
Stem, claret, pressed	40.00
Stem, oyster cocktail, pressed	25.00
Stem, sherbet, pressed	15.00
Stem, saucer champagne, pressed	22.00
Stem, wine, pressed	32.00
Stem, 1 oz., cordial, blown	160.00
Stem, 2 oz., sherry, blown	90.00
Stem, 2½ oz., wine, blown	80.00
Stem, 3½ oz., cocktail, blown	35.00
Stem, 4 oz., claret, blown	55.00
Stem, 4 oz., oyster cocktail, blown	30.00
Stem, 5 oz., saucer champagne, blown	25.00
Stem, 5 oz., sherbet, blown	20.00
Stem, 8 oz., luncheon, low stem....................	30.00
Stem, 8 oz., tall stem	40.00
Sugar	20.00
Sugar, indiv.	12.50
Tray, for indiv. sugar & creamer	20.00
Tray, 10½", oblong	30.00
Tray, 11", 3 part, relish	40.00
Tray, 12", celery & olive, divided..................	35.00
Tray, 12", celery	35.00
Tumbler, 2½ oz., bar, pressed.......................	35.00
Tumbler, 5 oz., juice, blown	30.00
Tumbler, 5 oz., soda, ftd., pressed	28.00
Tumbler, 8 oz., (#1469¾), pressed	24.00
Tumbler, 8 oz., old-fashioned, pressed............	26.00
Tumbler, 8 oz., soda, blown	32.00
Tumbler, 10 oz., (#1469½), pressed	40.00
Tumbler, 12 oz., ftd., soda, pressed	45.00
Tumbler, 12 oz., soda, (#1469½) pressed..........	45.00
Tumbler, 13 oz., iced tea, blown....................	28.00
Vase, #1 indiv., cuspidor shape	30.00
Vase, #2 indiv., cupped top...........................	35.00
Vase, #3 indiv., flared rim	27.50
Vase, #4 indiv., fan out top	45.00
Vase, #5 indiv., scalloped top	45.00
Vase, 3½"	22.00
Vase, 6" (also flared)...................................	20.00
Vase, 8"..	65.00
Vase, 8", triangular (#1469¾)	85.00

ROSALIE, or #731, Cambridge Glass Company, Late 1920's – 1930's

Colors: blue, green, Heatherbloom, pink, red, amber, bluebell, crystal, topaz

There are a wealth of listings for Cambridge's #731 line known as Rosalie; but don't let those mislead you into thinking this 70-year-old ware is easily located. Most collectors concentrate on pink and green though amber could also be accumulated. Perhaps a small set of Willow Blue is possible; but Carmen, Bluebell, or Heatherbloom are colors that are perhaps too infrequently seen to be gathered into sets.

The piece in the foreground of the bottom photograph is called a wafer tray. A smaller version is a sugar cube tray. These items are gathered by other collectors than Cambridge buffs. Though not as plentiful as some patterns, Rosalie is an ideal inaugural pattern for someone to collect without taking out a loan.

	Blue Pink Green	Amber		Blue Pink Green	Amber
Bottle, French dressing	125.00	90.00	Gravy, double, w/platter	150.00	90.00
Bowl, bouillon, 2 hdld.	25.00	15.00	Ice bucket or pail	75.00	50.00
Bowl, cream soup	25.00	20.00	Icer, w/liner	60.00	45.00
Bowl, finger, w/liner	40.00	25.00	Ice tub	75.00	65.00
Bowl, finger, ftd., w/liner	40.00	30.00	Marmalade	110.00	85.00
Bowl, 3½", cranberry	35.00	25.00	Mayonnaise, ftd., w/liner	55.00	25.00
Bowl, 3⅝", w/cover, 3 pt	55.00	40.00	Nut, 2½", ftd.	60.00	45.00
Bowl, 5½", fruit	18.00	12.00	Pitcher, 62 oz., #955	225.00	175.00
Bowl, 5½", 2 hdld., bonbon	20.00	12.00	Plate, 6¾", bread/butter	7.00	5.00
Bowl, 6¼", 2 hdld., bonbon	22.50	15.00	Plate, 7", 2 hdld.	15.00	7.00
Bowl, 7", basket, 2 hdld.	30.00	20.00	Plate, 7½", salad	10.00	6.00
Bowl, 8½", soup	45.00	30.00	Plate, 8⅜"	15.00	10.00
Bowl, 8½", 2 hdld.	35.00	25.00	Plate, 9½", dinner	60.00	35.00
Bowl, 8½", w/cover, 3 pt	75.00	40.00	Plate, 11", 2 hdld.	30.00	20.00
Bowl, 10"	45.00	30.00	Platter, 12"	75.00	45.00
Bowl, 10", 2 hdld.	45.00	30.00	Platter, 15"	110.00	80.00
Bowl, 11"	45.00	30.00	Relish, 9", 2 pt.	25.00	15.00
Bowl, 11", basket, 2 hdld.	50.00	40.00	Relish, 11", 2 pt.	35.00	20.00
Bowl, 11½"	75.00	50.00	Salt dip, 1½", ftd.	60.00	40.00
Bowl, 12", decagon	100.00	80.00	Saucer	5.00	4.00
Bowl, 13", console	60.00		Stem, 1 oz., cordial, #3077	90.00	60.00
Bowl, 14", decagon	235.00	175.00	Stem, 3½ oz., cocktail, #3077	20.00	15.00
Bowl, 15", oval console	95.00	70.00	Stem, 6 oz., low sherbet, #3077	15.00	12.00
Bowl, 15", oval, flanged	95.00	70.00	Stem, 6 oz., high sherbet, #3077	18.00	14.00
Bowl, 15½", oval	110.00	75.00	Stem, 9 oz., water goblet, #3077	25.00	20.00
Candlestick, 4", 2 styles	30.00	20.00	Stem, 10 oz., goblet, #801	30.00	20.00
Candlestick, 5", keyhole	35.00	25.00	Sugar, ftd.	16.00	13.00
Candlestick, 6", 3-lite keyhole	55.00	35.00	Sugar shaker	250.00	210.00
Candy and cover, 6"	110.00	70.00	Tray for sugar shaker/creamer	30.00	20.00
Celery, 11"	35.00	20.00	Tray, ctr. hdld., for sugar/creamer	20.00	14.00
Cheese & cracker, 11" plate	65.00	40.00	Tray, 11", ctr. hdld.	30.00	20.00
Comport, 5½", 2 hdld.	30.00	15.00	Tumbler, 2½ oz., ftd., #3077	35.00	25.00
Comport, 5¾"	30.00	15.00	Tumbler, 5 oz., ftd., #3077	25.00	20.00
Comport, 6", ftd., almond	40.00	25.00	Tumbler, 8 oz., ftd. #3077	25.00	16.00
Comport, 6½", low ft.	40.00	25.00	Tumbler, 10 oz., ftd., #3077	27.00	20.00
Comport, 6½", high ft.	40.00	25.00	Tumbler, 12 oz., ftd., #3077	35.00	25.00
Comport, 6¾"	45.00	30.00	Vase, 5½", ftd.	50.00	30.00
Creamer, ftd.	17.00	12.00	Vase, 6"	65.00	45.00
Creamer, ftd., tall, ewer	35.00	25.00	Vase, 6½", ftd.	85.00	50.00
Cup	35.00	25.00	Wafer tray	110.00	75.00

ROSE, Etching #1515 on WAVERLY Blank #1519, A.H. Heisey & Co., 1949 – 1957

Colors: crystal

An abundance of Rose stems are being found; except for oyster cocktails and clarets which are rare. Cocktail icers and the Waverly ice bucket are in demand; but for some reason, pitchers are not selling at present. (I counted seven at last year's Heisey convention.) That 6" epernette on the triple candle has turned out to be one of the rarest pieces in Rose.

	Crystal		Crystal
Ash tray, 3"	37.50	Cocktail icer, w/liner, #3304, UNIVERSAL	275.00
Bell, dinner, #5072	150.00	Cocktail shaker, #4225, COBEL	180.00
Bottle, 8 oz., French dressing, blown, #5031	195.00	Comport, 6½", low ft., WAVERLY	60.00
Bowl, finger, #3309	95.00	Comport, 7", oval, ftd., WAVERLY	130.00
Bowl, 5½", ftd., mint	35.00	Creamer, ftd., WAVERLY	35.00
Bowl, 5¾", ftd., mint, CABOCHON	75.00	Creamer, indiv., WAVERLY	40.00
Bowl, 6", ftd., mint, QUEEN ANN	50.00	Cup, WAVERLY	55.00
Bowl, 6", jelly, 2 hdld., ftd., QUEEN ANN	55.00	Decanter, 1 pt., #4036½, #101 stopper	195.00
Bowl, 6", oval, lemon, w/cover, WAVERLY	325.00	Hurricane lamp, w/12" globe, #5080	325.00
Bowl, 6½", 2 pt., oval, dressing, WAVERLY	70.00	Hurricane lamp, w/12" globe,	
Bowl, 6½", ftd., honey/cheese, WAVERLY	60.00	PLANTATION	450.00
Bowl, 6½", ftd., jelly, WAVERLY	45.00	Ice bucket, dolp. ft., QUEEN ANN	295.00
Bowl, 6½", lemon, w/cover, QUEEN ANN	175.00	Ice tub, 2 hdld., WAVERLY	425.00
Bowl, 7", ftd., honey, WAVERLY	60.00	Mayonnaise, 5½", 2 hdld., WAVERLY	55.00
Bowl, 7", ftd., jelly, WAVERLY	45.00	Mayonnaise, 5½", div., 1 hdld., WAVERLY	55.00
Bowl, 7", lily, QUEEN ANN	50.00	Mayonnaise, 5½", ftd., WAVERLY	60.00
Bowl, 7", relish, 3 pt., round, WAVERLY	67.50	Oil, 3 oz., ftd., WAVERLY	165.00
Bowl, 7", salad, WAVERLY	55.00	Pitcher, 73 oz., #4164	575.00
Bowl, 7", salad dressings, QUEEN ANN	50.00	Plate, 7", salad, WAVERLY	20.00
Bowl, 9", ftd., fruit or salad, WAVERLY	175.00	Plate, 7", mayonnaise, WAVERLY	20.00
Bowl, 9", salad, WAVERLY	95.00	Plate, 8", salad, WAVERLY	30.00
Bowl, 9", 4 pt., rnd, relish, WAVERLY	90.00	Plate, 10½", dinner WAVERLY	155.00
Bowl, 9½", crimped, floral, WAVERLY	65.00	Plate, 10½", service, WAVERLY	75.00
Bowl, 10", gardenia, WAVERLY	70.00	Plate, 11", sandwich, WAVERLY	50.00
Bowl, 10", crimped, floral, WAVERLY	70.00	Plate, 11", demi-torte, WAVERLY	70.00
Bowl, 11", 3 pt., relish, WAVERLY	77.50	Plate, 12", ftd., salver, WAVERLY	225.00
Bowl, 11", 3 ftd., floral, WAVERLY	150.00	Plate, 15", ftd., cake, WAVERLY	300.00
Bowl, 11", floral, WAVERLY	67.50	Plate, 14", torte, WAVERLY	90.00
Bowl, 11", oval, 4 ftd., WAVERLY	150.00	Plate, 14", sandwich, WAVERLY	110.00
Bowl, 12", crimped, floral, WAVERLY	70.00	Plate, 14", ctr. hdld., sandwich, WAVERLY	215.00
Bowl, 13", crimped, floral, WAVERLY	110.00	Salt & pepper, ftd., pr., WAVERLY	65.00
Bowl, 13", floral, WAVERLY	100.00	Saucer, WAVERLY	10.00
Bowl, 13", gardenia, WAVERLY	80.00	Stem, #5072, 1 oz., cordial	165.00
Butter, w/cover, 6", WAVERLY	185.00	Stem, #5072, 3 oz., wine	115.00
Butter, w/cover, ¼ lb., CABOCHON	295.00	Stem, #5072, 3½ oz., oyster cocktail, ftd.	55.00
Candlestick, 1-lite, #112	40.00	Stem, #5072, 4 oz., claret	125.00
Candlestick, 2-lite, FLAME	100.00	Stem, #5072, 4 oz., cocktail	45.00
Candlestick, 3-lite, #142, CASCADE	80.00	Stem, #5072, 6 oz., sherbet	30.00
Candlestick, 3-lite, WAVERLY	90.00	Stem, #5072, 6 oz., saucer champagne	33.00
Candlestick, 5", 2-lite, #134, TRIDENT	75.00	Stem, #5072, 9 oz., water	42.00
Candlestick, 6", epergnette, deep,		Sugar, indiv., WAVERLY	40.00
WAVERLY	400.00	Sugar, ftd., WAVERLY	35.00
Candy, w/cover, 5", ftd., WAVERLY	180.00	Tumbler, #5072, 5 oz., ftd., juice	55.00
Candy, w/cover, 6", low, bowknot cover	170.00	Tumbler, #5072, 12 oz., ftd., tea	65.00
Candy, w/cover, 6¼", #1951, CABOCHON	155.00	Tray, indiv. creamer/sugar, QUEEN ANN	55.00
Celery tray, 12", WAVERLY	60.00	Vase, 3½", ftd., violet, WAVERLY	110.00
Celery tray, 13", WAVERLY	67.50	Vase, 4", ftd., violet, WAVERLY	120.00
Cheese compote, 4½", & cracker (11" plate)		Vase, 7", ftd., fan, WAVERLY	120.00
WAVERLY	145.00	Vase, 8", #4198	120.00
Cheese compote, 5½", & cracker (12" plate)		Vase, 8", sq., ftd., urn	140.00
QUEEN ANNE	145.00	Vase, 10", #4198	200.00
Chocolate, w/cover, 5", WAVERLY	150.00	Vase, 10", sq., ftd, urn	140.00
Cigarette holder, #4035	125.00	Vase, 12", sq., ftd., urn	225.00

ROSE POINT, Cambridge Glass Company, 1936 – 1953

Colors: crystal; some crystal with gold

A major problem confronting new collectors is recognizing different blanks on which Rose Point is found. With the shelf shots on page 169, I am trying to clarify both blank and stemware.

Row 1: #3400 cup and saucer, #3900 plate, #3400 plate, #3900 cup and saucer

Row 2: #3500 cup and saucer, plate, cereal, individual sugar and creamer

Row 3: water goblet, ftd. iced tea, ftd. water tumbler, tall sherbet, cocktail, low sherbet, oyster cocktail

Row 4: cocktail icer, claret, parfait, ftd. juice, wine, cordial, short wine, brandy

In that last row be sure to notice the difference between the juice tumbler and the parfait. Many mistakes have been made in identifying them. There is a $40.00 difference in pricing; so, it pays to know which is which!

Rose Point is the most collected pattern in Cambridge. There were so many different blanks used to make the pattern that each collector can decide which shape suits his fancy; and thus, not everyone is always looking for the same pieces! Sometimes diversity is a good thing! Throughout the photographs are many unusual and rare pieces; but to show them, I have little space to discuss them. Look carefully, and enjoy!

	Crystal		Crystal
Ash tray, stack set on metal pole, #1715	225.00	Bowl, 9½", ftd., w/hdl. (#3500/115)	125.00
Ash tray, 2½", sq. #721	32.50	Bowl, 9½", 2 hdld. (#3400/34)	67.50
Ash tray, 3¼" (#3500/124)	32.50	Bowl, 9½", 2 part, blown (#225)	395.00
Ash tray, 3¼", sq. (#3500/129)	55.00	Bowl, 2 hdld. (#3400/1185)	70.00
Ash tray, 3½" (#3500/125)	35.00	Bowl, 10", 2 hdld. (#3500/28)	77.50
Ash tray, 4" (#3500/126)	40.00	Bowl, 10", 4 tab ftd., flared (#3900/54)	65.00
Ash tray, 4", oval (#3500/130)	85.00	Bowl, 10½", crimp edge, #1351	85.00
Ash tray, 4¼" (#3500/127)	45.00	Bowl, 10½", flared (#3400/168)	65.00
Ash tray, 4½" (#3500/128)	50.00	Bowl, 10½", 3 part, #222	250.00
Ash tray, 4½", oval (#3500/131)	65.00	Bowl, 10½", 3 part (#1401/122)	250.00
Basket, 3", favor (#3500/79)	295.00	Bowl, 11", ftd. (#3500/16)	110.00
Basket, 5", 1 hdld. (#3500/51)	225.00	Bowl, 11", ftd., fancy edge (#3500/19)	135.00
Basket, 6", 1 hdld. (#3500/52)	265.00	Bowl, 11", 4 ftd., oval (#3500/109)	325.00
Basket, 6", 2 hdld. (#3400/1182)	36.00	Bowl, 11", 4 ftd., shallow, fancy edge	
Basket, 6", sq., ftd., 2 hdld (#3500/55)	39.00	(#3400/48)	95.00
Basket, 7", 1 hdld., #119	410.00	Bowl, 11", fruit (#3400/1188)	100.00
Basket, 7", wide (#3500/56)	50.00	Bowl, 11", low foot (#3400/3)	155.00
Basket, sugar, w/handle and tongs (#3500/13)	285.00	Bowl, 11", tab hdld. (#3900/34)	75.00
Bell, dinner, #3121	150.00	Bowl, 11½", ftd., w/tab hdl. (#3900/28)	75.00
Bowl, 3", 4 ftd., nut (#3400/71)	70.00	Bowl, 12", crimped, pan (Pristine #136)	295.00
Bowl, 3½", bonbon, cupped, deep (#3400/204)	80.00	Bowl, 10", salad (Pristine #427)	145.00
Bowl, 3½", cranberry (#3400/70)	85.00	Bowl, 12", 4 ftd., oval (#3400/1240)	115.00
Bowl, 5", hdld. (#3500/49)	35.00	Bowl, 12", 4 ftd., oval, w/"ears" hdl.	
Bowl, 5" fruit (#3500/10)	45.00	(#3900/65)	85.00
Bowl, 5" fruit, blown #1534	80.00	Bowl, 12", 4 ftd., fancy rim oblong (#3400/160)	90.00
Bowl, 5¼" fruit (#3400/56)	45.00	Bowl, 12", 4 ftd., flared (#3400/4)	75.00
Bowl, 5½", nappy (#3400/56)	45.00	Bowl, 12", 4 tab ftd., flared (#3900/62)	77.50
Bowl, 5½", 2 hdld., bonbon (#3400/1179)	35.00	Bowl, 12", ftd., (#3500/17)	115.00
Bowl, 5½", 2 hdld., bonbon (#3400/1180)	32.00	Bowl, 12", ftd., oblong (#3500/118)	160.00
Bowl, 6", bonbon, crimped (#3400/203)	85.00	Bowl, 12", ftd., oval w/hdl. (#3500/21)	210.00
Bowl, 6", bonbon, cupped, shallow (#3400/205)	80.00	Bowl, 12½", flared, rolled edge (#3400/2)	155.00
Bowl, 6", cereal (#3400/53)	85.00	Bowl, 12½", 4 ftd., #993	90.00
Bowl, 6", cereal (#3400/10)	85.00	Bowl, 13", #1398	115.00
Bowl, 6", cereal (#3500/11)	85.00	Bowl, 13", 4 ftd., narrow, crimped (#3400/47)	125.00
Bowl, 6", hdld. (#3500/50)	45.00	Bowl, 13", flared (#3400/1)	70.00
Bowl, 6", 2 hdld. (#1402/89)	42.00	Bowl, 14", 4 ftd., crimp edge, oblong, #1247	145.00
Bowl, 6", 2 hdld., ftd., bonbon (#3500/54)	35.00	Bowl, 18", crimped, pan, (Pristine #136)	595.00
Bowl, 6", 4 ftd., fancy rim (#3400/136)	145.00	Bowl, cream soup, w/liner (#3400)	155.00
Bowl, 6½" bonbon, crimped (#3400/202)	85.00	Bowl, cream soup, w/liner (#3500/2)	165.00
Bowl, 7", bonbon, crimped, shallow		Bowl, finger, w/liner, #3106	95.00
(#3400/201)	115.00	Bowl, finger, w/liner, #3121	95.00
Bowl, 7", tab hdld., ftd., bonbon (#3900/130)	37.00	Butter, w/cover, round, #506	185.00
Bowl, 8", ram's head, squared (#3500/27)	335.00	Butter, w/cover, 5" (#3400/52)	175.00
Bowl, 8½", rimmed soup, #361	250.00	Butter dish, ¼ lb. (#3900/52)	295.00
Bowl, 8½", 3 part, #221	165.00	Candelabrum, 2-lite w/bobeches & prisms,	
Bowl, 9", 4 ftd., (#3400/135)	210.00	#1268	135.00
Bowl, 9", ram's head (#3500/25)	345.00	Candelabrum, 2-lite (#3500/94)	100.00
Bowl, 9½", pickle (like corn), #477	50.00	Candelabrum, 3-lite, #1338	65.00

ROSE POINT

	Crystal
Candelabrum, 5½", 3-lite w/#19 bobeche & #1 prisms, #1545	125.00
Candelabrum, 6½", 2-lite, w/bobeches & prisms, (Martha #496)	165.00
Candle, torchere, cup ft. (#3500/90)	180.00
Candle, torchere, flat ft. (#3500/88)	175.00
Candlestick, (Pristine #500)	135.00
Candlestick, sq. base & lites (#1700/501)	175.00
Candlestick, 2½" (#3500/108)	33.00
Candlestick, 3½", #628	38.00
Candlestick, 4", #627	55.00
Candlestick, 4", ram's head (#3500/74)	100.00
Candlestick, 5", 1-lite keyhole (#3400/646)	33.00
Candlestick, 5", inverts to comport (#3900/68)	57.50
Candlestick, 5½", 2-lite (Martha #495)	65.00
Candlestick, 6" (#3500/31)	90.00
Candlestick, 6", 2-lite keyhole (#3400/647)	40.00
Candlestick, 6", 2-lite (#3900/72)	45.00
Candlestick, 6", 3-lite (#3900/74)	50.00
Candlestick, 6", 3-lite keyhole (#3400/638)	50.00
Candlestick, 6", 3-tiered lite, #1338	75.00
Candlestick, 6½", Calla Lily, #499	95.00
Candlestick, 7", #3121	75.00
Candlestick, 7½", w/prism (Martha #497)	135.00
Candy box, w/cover, 5", apple shape, #316	900.00
Candy box, w/cover, 5⅜", #1066 stem	155.00
Candy box, w/cover, 5⅜", tall stem, (#3121/3)	150.00
Candy box, w/cover, 5⅜", short stem, (#3121/4)	160.00
Candy box, w/cover, blown, 5⅜" (#3500/103)	165.00
Candy box, w/cover, 6", ram's head (#3500/78)	265.00
Candy box, w/rose finial, 6", 3 ftd., #300	275.00
Candy box, w/cover, 7" (#3400/9)	145.00
Candy box, w/cover, 7", round, 3 pt. #103	165.00
Candy box, w/cover, 8", 3 pt. (#3500/57)	85.00
Candy box, w/cover, rnd. (#3900/165)	115.00
Celery, 12" (#3400/652)	47.50
Celery, 12" (#3500/652)	50.00
Celery, 12", 5 pt. (#3400/67)	80.00
Celery, 14", 4 pt., 2 hdld. (#3500/97)	155.00
Celery & relish, 9", 3 pt. (#3900/125)	55.00
Celery & relish, 12", 3 pt. (#3900/126)	65.00
Celery & relish, 12", 5 pt. (#3900/120)	70.00
Cheese (5" comport) & cracker (13" plate) (#3900/135)	120.00
Cheese (5½" comport) & cracker (11½" plate) (#3400/6)	120.00
Cheese (6" comport) & cracker (12" plate) (#3500/162)	140.00
Cheese dish, w/cover, 5", #980	450.00
Cigarette box, w/cover, #615	125.00
Cigarette box, w/cover, #747	155.00
Cigarette holder, oval, w/ash tray ft., #1066	167.00
Cigarette holder, round, w/ash tray ft., #1337	150.00
Coaster, 3½", #1628	55.00
Cocktail icer, 2 pc. (#3600)	75.00
Cocktail shaker, metal top (#3400/157)	175.00
Cocktail shaker, metal top (#3400/175)	150.00
Cocktail shaker, 12 oz., metal top, #97	310.00
Cocktail shaker, 32 oz., w/glass stopper, #101	195.00
Cocktail shaker, 46 oz., metal top, #98	185.00
Cocktail shaker, 48 oz., glass stopper, #102	175.00
Comport, 5" (#3900/135)	45.00

	Crystal
Comport, 5", 4 ftd., (#3400/74)	70.00
Comport, 5½", scalloped edge (#3900/136)	57.50
Comport, 5⅜", blown (#3500/101)	62.50
Comport, 5⅜", blown, #3121 stem	60.00
Comport, 5⅜", blown, #1066 stem	67.50
Comport, 6" (#3500/36)	125.00
Comport, 6" (#3500/111)	150.00
Comport, 6", 4 ftd., (#3400/13)	40.00
Comport, 7", 2 hdld. (#3500/37)	125.00
Comport, 7", keyhole (#3400/29)	135.00
Comport, 7", keyhole, low (#3400/28)	85.00
Creamer (#3400/68)	20.00
Creamer (#3500/14)	22.00
Creamer, flat #137	120.00
Creamer, flat, #944	145.00
Creamer, ftd., (#3400/16)	90.00
Creamer, ftd., (#3900/41)	20.00
Creamer, indiv. (#3500/15) pie crust edge	25.00
Creamer, indiv. (#3900/40) scalloped edge	20.00
Cup, 3 styles (#3400/54, #3500/1, #3900/17)	30.00
Cup, 5 oz., punch, #488	37.50
Cup, after dinner (#3400/69)	265.00
Decanter, 12 oz., ball, w/stopper (#3400/119)	250.00
Decanter, 14 oz., ftd., #1320	425.00
Decanter, 26 oz., sq., #1380	425.00
Decanter, 28 oz., tall, #1372	595.00
Decanter, 28 oz., w/stopper, #1321	325.00
Decanter, 32 oz., ball, w/stopper (#3400/92)	395.00
Dressing bottle, flat, #1263	295.00
Dressing bottle, ftd., #1261	315.00
Epergne (candle w/vases) (#3900/75)	225.00
Grapefruit, w/liner, #187	115.00
Hat, 5", #1704	435.00
Hat, 6", #1703	435.00
Hat, 8", #1702	495.00
Hat, 9", #1701	595.00
Honey dish, w/cover (#3500/139)	295.00
Hot plate or trivet	75.00
Hurricane lamp, w/prisms, #1613	335.00
Hurricane lamp, candlestick base, #1617	225.00
Hurricane lamp, keyhole base, w/prisms, #1603	225.00
Hurricane lamp, 8", etched chimney, #1601	250.00
Hurricane lamp, 10", etched chimney & base, #1604	295.00
Ice bucket (#1402/52)	210.00
Ice bucket, w/chrome hand. (#3900/671)	155.00
Ice pail, #1705	225.00
Ice pail (#3400/851)	125.00
Ice tub, (Pristine), #671	225.00
Icer, cocktail, #968 or #18	75.00
Marmalade, 8 oz., #147	155.00
Marmalade, w/cover, 7 oz., ftd., #157	175.00
Mayonnaise (sherbet type w/ladle) #19	55.00
Mayonnaise, div., w/liner & 2 ladles (#3900/111)	77.50
Mayonnaise, 3 pc. (#3400/11)	67.50
Mayonnaise, 3 pc. (#3900/129)	65.00
Mayonnaise, w/liner & ladle (#3500/59)	75.00
Mustard, 3 oz., #151	150.00
Mustard, 4½ oz., ftd., #1329	325.00
Oil, 2 oz., ball, w/stopper (#3400/96)	77.50

ROSE POINT

Item	Crystal
Oil, 6 oz., ball, w/stopper (#3400/99)	125.00
Oil, 6 oz., hdld (#3400/193)	100.00
Oil, 6 oz., loop hdld., w/stopper (#3900/100)	135.00
Oil, 6 oz., w/stopper, ftd., hdld. (#3400/161)	225.00
Pickle, 9" (#3400/59)	65.00
Pickle or relish, 7", (#3900/123)	35.00
Pitcher, 20 oz., (#3900/117)	235.00
Pitcher, 20 oz. w/ice lip, #70	235.00
Pitcher, 32 oz. (#3900/118)	295.00
Pitcher, 32 oz. martini (slender) w/metal insert, (#3900/114)	450.00
Pitcher, 60 oz., martini, #1408	1,900.00
Pitcher, 76 oz. (#3900/115)	195.00
Pitcher, 76 oz., ice lip (#3400/100)	200.00
Pitcher, 76 oz., ice lip (#3400/152)	285.00
Pitcher, 80 oz., ball (#3400/38)	195.00
Pitcher, 80 oz., ball (#3900/116)	210.00
Pitcher, 80 oz., Doulton (#3400/141)	275.00
Pitcher, nite set, 2 pc., w/tumbler insert top, #103	595.00
Plate, 6", bread/butter (#3400/60)	13.50
Plate, 6", bread/butter (#3500/3)	15.00
Plate, 6", 2 hdld. (#3400/1181)	20.00
Plate, 6⅛" canape #693	160.00
Plate, 6½", bread/butter (#3900/20)	13.50
Plate, 7½" (#3500/4)	15.00
Plate, 7½", salad (#3400/176)	15.00
Plate, 8", salad (#3900/22)	20.00
Plate, 8", 2 hdld., ftd., (#3500/161)	42.50
Plate, 8", tab hdld., ftd., bonbon (#3900/131)	40.00
Plate, 8½", breakfast (#3400/62)	20.00
Plate, 8½", salad (#3500/5)	20.00
Plate, 9½" crescent salad #485	240.00
Plate, 9½", luncheon (#3400/63)	40.00
Plate, 10½", dinner (#3400/64)	130.00
Plate, 10½" dinner (#3900/24)	130.00
Plate, 11", 2 hdld. (#3400/35)	50.00
Plate, 12", 4 ftd., service (#3900/26)	70.00
Plate, 12", ftd. (#3500/39)	90.00
Plate, 12½", 2 hdld. (#3400/1186)	65.00
Plate, 13", rolled edge, ftd. (#3900/33)	70.00
Plate, 13", 4 ftd., torte (#3500/110)	125.00
Plate, 13", ftd., cake (Martha #170)	240.00
Plate, 13", torte (#3500/38)	185.00
Plate, 13½", #242	150.00
Plate, 13½", rolled edge, #1397	70.00
Plate, 13½", tab hdld., cake (#3900/35)	70.00
Plate, 14", rolled edge (#3900/166)	65.00
Plate, 14", service (#3900/167)	75.00
Plate, 14", torte (#3400/65)	130.00
Plate, 18", punch bowl liner (Martha #129)	500.00
Punch bowl, 15", Martha #478	3,500.00
Punch set, 15-pc. (Martha)	4,500.00
Relish, 5½", 2 pt. (#3500/68)	25.00
Relish, 5½", 2 pt., hdld. (#3500/60)	30.00
Relish, 6", 2 pt. (#3400/90)	32.50
Relish, 6", 2 pt., 1 hdl. (#3400/1093)	85.00
Relish, 6½", 3 pt. (#3500/69)	32.50
Relish, 6½", 3 pt., hdld. (#3500/61)	37.50
Relish, 7", 2 pt. (#3900/124)	37.50
Relish, 7½", 3 pt., center hdld. (#3500/71)	135.00

Item	Crystal
Relish, 7½", 4 pt. (#3500/70)	37.50
Relish, 7½", 4 pt., 2 hdld. (#3500/62)	55.00
Relish, 8", 3 pt., 3 hdld. (#3400/91)	37.50
Relish, 10", 2 hdld. (#3500/85)	70.00
Relish, 10", 3 pt., 2 hdld. (#3500/86)	52.50
Relish, 10", 3 pt., 4 ftd., 2 hdld. (#3500/64)	52.50
Relish, 10", 4 pt., 4 ftd., (#3500/65)	62.50
Relish, 10", 4 pt., 2 hdld. (#3500/87)	60.00
Relish, 11", 2 pt., 2 hdld. (#3400/89)	80.00
Relish, 11", 3 pt. (#3400/200)	57.50
Relish, 12", 5 pt. (#3400/67)	75.00
Relish, 12", 5 pt., (Pristine #419)	235.00
Relish, 12", 6 pc. (#3500/67)	225.00
Relish, 14", w/cover, 4 pt., 2 hdld. (#3500/142)	450.00
Relish, 15", 4 pt., hdld. (#3500/113)	195.00
Salt & pepper, egg shape, pr., #1468	90.00
Salt & pepper, individual, rnd., glass base, pr., #1470	85.00
Salt & pepper, individual, w/chrome tops, pr., #360	70.00
Salt & pepper, lg., rnd., glass base, pr., #1471	85.00
Salt & pepper, w/chrome tops, pr., #395	175.00
Salt & pepper, w/chrome tops, pr. (#3400/37)	175.00
Salt & pepper, w/chrome tops, pr., ftd. (#3400/77)	55.00
Salt & pepper w/chrome tops, pr., flat (#3900/1177)	45.00
Sandwich tray, 11", center handled (#3400/10)	140.00
Saucer, after dinner (#3400/69)	55.00
Saucer, 3 styles (#3400, #3500, #3900)	5.00
Stem, #3104, 3½ oz., cocktail	275.00
Stem, #3106, ¾ oz., brandy	115.00
Stem, #3106, 1 oz., cordial	115.00
Stem, #3106, 1 oz., pousse cafe	125.00
Stem, #3106, 2 oz., sherry	45.00
Stem, #3106, 2½ oz., wine	45.00
Stem, #3106, 3 oz., cocktail	35.00
Stem, #3106, 4½ oz., claret	50.00
Stem, #3106, 5 oz., oyster cocktail	32.50
Stem, #3106, 7 oz., high sherbet	30.00
Stem, #3106, 7 oz., low sherbet	25.00
Stem, #3106, 10 oz., water goblet	35.00
Stem, #3121, 1 oz., brandy	125.00
Stem, #3121, 1 oz., cordial	70.00
Stem, #3121, 3 oz., cocktail	32.50
Stem, #3121, 3½ oz., wine	60.00
Stem, #3121, 4½ oz., claret	90.00
Stem, #3121, 4½ oz., low oyster cocktail	37.50
Stem, #3121, 5 oz., low ft. parfait	75.00
Stem, #3121, 6 oz., low sherbet	20.00
Stem, #3121, 6 oz., tall sherbet	22.00
Stem, #3121, 10 oz., water	30.00
Stem, #3500, 1 oz., cordial	70.00
Stem, #3500, 2½ oz., wine	57.50
Stem, #3500, 3 oz., cocktail	35.00
Stem, #3500, 4½ oz., claret	80.00
Stem, #3500, 4½ oz., low oyster cocktail	37.50
Stem, #3500, 5 oz., low ft. parfait	75.00
Stem, #3500, 7 oz., low ft. sherbet	18.00
Stem, #3500, 7 oz., tall sherbet	24.00
Stem, #3500, 10 oz. water	30.00

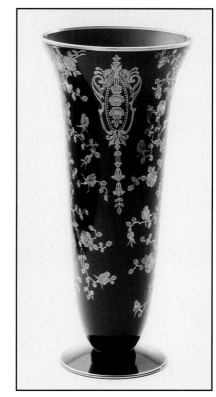

ROSE POINT

	Crystal
Stem, #37801, 4 oz., cocktail	45.00
Stem, #7801, 4 oz. cocktail, plain stem	40.00
Stem, #7966, 1 oz., cordial, plain ft.	135.00
Stem, #7966, 2 oz., sherry, plain ft.	95.00
Sugar (#3400/68)	20.00
Sugar (#3500/14)	20.00
Sugar, flat, #137	110.00
Sugar, flat, #944	135.00
Sugar, ftd. (#3400/16)	85.00
Sugar, ftd. (#3900/41)	20.00
Sugar, indiv. (#3500/15) pie crust edge	22.50
Sugar, indiv. (#3900/40) scalloped edge	21.50
Syrup, w/drip stop top, #1670	385.00
Tray, 6", 2 hdld., sq. (#3500/91)	170.00
Tray, 12", 2 hdld., oval, service (#3500/99)	225.00
Tray, 12", rnd. (#3500/67)	165.00
Tray, 13", 2 hdld., rnd. (#3500/72)	165.00
Tray, sugar/creamer, (#3900/37)	25.00
Tumbler, #498, 2 oz., straight side	110.00
Tumbler, #498, 5 oz., straight side	47.50
Tumbler, #498, 8 oz., straight side	47.50
Tumbler, #498, 10 oz., straight side	47.50
Tumbler, #498, 12 oz., straight side	52.00
Tumbler, #3000, 3½ oz., cone, ftd.	95.00
Tumbler, #3000, 5 oz., cone, ftd.	115.00
Tumbler, #3106, 3 oz., ftd.	30.00
Tumbler, #3106, 5 oz., ftd.	30.00
Tumbler, #3106, 9 oz., ftd.	30.00
Tumbler, #3106, 12 oz., ftd.	35.00
Tumbler, #3121, 2½ oz., ftd.	67.50

	Crystal
Tumbler, #3121, 5 oz., low ft., juice	35.00
Tumbler, #3121, 10 oz., low ft., water	29.00
Tumbler, #3121, 12 oz., low ft., ice tea	32.50
Tumbler, #3400/1341, 1 oz., cordial	100.00
Tumbler, #3400/92, 2½ oz.	110.00
Tumbler, #3400/38, 5 oz.	95.00
Tumbler, #3400/38, 12 oz.	55.00
Tumbler, #3900/115, 13 oz.	45.00
Tumbler, #3500, 2½ oz., ftd.	60.00
Tumbler, #3500, 5 oz., low ft., juice	40.00
Tumbler, #3500, 10 oz., low ft., water	27.50
Tumbler, #3500, 13 oz., low ftd.	35.00
Tumbler, #3500, 12 oz., tall ft., ice tea	32.50
Tumbler, #7801, 5 oz., ftd.	40.00
Tumbler, #7801, 12 oz., ftd., ice tea	55.00
Tumbler, #3900/117, 5 oz.	50.00
Tumbler, #3400/115, 13 oz.	50.00
Urn, 10", w/cover (#3500/41)	525.00
Urn, 12", w/cover (#3500/42)	650.00
Vase, 5", #1309	70.00
Vase, 5", globe (#3400/102)	75.00
Vase, 5", ftd., #6004	50.00
Vase, 6", high ftd., flower, #6004	55.00
Vase, 6", #572	140.00
Vase, 6½", globe (#3400/103)	85.00
Vase, 7", ivy, ftd., ball, #1066	250.00
Vase, 8", #1430	155.00
Vase, 8", flat, flared, #797	130.00
Vase, 8", ftd. (#3500/44)	125.00
Vase, 8", high ftd., flower, #6004	60.00
Vase, 9", ftd., keyhole, #1237	95.00
Vase, 9", ftd., #1620	125.00
Vase, 9½" ftd., keyhole, #1233	85.00
Vase, 10", ball bottom, #400	185.00
Vase, 10", bud, #1528	80.00
Vase, 10", cornucopia (#3900/575)	195.00
Vase, 10", flat, #1242	135.00
Vase, 10", ftd., #1301	75.00
Vase, 10", ftd., #6004	75.00
Vase, 10", ftd. (#3500/45)	175.00
Vase, 10", slender, #274	55.00
Vase, 11", ftd., flower, #278	125.00
Vase, 11", ped. ftd., flower, #1299	155.00
Vase, 12", ftd., #6004	95.00
Vase, 12", ftd., keyhole, #1234	95.00
Vase, 12", ftd., keyhole, #1238	155.00
Vase, 13", ftd., flower, #279	225.00
Vase 18", #1336	2,000.00
Vase, sweet pea, #629	265.00

ROYAL, Plate Etching #273, Fostoria Glass Company, 1925 – 1932

Colors: amber, black, blue, green

Royal is a Fostoria pattern often confused with Vesper since both etchings are similar, both are found on the #2350 blank and both appeared in the same colors. There are not as many collectors for Royal as there are Vesper, possibly due to a more limited distribution of Royal. New collectors should find Royal more agreeably priced.

Rarely found pieces include the covered cheese, cologne bottle, and the pitchers. Amber and green can be collected in sets; but only a few pieces can be found in blue and black. Fostoria's blue color found with Royal etching was called "Blue" as opposed to the "Azure" blue which is a lighter color found with June, Kashmir, and Versailles etchings. It is a shame that there is so little available of this very attractive blue color!

Although some production of Royal presumably continued until 1934, the January 1, 1933, Fostoria catalog no longer listed pieces as being for sale. I am adjusting my cutoff date for production to 1932. If you have access to a May, 1928, copy of *House and Garden,* there is an interesting Fostoria advertisement there showing Royal.

	*Amber, Green		*Amber, Green
Ash tray, #2350, 3½"	22.50	Ice bucket, #2378	55.00
Bowl, #2350, bouillon, flat	12.50	Mayonnaise, #2315	25.00
Bowl, #2350½, bouillon, ftd.	13.00	Pickle, 8", #2350	20.00
Bowl, #2350, cream soup, flat	16.00	Pitcher, #1236	365.00
Bowl, #2350½, cream soup, ftd.	18.00	Pitcher, #5000, 48 oz.	265.00
Bowl, #869, 4½", finger	18.00	Plate, 8½", deep soup/underplate	35.00
Bowl, #2350, 5½", fruit	12.00	Plate, #2350, 6", bread/butter	3.00
Bowl, #2350, 6½", cereal	20.00	Plate, #2350, 7½", salad	4.00
Bowl, #2267, 7", ftd.	32.00	Plate, #2350, 8½", luncheon	8.00
Bowl, #2350, 7¾", soup	22.00	Plate, #2321, 8¾, Maj Jongg (canape)	35.00
Bowl, #2350, 8", nappy	30.00	Plate, #2350, 9½", small dinner	13.00
Bowl, #2350, 9", nappy	32.00	Plate, #2350, 10½", dinner	30.00
Bowl, #2350, 9", oval, baker	37.50	Plate, #2350, 13", chop	30.00
Bowl, #2324, 10", ftd.	45.00	Plate, #2350, 15", chop	40.00
Bowl, #2350, 10", salad	35.00	Platter, #2350, 10½"	30.00
Bowl, #2350, 10½", oval, baker	45.00	Platter, #2350, 12"	45.00
Bowl, #2315, 10½", ftd.	45.00	Platter, #2350, 15½"	85.00
Bowl, #2329, 11", console	22.00	Salt and pepper, #5100, pr.	60.00
Bowl, #2297, 12", deep	22.00	Sauce boat, w/liner	125.00
Bowl, #2329, 13", console	30.00	Saucer, #2350/#2350½	3.00
Bowl, #2324, 13", ftd.	50.00	Saucer, #2350, demi	5.00
Bowl, #2371, 13", oval, w/flower frog	110.00	Server, #2287, 11", center hdld.	25.00
Butter, w/cover #2350	250.00	Stem, #869, ¾ oz., cordial	65.00
Candlestick, #2324, 4"	15.00	Stem, #869, 2¾ oz., wine	30.00
Candlestick, #2324, 9"	50.00	Stem, #869, 3 oz., cocktail	22.50
Candy, w/cover, #2331, 3 part	75.00	Stem, #869, 5½ oz., oyster cocktail	15.00
Candy, w/cover, ftd., ½ lb.	165.00	Stem, #869, 5½ oz., parfait	30.00
Celery, #2350, 11"	25.00	Stem, #869, 6 oz., low sherbet	12.50
Cheese, w/cover/plate #2276 (plate 11")	125.00	Stem, #869, 6 oz., high sherbet	16.00
Cologne, #2322, tall	50.00	Stem, #869, 9 oz., water	20.00
Cologne, #2323, short	45.00	Sugar, flat, w/lid	155.00
Cologne/powder jar combination	210.00	Sugar, #2315, ftd., flat	17.00
Comport, #1861½, 6", jelly	25.00	Sugar, #2350½, ftd.	12.00
Comport, #2327, 7"	28.00	Sugar lid, #2350½	100.00
Comport, #2358, 8" wide	30.00	Tumbler, #869, 5 oz., flat	22.50
Creamer, flat	14.00	Tumbler, #859, 9 oz., flat	25.00
Creamer, #2315½, ftd., fat	18.00	Tumbler, #859, 12 oz., flat	30.00
Creamer, #2350½, ftd.	13.00	Tumbler, #5000, 2½ oz., ftd.	30.00
Cup, #2350, flat	12.00	Tumbler, #5000, 5 oz., ftd.	14.00
Cup, #2350½, ftd.	13.00	Tumbler, #5000, 9 oz., ftd.	16.00
Cup, #2350, demi	25.00	Tumbler, #5000, 12 oz., ftd.	25.00
Egg cup, #2350	27.50	Vase, #2324, urn, ftd.	80.00
Grapefruit, w/insert	80.00	Vase, #2292, flared	90.00

* Add 50% more for blue or black!

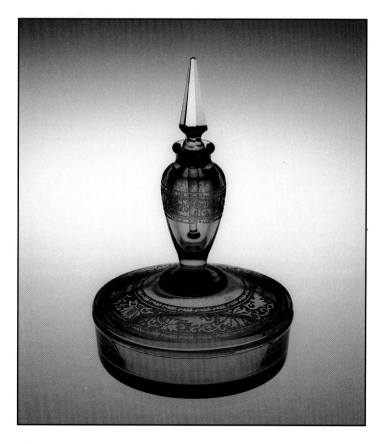

RUBA ROMBIC, Consolidated Lamp and Glass Company, 1928 – 1933

Colors: Smokey topaz, Jungle green, French Crystal, Silver grey, Lilac, Sunshine, Jade; some milk glass, Apple green, black, French Opalescent

Prices for Ruba Rhombic have remained rather steady. Several large accumulations have been sold. This is a very specialized market and not all dealers have an outlet where they can sell at the prices listed below. Collectors of Consolidated glass may not number in the thousands as do collectors of other glass company products, but they make up for lack of numbers with a fervor to own their glassware. I have not seen as much zeal to obtain such a limited production in quite a while!

You may see little of this pattern in your shopping; but if you do, please note that a piece or two found at the right price could make your day! The color shown here is Smokey Topaz, priced below with the Jungle Green.

If you look up rombic, you will find that it means irregular in shape, an apropos name! I've found collectors either love or hate it. There seems to be no in between!

This pattern was displayed sporadically for years at Depression glass shows; but in the last few years, advanced Art Deco collectors and museums have started displaying Ruba Rombic, and prices have soared out of the reach of the average collector. Those who bought Ruba Rhombic before this upsurge in collecting can make a substantial profit on their collections now.

The cased color column in the prices below includes three colors. They are: Lilac (lavender), Sunshine (yellow), and Jade (green). The French crystal is a white, applied color except that the raised edges are crystal with no white coloring at all. The Silver is sometimes referred as Gray Silver.

	Smokey Topaz/ Jungle Green	Cased Colors	French Opal/ French Crystal/ Silver		Smokey Topaz/ Jungle Green	Cased Colors	French Opal/ French Crystal/ Silver
Ash tray, 3½"	800.00	1000.00	1200.00	Light, wall sconce		1500.00	1500.00
Bon bon, flat, 3 part	250.00	350.00	400.00	Pitcher, 8¼"	2500.00	3000.00	4000.00
Bottle, decanter, 9"	1800.00	2200.00	2500.00	Plate, 7"	75.00	100.00	150.00
Bottle, perfume, 4¾"	1200.00	1500.00	1800.00	Plate, 8"	75.00	100.00	150.00
Bottle, toilet, 7½"	1800.00	2200.00	2500.00	Plate, 10"	250.00	275.00	300.00
Bowl, 3", almond	225.00	250.00	300.00	Plate, 15"	2000.00	2200.00	2400.00
Bowl, 8", cupped	1500.00	1800.00	2000.00	Relish, 2 part	350.00	450.00	500.00
Bowl, 9", flared	1500.00	1800.00	2000.00	Sugar	200.00	250.00	300.00
Bowl, 12", oval	1800.00	2200.00	2500.00	Sundae	100.00	135.00	150.00
Bowl, bouillon	175.00	250.00	275.00	Tray for decanter set	2000.00	2250.00	2500.00
Bowl, finger	95.00	125.00	140.00	Tumbler, 2 oz., flat, 2¾"	100.00	125.00	150.00
Box, cigarette 3½" x 4¼"	850.00	1250.00	1500.00	Tumbler, 3 oz., ftd	125.00	150.00	175.00
Box, powder, 5", round	850.00	1250.00	1500.00	Tumbler, 9 oz., flat	125.00	175.00	200.00
Candlestick, 2½" high, pr.	500.00	650.00	750.00	Tumbler, 10 oz., ftd.	175.00	300.00	350.00
Celery, 10", 3 part	1000.00	1250.00	1400.00	Tumbler, 12 oz., flat	175.00	300.00	350.00
Comport, 7", wide	1000.00	1250.00	1400.00	Tumbler, 15 oz., ftd., 7"	350.00	450.00	500.00
Creamer	200.00	250.00	300.00	Vase, 6"	850.00	1000.00	1500.00
Light, ceiling fixture, 10"		1500.00	1500.00	Vase, 9½"	2000.00	3000.00	5000.00
Light, ceiling fixture, 16"		2500.00	2500.00	Vase, 16"	10000.00	12000.00	12000.00
Light, table light		1200.00	1200.00				

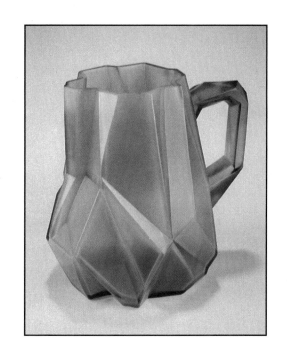

SANDWICH, #41, Duncan & Miller Glass Company, 1924 – 1955

Colors: crystal, amber, pink, green, red, cobalt blue

Lancaster Colony persists in making some Sandwich pieces in their lines today. The bright blue, green, and amberina color combinations are from Duncan moulds (made by Indiana) and were sold by Montgomery Ward in the early 1970's. Tiffin also made some Sandwich pieces in milk glass out of the same Duncan moulds. Stemware abounds and is as economical to use as most currently made stemware. I have included some original Duncan catalog reprints on pages 183 – 185. Hopefully, these will add to your pleasure!

	Crystal		Crystal
Ash tray, 2½" x 3¾", rect.	10.00	Bowl, 10", lily, vertical edge	50.00
Ash tray, 2⅔", sq.	8.00	Bowl, 11", cupped nut	52.50
Basket, 6½", w/loop hdld.	115.00	Bowl, 11½", crimped flower	55.00
Basket, 10", crimped, w/loop hdl.	165.00	Bowl, 11½", gardenia	45.00
Basket, 10", oval, w/loop hdl.	165.00	Bowl, 11½", ftd., crimped fruit	60.00
Basket, 11½", w/loop hdl.	225.00	Bowl, 12", fruit, flared edge	45.00
Bonbon, 5", heart shape, w/ring hdl.	15.00	Bowl, 12", shallow salad	40.00
Bonbon, 5½", heart shape, hdld.	15.00	Bowl, 12", oblong console	40.00
Bonbon, 6", heart shape, w/ring hdl.	20.00	Bowl, 12", epergne, w/ctr. hole	95.00
Bonbon, 7½", ftd., w/cover	40.00	Butter, w/cover, ¼ lb.	37.50
Bowl, 2½", salted almond	10.00	Cake stand, 11½", ftd., rolled edge	90.00
Bowl, 3½", nut	10.00	Cake stand, 12", ftd., rolled edge, plain	
Bowl, 4", finger	12.50	pedestal	75.00
Bowl, 5½", hdld.	15.00	Cake stand, 13", ftd., plain pedestal	75.00
Bowl, 5½", ftd., grapefruit, w/rim liner	16.00	Candelabra, 10", 1-lite, w/bobeche & prisms	75.00
Bowl, 5½", ftd., grapefruit, w/fruit cup liner	16.00	Candelabra, 10", 3-lite, w/bobeche & prisms	175.00
Bowl, 5", 2 pt., nappy	12.00	Candelabra, 16", 3-lite, w/bobeche & prisms	235.00
Bowl, 5", ftd., crimped ivy	27.50	Candlestick, 4", 1-lite	14.00
Bowl, 5", fruit	10.00	Candlestick, 4", 1-lite, w/bobeche & stub.	
Bowl, 5", nappy, w/ring hdl.	12.00	prisms	32.50
Bowl, 6", 2 pt., nappy	14.00	Candlestick, 5", 3-lite	45.00
Bowl, 6", fruit salad	12.00	Candlestick, 5", 3-lite, w/bobeche & stub.	
Bowl, 6", grapefruit, rimmed edge	16.00	prisms	110.00
Bowl, 6", nappy, w/ring hdl.	17.50	Candlestick, 5", 2-lite, w/bobeche & stub.	
Bowl, 10", salad, deep	70.00	prisms	85.00
Bowl, 10", 3 pt., fruit	80.00	Candlestick, 5", 2-lite	30.00

SANDWICH

	Crystal
Candy, 6" square	365.00
Candy box, w/cover, 5", flat	40.00
Candy jar, w/cover, 8½", ftd.	55.00
Cheese, w/cover (cover 4¾", plate 8")	110.00
Cheese/cracker (3" compote, 13" plate)	55.00
Cigarette box, w/cover, 3½"	22.00
Cigarette holder, 3", ftd.	27.50
Coaster, 5"	12.00
Comport, 2¼"	15.00
Comport, 3¼", low ft., crimped candy	20.00
Comport, 3¼", low ft., flared candy	17.50
Comport, 4¼", ftd.	20.00
Comport, 5", low ft.	20.00
Comport, 5½", ftd., low crimped	25.00
Comport, 6", low ft., flared	22.50
Condiment set (2 cruets; 3¾" salt & pepper; 4 pt. tray)	100.00
Creamer, 4", 7 oz., ftd.	9.00
Cup, 6 oz., tea	10.00
Epergne, 9", garden	110.00
Epergne, 12", 3 pt., fruit or flower	235.00
Jelly, 3", indiv.	7.00
Mayonnaise set, 3 pc.: ladle, 5" bowl, 7" plate	32.00
Oil bottle, 5¾"	35.00
Pan, 6¾" x 10½", oblong, camelia	60.00
Pitcher, 13 oz., metal top	60.00
Pitcher, w/ice lip, 8", 64 oz.	130.00
Plate, 3", indiv. jelly	6.00
Plate, 6", bread/butter	6.00
Plate, 6½", finger bowl liner	8.00
Plate, 7", dessert	7.50
Plate, 8", mayonnaise liner, w/ring	7.00
Plate, 8", salad	10.00
Plate, 9½", dinner	35.00
Plate, 11½", hdld., service	37.50
Plate, 12", torte	45.00
Plate, 12", ice cream, rolled edge	55.00
Plate, 12", deviled egg	65.00
Plate, 13", salad dressing, w/ring	32.00
Plate, 13", service	50.00
Plate, 13", service, rolled edge	55.00
Plate, 13", cracker, w/ring	30.00
Plate, 16", lazy susan, w/turntable	100.00
Plate, 16", hostess	100.00
Relish, 5½", 2 pt., rnd., ring hdl.	15.00
Relish, 6", 2 pt., rnd., ring hdl.	17.00
Relish, 7", 2 pt., oval	20.00
Relish, 10", 4 pt., hdld.	25.00

	Crystal
Relish, 10", 3 pt., oblong	27.50
Relish, 10½", 3 pt., oblong	27.50
Relish, 12", 3 pt.	37.50
Salad dressing set: (2 ladles; 5" ftd. mayonnaise; 13" plate w/ring)	80.00
Salad dressing set: (2 ladles; 6" ftd. div. bowl; 8" plate w/ring)	65.00
Salt & pepper, 2½", w/glass tops, pr.	18.00
Salt & pepper, 2½", w/metal tops, pr.	18.00
Salt & pepper, 3¾", w/metal top (on 6" tray), 3 pc.	30.00
Saucer, 6", w/ring	4.00
Stem, 2½", 6 oz., ftd., fruit cup/jello	11.00
Stem, 2¾", 5 oz., ftd., oyster cocktail	15.00
Stem, 3½", 5 oz., sundae (flared rim)	12.00
Stem, 4¼", 3 oz., cocktail	15.00
Stem, 4¼", 5 oz., ice cream	12.50
Stem, 4¼", 3 oz., wine	20.00
Stem, 5¼", 4 oz., ftd., parfait	30.00
Stem, 5¼", 5 oz., champagne	20.00
Stem, 6", 9 oz., goblet	18.50
Sugar, 3¼", ftd., 9 oz.	8.00
Sugar, 5 oz.	7.50
Sugar (cheese) shaker, 13 oz., metal top	65.00
Tray, oval (for sugar/creamer)	10.00
Tray, 6" mint, rolled edge, w/ring hdl.	17.50
Tray, 7", oval, pickle	15.00
Tray, 7", mint, rolled edge, w/ring hdl.	20.00
Tray, 8", oval	18.00
Tray, 8", for oil/vinegar	20.00
Tray, 10", oval, celery	18.00
Tray, 12", fruit epergne	50.00
Tray, 12", ice cream, rolled edge	45.00
Tumbler, 3¾", 5 oz., ftd., juice	12.00
Tumbler, 4¾", 9 oz., ftd., water	14.00
Tumbler, 5¼", 13 oz., flat, iced tea	20.00
Tumbler, 5¼", 12 oz., ftd., iced tea	17.50
Urn, w/cover, 12", ftd.	135.00
Vase, 3", ftd., crimped	17.50
Vase, 3", ftd., flared rim	15.00
Vase, 4", hat shape	20.00
Vase, 4½", flat base, crimped	25.00
Vase, 5", ftd., flared rim	22.50
Vase, 5", ftd., crimped	25.00
Vase, 5", ftd., fan	40.00
Vase, 7½", epergne, threaded base	60.00
Vase, 10", ftd.	65.00

DUNCAN

EARLY AMERICAN SANDWICH

No. 41 PATTERN

Washington, Pa.   1-1-43

THE DUNCAN & MILLER GLASS CO.

No. 41
9 oz. Goblet
Height—6"

No. 41
5 oz. Saucer
Champagne
Height—5¼"

No. 41
3 oz. Wine
Height—4½"

No. 41
3 oz. Cocktail
Height—4¼"

No. 41
5 oz. Ice Cream
Height—4¼"

No. 41
5 oz. Flared Sundae
Height—3½"

No. 41
3 in. Ind. Jelly

No. 41
6 oz. Fruit Cup or Jello
Height—2½"

No. 41
5 oz. Oyster Cocktail
Height—2¾"

No. 41
13 oz. Ice Tea
Tumbler—Straight
Height—5¼"

No. 41
½ gal. Ice Lip Jug
Height—8"

No. 41
12 oz. Ftd. Ice Tea
Height—5½"

No. 41
9 oz. Ftd. Tumbler
Height—4¼"

No. 41
5 oz. Ftd. Orange Juice
Height—3¼"

No. 41
4 oz. Parfait
Height—5¼"

DUNCAN

EARLY AMERICAN SANDWICH

No. 41 PATTERN

Genuine Duncan

THE DUNCAN & MILLER GLASS CO. Washington, Pa. 1-1-43

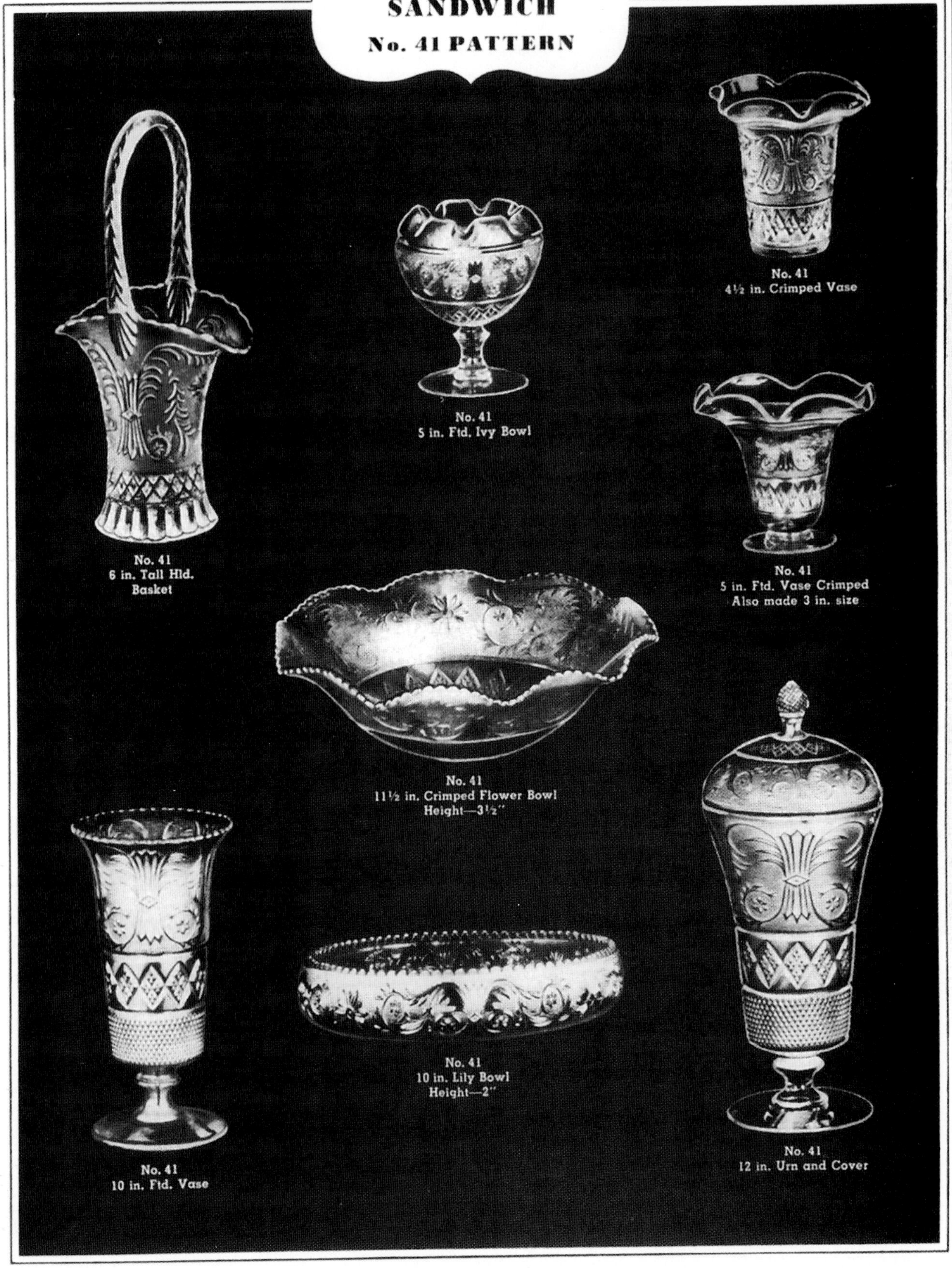

No. 41
4½ in. Crimped Vase

No. 41
5 in. Ftd. Ivy Bowl

No. 41
6 in. Tall Hld. Basket

No. 41
5 in. Ftd. Vase Crimped
Also made 3 in. size

No. 41
11½ in. Crimped Flower Bowl
Height—3½"

No. 41
10 in. Lily Bowl
Height—2"

No. 41
10 in. Ftd. Vase

No. 41
12 in. Urn and Cover

DUNCAN

EARLY AMERICAN SANDWICH
No. 41 PATTERN

Washington, Pa.   1-1-43

THE DUNCAN & MILLER GLASS CO.

No. 1-B-41—3 Light
Candelabrum W/U Prisms
Height—10"   Width—13"
2 Bobeches

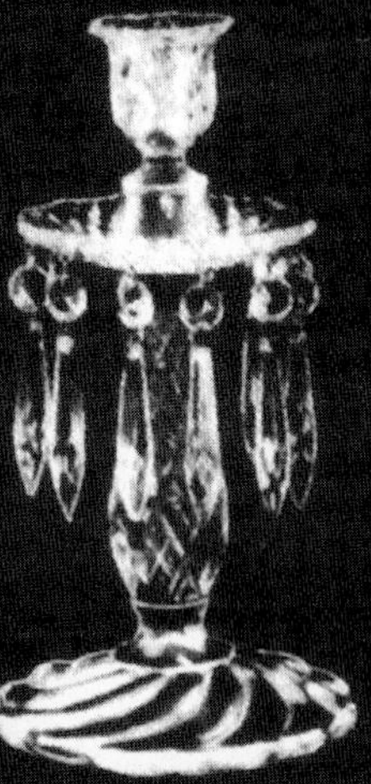

No. 1-41—1 Light
Candelabrum W/U Prisms
Height—10"

No. 1-41—1 Light
Hurricane Lamp Candelabrum
W/Prisms
Height—15"

No. 1-C-41—3 Light
Candelabrum W/U Prisms
Height—16"   Width—13"
3 Bobeches

SATURN, Blank #1485, A.H. Heisey & Co.

Colors: crystal, "Zircon" or "Limelight" green, "Dawn"

"Limelight" and "Zircon" are the same color. Originally made in 1937, this color was called "Zircon." In 1955, it was made again by Heisey, but called "Limelight." Zircon prices are continuing their upward spiral with crystal prices of Saturn holding steady. That Zircon mustard paddle is quite difficult to find! You can tell by the price.

	Crystal	Zircon/ Limelight
Ash tray	10.00	150.00
Bitters bottle, w/short tube, blown	35.00	
Bowl, baked apple	7.00	75.00
Bowl, finger	5.00	
Bowl, rose, lg.	40.00	
Bowl, 4½", nappy	5.00	
Bowl, 5", nappy	7.00	90.00
Bowl, 5", whipped cream	15.00	150.00
Bowl, 7", pickle	15.00	
Bowl, 9", 3 part, relish	17.50	
Bowl, 10", celery	15.00	
Bowl, 11", salad	40.00	140.00
Bowl, 12", fruit, flared rim	35.00	100.00
Bowl, 13", floral, rolled edge	37.00	
Bowl, 13", floral	37.00	
Candelabrum, w/"e" ball drops, 2-lite	125.00	500.00
Candle block, 2-lite	95.00	350.00
Candlestick, 3", ftd., 1-lite	30.00	500.00
Comport, 7"	50.00	550.00
Creamer	17.00	180.00
Cup	10.00	150.00
Hostess Set, 8 pc. (low bowl w/ftd. ctr. bowl, 3 toothpick holders & clips)	55.00	300.00
Marmalade, w/cover	45.00	500.00
Mayonnaise	8.00	80.00
Mustard, w/cover and paddle	60.00	350.00
Oil bottle, 3 oz.	55.00	500.00
Pitcher, 70 oz., w/ice lip, blown	65.00	500.00
Pitcher, juice	40.00	300.00
Plate, 6"	3.00	35.00
Plate, 7", bread	5.00	45.00
Plate, 8", luncheon	7.00	55.00
Plate, 13", torte	25.00	
Plate, 15", torte	30.00	
Salt & pepper, pr.	45.00	550.00
Saucer	5.00	30.00
Stem, 3 oz., cocktail	10.00	60.00
Stem, 4 oz., fruit cocktail or oyster cocktail, no ball in stem, ftd.	8.00	75.00
Stem, 4½ oz., sherbet	5.00	70.00
Stem, 5 oz., parfait	10.00	110.00
Stem, 6 oz., saucer champagne	5.00	95.00
Stem, 10 oz.	18.00	100.00
Sugar	17.00	180.00
Sugar shaker (pourer)	80.00	
Sugar, w/cover, no handles	25.00	
Tray, tidbit, 2 sides turned as fan	25.00	80.00
Tumbler, 5 oz., juice	7.00	120.00
Tumbler, 7 oz., old-fashioned	10.00	
Tumbler, 8 oz., old-fashioned	10.00	
Tumbler, 9 oz., luncheon	12.00	
Tumbler, 10 oz.	17.50	70.00
Tumbler, 12 oz., soda	10.00	150.00
Vase, violet	22.00	130.00
Vase, 8½", flared	25.00	175.00
Vase, 8½", straight	25.00	175.00
Vase, 10½"		230.00

SEVILLE, Fostoria Glass Company, 1926 – 1931

Colors: amber, green

Seville is a Fostoria pattern that has mostly been neglected by the collecting world. It would be an economical Elegant pattern to collect though there is not a great deal of it to go around. Green would be easier to obtain than amber. The butter dish, pitcher, grapefruit and liner, and sugar lid are all troublesome to find; be on the lookout for them.

For comparison, the bouillon and liner are at the right of the cream soup and liner in the top picture. The stemmed piece at bottom (between the shaker and the cup and saucer) is a grapefruit liner. Most Fostoria patterns have the design on both the grapefruit and the liner.

	Amber	Green
Ash tray, #2350, 4"	17.50	22.50
Bowl, #2350, fruit, 5½"	10.00	12.00
Bowl, #2350, cereal, 6½"	18.00	20.00
Bowl, #2350, soup, 7¾"	20.00	25.00
Bowl, #2315, low foot, 7"	16.00	18.00
Bowl, #2350, vegetable	20.00	25.00
Bowl, #2350, nappy, 9"	30.00	35.00
Bowl, #2350, oval, baker, 9"	25.00	30.00
Bowl, #2315, flared, 10½", ftd.	25.00	30.00
Bowl, #2350, oval, baker, 10½"	35.00	40.00
Bowl, 10", ftd.	35.00	40.00
Bowl, #2350, salad, 10"	30.00	35.00
Bowl, #2329, rolled edge, console, 11"	27.50	32.50
Bowl, #2297, deep, flared, 12"	30.00	32.50
Bowl, #2371, oval, console, 13"	35.00	40.00
Bowl, #2329, rolled edge, console, 13"	30.00	32.50
Bowl, #2350, bouillon, flat	13.50	15.00
Bowl, #2350½, bouillon, ftd.	14.00	16.00
Bowl, #2350, cream soup, flat	14.50	16.00
Bowl, #2350½, cream soup, ftd.	15.50	17.00
Bowl, #869/2283, finger, w/6" liner	20.00	22.00
Butter, w/cover, #2350, round	185.00	235.00
Candlestick, #2324, 2"	18.00	22.00
Candlestick, #2324, 4"	15.00	20.00
Candlestick, #2324, 9"	30.00	35.00
Candy jar, w/cover, #2250, ½ lb., ftd.	95.00	120.00
Candy jar, w/cover, #2331, 3 pt., flat	65.00	80.00
Celery, #2350, 11"	15.00	17.50
Cheese and cracker, #2368, (11" plate)	40.00	45.00
Comport, #2327, 7½", (twisted stem)	20.00	25.00

	Amber	Green
Comport, #2350, 8"	27.50	35.00
Creamer, #2315½, flat, ftd.	13.50	15.00
Creamer, #2350½, ftd.	12.50	13.50
Cup, #2350, after dinner	25.00	30.00
Cup, #2350, flat	10.00	12.50
Cup, #2350½, ftd.	10.00	12.50
Egg cup, #2350	30.00	35.00
Grapefruit, #945½, blown	40.00	45.00
Grapefruit, #945½, liner, blown	30.00	35.00
Grapefruit, #2315, molded	25.00	30.00
Ice bucket, #2378	50.00	55.00
Pickle, #2350, 8"	13.50	15.00
Pitcher, #5084, ftd.	235.00	265.00
Plate, #2350, bread and butter, 6"	3.50	4.00
Plate, #2350, salad, 7½"	5.00	5.50
Plate, #2350, luncheon, 8½"	6.00	6.50
Plate, #2321, Maj Jongg (canape), 8¾"	35.00	40.00
Plate, #2350, sm. dinner, 9½"	12.00	13.50
Plate, #2350, dinner, 10½"	32.50	40.00
Plate, #2350, chop, 13¾"	30.00	35.00
Plate, #2350, round, 15"	35.00	40.00
Plate, #2350, cream soup liner	5.00	6.00
Platter, #2350, 10½"	22.50	25.00
Platter, #2350, 12"	35.00	40.00
Platter, #2350, 15"	70.00	80.00
Salt and pepper shaker, #5100, pr.	60.00	65.00
Sauce boat liner, #2350	25.00	27.50
Sauce boat, #2350	55.00	72.50
Saucer, #2350	3.00	3.00
Saucer, after dinner, #2350	5.00	5.00
Stem, #870, cocktail	15.00	16.00
Stem, #870, cordial	65.00	70.00
Stem, #870, high sherbet	15.00	16.00
Stem, #870, low sherbet	12.50	13.50
Stem, #870, oyster cocktail	16.50	17.50
Stem, #870, parfait	30.00	35.00
Stem, #870, water	20.00	22.50
Stem, #870, wine	22.50	25.00
Sugar cover, #2350½	80.00	100.00
Sugar, fat, ftd., #2315	13.50	14.50
Sugar, ftd., #2350½	12.50	13.50
Tray, 11", center handled, #2287	27.50	30.00
Tumbler, #5084, ftd., 2 oz.	35.00	37.50
Tumbler, #5084, ftd., 5 oz.	13.50	15.00
Tumbler, #5084, ftd., 9 oz.	15.00	16.50
Tumbler, #5084, ftd., 12 oz.	18.00	20.00
Urn, small, #2324	75.00	95.00
Vase, #2292, 8"	55.00	65.00

"SPIRAL FLUTES," Duncan & Miller Glass Company, Introduced 1924

Colors: amber, green, pink, crystal

"Spiral Flutes" has been predominantly ignored by collectors. Several pieces are readily found; namely the 6¾" flanged bowls, 7 oz. footed tumblers, and 7½" plates; after that, there is little found effortlessly. Green can be collected more easily than any other color. Amber and crystal sets can be put together, but few try!

	Amber, Green, Pink		Amber, Green, Pink
Bowl, 2", almond	12.00	Ice tub, handled	50.00
Bowl, 3¾", bouillon	15.00	Lamp, 10½", countess	265.00
Bowl, 4⅜", finger	6.00	Mug, 6½", 9 oz., handled	27.50
Bowl, 4¾", ftd., cream soup	15.00	Mug, 7", 9 oz., handled	35.00
Bowl, 4" w., mayonnaise	17.50	Oil, w/stopper, 6 oz.	175.00
Bowl, 5", nappy	6.00	Pickle, 8⅝"	12.00
Bowl, 6½", cereal, sm. flange	32.50	Pitcher, ½ gal.	175.00
Bowl, 6¾", grapefruit	7.50	Plate, 6", pie	3.00
Bowl, 6", handled nappy	22.00	Plate, 7½", salad	4.00
Bowl, 6", handled nappy, w/cover	85.00	Plate, 8⅜", luncheon	4.00
Bowl, 7", nappy	15.00	Plate, 10⅜", dinner	22.50
Bowl, 7½", flanged (baked apple)	22.50	Plate, 13⅝", torte	27.50
Bowl, 8", nappy	17.50	Plate, w/star, 6", (fingerbowl item)	6.00
Bowl, 8½", flanged (oyster plate)	22.50	Platter, 11"	35.00
Bowl, 9", nappy	27.50	Platter, 13"	45.00
Bowl, 10", oval, veg., two styles.	45.00	Relish, 10" x 7⅜", oval, 3 pc. (2 inserts)	85.00
Bowl, 10½", lily pond	40.00	Saucer	3.00
Bowl, 11¾" w. x 3¾" t., console, flared	30.00	Saucer, demi	5.00
Bowl, 11", nappy	30.00	Seafood sauce cup, 3" w. x 2½" h.	25.00
Bowl, 12", cupped console	30.00	Stem, 3¾", 3½ oz., wine	17.50
Candle, 3½"	15.00	Stem, 3¾", 5 oz., low sherbet	8.00
Candle, 7½"	55.00	Stem, 4¾", 6 oz., tall sherbet	12.00
Candle, 9½"	75.00	Stem, 5⅝", 4½ oz., parfait	17.50
Candle, 11½"	110.00	Stem, 6¼", 7 oz., water	17.50
Celery, 10¾" x 4¾"	17.50	Sugar, oval	8.00
* Chocolate jar, w/cover	250.00	Sweetmeat, w/cover, 7½"	110.00
Cigarette holder, 4"	32.00	Tumbler, 3⅜", ftd., 2½ oz., cocktail (no stem)	7.00
Comport, 4⅜"	15.00	Tumbler, 4¼", 8 oz., flat	30.00
Comport, 6⅝"	17.50	Tumbler, 4⅜", ftd., 5½ oz., juice (no stem)	14.00
Comport, 9", low ft., flared	55.00	Tumbler, 4¾", 7 oz., flat, soda	35.00
Console stand, 1½" h. x 4⅝" w.	12.00	Tumbler, 5⅛", ftd., 7 oz., water (1 knob)	8.00
Creamer, oval	8.00	Tumbler, 5⅛", ftd., 9 oz., water (no stem)	20.00
Cup	9.00	Tumbler, 5½", 11 oz., gingerale	65.00
Cup, demi	25.00	Vase, 6½"	12.00
* Fernery, 10" x 5½", 4 ftd., flower box	365.00	Vase, 8½"	17.50
Grapefruit, ftd.	20.00	Vase, 10½"	25.00

*Crystal, $135.00

STANHOPE, #1483, A.H. Heisey Co., 1936 – 1941

Colors: crystal, some blown stemware in Zircon

Deco collectors find Heisey's Stanhope to their liking. As with New Era, this has increased competition for this pattern. Notice that prices have surged in almost all areas except stemware!

The black and red insert handles (round knobs) are whimsical to some; but others think they look majestic. For those who asked, the T knobs (insert handles) are like wooden dowel rods that act as horizontal handles.

Some people believe the salad bowl shown at the bottom is a punch bowl; but it is not!

	Crystal
Ash tray, indiv.	20.00
Bottle, oil, 3 oz. w or w/o rd. knob	275.00
Bowl, 6" mint, 2 hdld., w or w/o rd. knobs	20.00
Bowl, 6" mint, 2 pt., 2 hdld., w or w/o rd. knobs	20.00
Bowl, 11" salad	65.00
Bowl, finger #4080 (blown, plain)	10.00
Bowl, floral, 11", 2 hdld. w or w/o "T" knobs	60.00
Candelabra, 2-lite, w bobeche & prisms	160.00
Candy box & lid, rnd., w or w/o rd. knob	180.00
Cigarette box & lid, w or w/o rd. knob	55.00
Creamer, 2 hdld., w or w/o rd. knobs	25.00
Cup, w or w/o rd. knob	15.00
Ice tub, 2 hdld., w or w/o "T" knobs	50.00
Jelly, 6", 1 hdld., w or w/o rd. knobs	25.00
Jelly, 6", 3 pt., 1 hdld., w or w/o rd. knobs	25.00
Nappy, 4½", 1 hdld. w or w/o rd. knob	15.00
Nut, indiv., 1 hdld., w or w/o rd. knob	30.00
Plate, 7"	10.00
Plate, 12" torte, 2 hdld. w or w/o "T" knobs	30.00
Plate, 15" torte, rnd. or salad liner	32.50
Relish, 11" triplex buffet, 2 hdld., w or w/o "T" knobs	30.00
Relish, 12" 4 pt., 2 hdld., w or w/o "T" knobs	45.00
Relish, 12", 5 pt., 2 hdld. w or w/o "T" knobs	45.00
Salt & pepper, #60 top	45.00
Saucer	5.00
Stem, 1 oz. cordial #4083 (blown)	70.00
Stem, 2½ oz. pressed wine	20.00
Stem, 2½ oz. wine, #4083	25.00
Stem, 3½ oz. cocktail #4083	20.00
Stem, 3½ oz. pressed cocktail	10.00
Stem, 4 oz. claret #4083	25.00
Stem, 4 oz. oyster cocktail #4083	10.00
Stem, 5½ oz. pressed saucer champagne	15.00
Stem, 5½ oz. saucer champagne #4083	15.00
Stem, 9 oz. pressed goblet	35.00
Stem, 10 oz. goblet #4083	22.50
Stem, 12 oz. pressed soda	25.00
Sugar, 2 hdld., w or w/o rd. knobs	25.00
Tray, 12" celery, 2 hdld. w or w/o "T" knobs	25.00
Tumbler, 5 oz. soda #4083	20.00
Tumbler, 8 oz. soda #4083	22.50
Tumbler, 12 oz. soda #4083	25.00
Vase, 7" ball	60.00
Vase, 9", 2 hdld., w or w/o "T" knobs	65.00

SUN RAY, Line #2510, Fostoria Glass Company, 1935 – 1944

Colors: crystal, red, blue, green, yellow

Sunray is one Fostoria pattern that is included here by collector requests. It took some time to acquire enough pieces and pricing, but here are the results. I only price crystal; but be aware there are pieces to be found in red, blue, green, and yellow. I have included a sample of each color except red in my photos.

The cream soup is tab handled. By putting a lid on the cream soup, one makes an onion soup according to Fostoria's catalogs.

Notice the two tumblers in the upper photograph. One has frosted panels and the other is clear. Pieces with frosted panels were called Glacier by Fostoria and sold as a separate pattern. Some Sunray enthusiasts are willing to mix the two, but most gather one or the other. Personally, I think the frosting adds to the overall design. Prices for both patterns are about the same.

	Crystal		Crystal
Almond, ftd., ind.	12.00	Pitcher, 64 oz., ice lip	185.00
Ash tray, ind., 2510½	8.00	Plate, 6"	5.00
Ash tray, square	10.00	Plate, 7½"	8.00
Bon bon, hdld.	16.00	Plate, 8½"	12.00
Bon bon. 3-toed	17.50	Plate, 9½"	28.00
Bowl, 5", fruit	8.00	Plate, 11", torte	35.00
Bowl, 9½", flared	30.00	Plate, 12", sandwich	35.00
Bowl, 12", salad	35.00	Plate, 15", torte	65.00
Bowl, 13", rolled edge	40.00	Plate, 16"	70.00
Bowl, custard, 2¼", high	12.00	Relish, 2-part	16.00
Bowl, hdld.	35.00	Relish, 3-part	20.00
Butter w/lid, ¼ lb.	25.00	Relish, 4-part	22.00
Candelabra, 2 light	45.00	Salt dip	9.00
Candlestick, 3"	18.00	Saucer	3.00
Candlestick, 5½"	25.00	Shaker, 4", pr.	45.00
Candlestick, duo	35.00	Shaker, individual, 2¼", 2510½	15.00
Candy jar w/cover	45.00	Stem, 3½", 5½ oz., sherbet, low	9.00
Celery, hdld.	22.00	Stem, 3¼", 3½ oz., fruit cocktail	12.00
Cigarette and cover	22.00	Stem, 3", 4 oz., cocktail, ftd.	12.00
Cigarette box, oblong	25.00	Stem, 4⅞", 4½ oz., claret	25.00
Coaster, 4"	6.00	Stem, 5¾", 9 oz., goblet	16.00
Comport	18.00	Sugar, ftd.	12.00
Cream soup	25.00	Sugar, individual	12.00
Cream soup liner	8.00	Sweetmeat, hdld., divided	30.00
Cream, ftd.	12.00	Tray, 6½", ind sug/cream	10.00
Cream, individual	12.00	Tray, 10½", oblong	25.00
Cup	12.00	Tray, 10", square	35.00
Decanter w/stopper, 18 oz.	40.00	Tray, condiment, 8½"	35.00
Decanter w/stopper, oblong, 26 oz.	55.00	Tray, oval hdld.	25.00
Ice bucket, no handle	45.00	Tumbler, 2¼", 2 oz., whiskey. 2510½	12.00
Ice bucket w/handle	50.00	Tumbler, 3½", 5 oz., juice, 2510½	12.50
Jelly	16.00	Tumbler, 3½", 6 oz., old fashion, 2510½	14.00
Jelly w/cover	28.00	Tumbler, 4⅛", 9 oz., table, 2510½	13.00
Mayonnaise w/liner, ladle	35.00	Tumbler, 4¾", 9 oz., ftd. table	14.00
Mustard w/cover, spoon	30.00	Tumbler, 4⅝", 5 oz., ftd. juice	15.00
Nappy, hdld., flared	13.00	Tumbler, 5¼", 13 oz., ftd. tea	18.00
Nappy, hdld., reg.	12.00	Tumbler, 5⅛", 13 oz., tea, 2510½	22.00
Nappy, hdld., square	14.00	Vase, 3½", rose bowl	22.00
Nappy, hdld., tri-corner	15.00	Vase, 5", rose bowl	30.00
Oil bottle w/stopper, 3 oz.	32.00	Vase, 6", crimped	37.50
Onion soup w/cover	35.00	Vase, 7"	50.00
Pickle, hdld.	22.00	Vase, 9", sq. ftd.	55.00
Pitcher, 16 oz., cereal	40.00	Vase, sweetpea	65.00
Pitcher, 64 oz.	150.00		

SUNRISE MEDALLION, "Dancing Girl," #758, Morgantown Glass Works,
Late 1920's – Early 1930's

Colors: pink, green, blue, crystal

More collectors are beginning to use the official name Sunrise Medallion, (etching #758) for this Morgantown pattern that had previously been dubbed "Dancing Girl" by collectors.

Measurements in most catalogues were in ounces only. The twisted stem items (#7642½) are slightly taller than their plain stem (#7630) counterparts. Measurements given below are mainly from the #7630 line. Twisted stemware champagne and waters are the only #7642½ stems I have been able to find. If you have others, I would appreciate having measurements.

Oyster cocktails, which look more like juice or bar tumblers to me, have surfaced in several coastal areas. In any case, these stand 2⁷⁄₁₆" to 2⁹⁄₁₆" tall and hold 4 ozs. Both green and pink sugar bowls pictured need creamers if you spot one for me!

Several newly listed items include a cone shaped sherbet and several sizes of tumblers. So far, few serving pieces have been found.

The address of the Morgantown Collectors of America is listed in the back of the book. If you would like more information about Morgantown Glass, please contact them!

	Crystal	Blue	Pink/ Green
Bowl, finger, ftd.		65.00	
Creamer		325.00	275.00
Cup	40.00	90.00	80.00
Parfait, 5 oz.	55.00	110.00	80.00
Pitcher		425.00	
Plate, 5⅞", sherbet..	6.00	12.50	10.00
Plate, 7½", salad	10.00	25.00	20.00
Plate, 8⅜"...	12.50	30.00	22.50
Saucer..	15.00	22.50	17.50
Sherbet, cone...	20.00		
Stem, 1½ oz., cordial	110.00	265.00	185.00
Stem, 2½ oz., wine...	45.00	85.00	55.00
Stem, 6¼", 7 oz., champagne (twist stem, 6¾")...........	25.00	45.00	30.00
Stem, 6⅛", cocktail...	30.00	65.00	40.00
Stem, 7¾", 9 oz., water (twist stem, 8¼")	35.00	70.00	45.00
Sugar...		300.00	250.00
Tumbler, 2½", 4 oz, ftd...	25.00	150.00	
Tumbler, 3½", 4 oz., ftd..			35.00
Tumbler, 4¼", 5 oz., ftd..	45.00	55.00	35.00
Tumbler, 4¼", flat..	20.00		
Tumbler, 4¾", 9 oz., ftd..	20.00	60.00	40.00
Tumbler, 5½", 11 oz., ftd..	35.00	85.00	65.00
Tumbler, 5½", flat..	25.00		
Vase, 6" tall, 5" wide			350.00
Vase, 10", slender, bud...	65.00		250.00
Vase, 10", bulbous bottom			295.00

TEAR DROP, #301, Duncan & Miller Glass Company, 1936 – 1955

Colors: crystal

Tear Drop stemware continues to be plentiful! Few collectors need any to finish sets. Mint condition dinner plates and supplementary serving pieces are not as easily located. Cordials are readily available when compared to finding cordials in other Duncan patterns! This is an excellent inaugural pattern for beginners.

Reprints of original Duncan catalogs are included on pages 201 – 203.

	Crystal		Crystal
Ash tray, 3" indiv.	6.00	Coaster/ashtray, 3", rolled edge	7.00
Ash tray, 5"	8.00	Comport, 4¾", ftd.	12.00
Bonbon, 6", 4 hdld.	12.00	Comport, 6", low foot., hdld.	15.00
Bottle, w/stopper, 12", bar	135.00	Condiment set: 5 pc. (salt/pepper, 2	
Bowl, 4¼", finger	7.00	3 oz. cruets, 9", 2 hdld. tray)	100.00
Bowl, 5", fruit nappy	6.00	Creamer, 3 oz.	5.00
Bowl, 5", 2 hdld., nappy	8.00	Creamer, 6 oz.	6.00
Bowl, 6", dessert, nappy	6.00	Creamer, 8 oz.	8.00
Bowl, 6", fruit, nappy	6.00	Cup, 2½ oz., demi	10.00
Bowl, 7", fruit, nappy	7.00	Cup, 6 oz., tea	6.00
Bowl, 7", 2 hdld., nappy	10.00	Flower basket, 12", loop hdl.	120.00
Bowl, 8" x 12", oval, flower	42.00	Ice bucket, 5½"	62.00
Bowl, 9", salad	25.00	Marmalade, w/cover, 4"	35.00
Bowl, 9", 2 hdld., nappy	20.00	Mayonnaise, 4½" (2 hdld. bowl, ladle,	
Bowl, 10", crimped console, 2 hdld.	27.50	6" plate)	27.50
Bowl, 10", flared, fruit	25.00	Mayonnaise set, 3 pc. (4½" bowl, ladle,	
Bowl, 11½", crimped, flower	30.00	8" hdld. plate)	32.50
Bowl, 11½", flared, flower	30.00	Mustard jar, w/cover, 4¼"	35.00
Bowl, 12", salad	40.00	Nut dish, 6", 2 pt.	10.00
Bowl, 12", crimped, low foot	37.00	Oil bottle, 3 oz.	20.00
Bowl, 12", ftd., flower	45.00	Olive dish, 4¼", 2 hdld., oval	15.00
Bowl, 12", sq., 4 hdld.	42.50	Olive dish, 6", 2 pt.	15.00
Bowl, 13", gardenia	35.00	Pickle dish, 6"	15.00
Bowl, 15½", 2½ gal. punch	100.00	Pitcher, 5", 16 oz., milk	50.00
Butter, w/cover, ¼ lb., 2 hdld.	22.00	Pitcher, 8½", 64 oz., w/ice lip	110.00
Cake salver, 13", ftd.	47.00	Plate, 6", bread/butter	4.00
Canape set: (6" plate w/ring, 4 oz., ftd.,		Plate, 6", canape	10.00
cocktail)	27.00	Plate, 7", 2 hdld., lemon	12.50
Candlestick, 4"	9.00	Plate, 7½", salad	5.00
Candlestick, 7", 2-lite, ball loop ctr.	18.00	Plate, 8½", luncheon	7.00
Candlestick, 7", lg. ball ctr. w/bobeches,		Plate, 10½", dinner	35.00
prisms	35.00	Plate, 11", 2 hdld.	27.50
Candy basket, 5½" x 7½", 2 hdld., oval	75.00	Plate, 13", 4 hdld.	25.00
Candy box, w/cover, 7", 2 pt., 2 hdld.	55.00	Plate, 13", salad liner, rolled edge	27.50
Candy box, w/cover, 8", 3 pt., 3 hdld.	60.00	Plate, 13", torte, rolled edge	30.00
Candy dish, 7½", heart shape	22.00	Plate, 14", torte	35.00
Celery, 11", 2 hdld.	15.00	Plate, 14", torte, rolled edge	35.00
Celery, 11", 2 pt., 2 hdld.	18.00	Plate, 16", torte, rolled edge	37.50
Celery, 12", 3 pt.	20.00	Plate, 18", lazy susan	75.00
Cheese & cracker (3½" comport, 11"		Plate, 18", punch liner, rolled edge	60.00
2 hdld. plate)	45.00		

TEAR DROP

	Crystal		Crystal
Relish, 7", 2 pt., 2 hdld.	15.00	Sugar, 8 oz.	8.00
Relish, 7½", 2 pt., heart shape	18.00	Sweetmeat, 5½", star shape, 2 hdld.	30.00
Relish, 9", 3 pt., 3 hdld.	27.50	Sweetmeat, 6½", ctr. hdld.	30.00
Relish, 11", 3 pt., 2 hdld.	27.50	Sweetmeat, 7", star shape, 2 hdld.	37.50
Relish, 12", 3 pt.	27.50	Tray, 5½", ctr. hdld. (for mustard jar)	11.00
Relish, 12", 5 pt., rnd.	27.50	Tray, 6", 2 hdld. (for salt/pepper)	10.00
Relish, 12", 6 pt., rnd.	27.50	Tray, 7¾", ctr. hdld. (for cruets)	12.50
Relish, 12", sq., 4 pt., 4 hdld.	27.50	Tray, 8", 2 hdld. (for oil/vinegar)	12.50
Salad set, 6" (compote, 11" hdld. plate)	37.50	Tray, 8", 2 hdld. (for sugar/creamer)	7.50
Salad set, 9", (2 pt. bowl, 13" rolled edge plate)	75.00	Tray, 10", 2 hdld (for sugar/creamer)	8.00
Salt & pepper, 5"	25.00	Tumbler, 2¼", 2 oz., flat, whiskey	17.00
Saucer, 4½", demi	3.00	Tumbler, 2¼", 2 oz., ftd., whiskey	12.00
Saucer, 6"	1.50	Tumbler, 3", 3 oz., ftd., whiskey	12.00
Stem, 2½", 5 oz., ftd., sherbet	5.00	Tumbler, 3¼", 3½ oz., flat, juice	6.00
Stem, 2¾", 3½ oz., ftd., oyster cocktail	7.50	Tumbler, 3¼", 7 oz., flat, old-fashioned	11.00
Stem, 3½", 5 oz., sherbet	6.00	Tumbler, 3½", 5 oz., flat, juice	6.00
Stem, 4", 1 oz., cordial	30.00	Tumbler, 4", 4½ oz., ftd., juice	8.00
Stem, 4½", 1¾ oz., sherry	30.00	Tumbler, 4¼", 9 oz., flat	8.00
Stem, 4½", 3½ oz., cocktail	15.00	Tumbler, 4½", 8 oz., flat, split	8.00
Stem, 4¾", 3 oz., wine	18.00	Tumbler, 4½", 9 oz., ftd.	8.00
Stem, 5", 5 oz., champagne	10.00	Tumbler, 4¾", 10 oz., flat, hi-ball	10.00
Stem, 5½", 4 oz., claret	17.50	Tumbler, 5", 8 oz., ftd., party	9.00
Stem, 5¾", 9 oz.	10.00	Tumbler, 5¼", 12 oz., flat, iced tea	15.00
Stem, 6¼", 8 oz., ale	15.00	Tumbler, 5¾", 14 oz., flat, hi-ball	17.50
Stem, 7", 9 oz.	14.00	Tumbler, 6", 14 oz., iced tea	17.50
Sugar, 3 oz.	5.00	Urn, w/cover, 9", ftd.	115.00
Sugar, 6 oz.	6.00	Vase, 9", ftd., fan	25.00
		Vase, 9", ftd., round	37.50

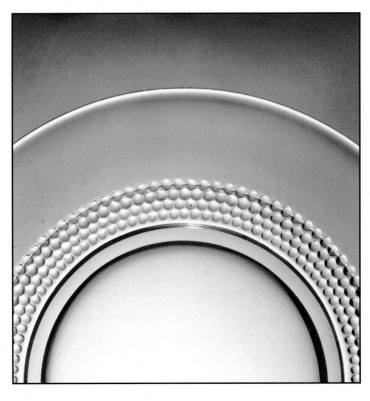

DUNCAN

TEAR DROPS
No. 5301 STEMWARE
No. 5300 TUMBLERS
(Lead Blown)

No. 5301—4½ oz. Ftd.
Orange Juice
Height—4"

No. 5301—3 oz. Ftd.
Whiskey or Cocktail
Height—3"

No. 5301—2 oz.
Ftd. Whiskey
Height—2¾"

No. 5301
½ Gal. Pitcher with Ice Guard Lip
Height—8½"

No. 5301
No. 5301—14 oz. Ftd.
Ice Tea or Hiball
Height—6"
Also made 12 oz.
Height—5½"

No. 5301
8 oz. Ftd. Split
or Party Glass
Height—5"

No. 5301—9 oz.
Ftd. Tumbler
Height—4½"

No. 5300—2 oz.
Whiskey
Height—2¼"

No. 5300—3½ oz.
Orange Juice
Height—3¼"

No. 5300—5 oz.
Orange Juice
Height—3½"

No. 5300
9 oz. Tumbler
Height—4¼"

No. 5300
10 oz. Hiball
Height—4¾"

No. 5300
14 oz. Hiball
Height—5¾"

No. 5300
12 oz. Ice Tea
Height—5¼"

No. 5300
8 oz. Split
Height—4½"

No. 5300
7 oz. Old Fashioned
Height—3¼"

Washington, Pa.   1-1-43

THE DUNCAN & MILLER GLASS CO.

201

DUNCAN

TEAR DROP
No. 301 PATTERN

No. 301
3 in. Individual Ash Tray

No. 301
3 in. Coaster or Ash Tray

No. 301
5 in. Ash Tray

No. 301
6 in. Canape Plate with Ring

No. 520½
4 oz. Ftd. Cocktail
Height, Cocktail—3½"

No. 301
Bar Bottle & Stopper
Height—12"

No. 301
6 in. Ice Bucket
Height—6½" Diameter—5½"

No. 301
6 in. Low Foot Comport
Height—4"

Washington, Pa.   1-1-43

THE DUNCAN & MILLER GLASS CO.

DUNCAN

TEAR DROP
Lead Blown Stemware
NO. 5301 PATTERN

Washington, Pa.   1-1-43

THE DUNCAN & MILLER GLASS CO.

No. 5301
9 oz. Goblet
Height—7"

No. 5301
5 oz. Saucer
Champagne
Height—5"

No. 5301
3½ oz.
Liquor Cocktail
Height—4½"

No. 5301
4 oz. Claret
Height—5½"

No. 5301
3 oz. Wine
Height—4¾"

No. 5301
1¾ oz. Sherry
Height—4½"

No. 5301
1 oz. Cordial
Height—4"

No. 5301
Finger Bowl
Height—2¼"
Diameter—4¼"

No. 5301
9 oz.
Luncheon Goblet
Height—5¾"

No. 5301
5 oz.
Ice Cream
Height—3½"

No. 5301
5 oz. Ftd.
Sherbet
Height—2½"

No. 5301
3½ oz. Ftd.
Oyster Cocktail
Height—2¾"

No. 5301
8 oz.
Ale Goblet
Height—6¼"

TERRACE, No. 111, Duncan & Miller Glass Company, 1937

Color: crystal, cobalt, red

Terrace is a Duncan pattern that collectors seek in color, but few buy in crystal. Most recognize Terrace as a blank on which First Love is found. I have been trying to buy enough Terrace to photograph for the book for four years! Many items still elude me.

Amber is available; but presently, few search for it. The gold decorated sugar and creamer pictured were bought from a dealer who had no idea what pattern they were! I thought they were intriguing, but I have since discovered that Terrace collectors are generally not very fond of decorated ware. Keep that in mind if you are collecting with future selling in mind!

	Crystal/ Amber	Cobalt/ Red		Crystal/ Amber	Cobalt/ Red
Ash tray, 3½" sq.	17.50	30.00	Plate, 11"	47.50	90.00
Ash tray, 4¾" sq.	22.00	95.00	Plate, 11", hdld.	40.00	
Bowl, 4¼", finger, #5111½	35.00	35.00	Plate, 11", hdld., cracker w/ring	40.00	95.00
Bowl, 6¾" x 4¼", ftd., flared rim	30.00		Plate, 11", hdld., sandwich	40.00	
Bowl, 8" sq. x 2½", hdld.	55.00		Plate, 12", torte, rolled edge	40.00	
Bowl, 9" x 4½", ftd.	42.00		*Plate, 13", cake, ftd.	75.00	180.00
Bowl, 9½" x 2½", hdld	45.00		Plate, 13", torte, flat edge	50.00	
Bowl, 10" x 3¾", ftd., flared rim	55.00		Plate, 13", torte, rolled edge	57.50	
* Bowl, 10¼" x 4¾", ftd.	75.00	125.00	Plate, 13¼", torte	57.50	175.00
Bowl, 11" x 3¼", flared rim	32.50		Relish, 6" x 1¾", hdld., 2 pt.	20.00	40.00
Butter or cheese, 7" sq. x 1¼"	115.00		Relish, 9", 4 pt.	35.00	75.00
Candle, 3", 1-lite	25.00	65.00	Relish, 10½" x 1½", hdld., 5 pt.	75.00	
Candle, 4", low	25.00		Relish, 12", 4 pt., hdld.	40.00	
Candlesticks, 1 lite, bobeche & prisms	175.00		Relish, 12", 5 pt., hdld.	50.00	
Candlesticks, 2 lite 7" x 9¼", bobeche & prisms	225.00		Relish, 12", 5 pt. w/lid	150.00	250.00
Candy urn w/lid	125.00	350.00	Salad dressing bowl, 2 pt., 5½" x 4¼"	45.00	95.00
Cheese stand, 3" x 5¼"	25.00	40.00	Saucer, sq	6.00	12.00
Cocktail shaker, metal lid	85.00	185.00	Saucer, demi	5.00	
Comport w/lid, 8¾" x 5½"	125.00	375.00	Stem, 3¾", 1 oz., cordial, #5111½	40.00	
Comport, 3½" x 4¾"W	30.00	75.00	Stem, 3¾", 4½ oz., oyster cocktail, #5111½	22.50	
Creamer, 3", 10 oz.	18.00	40.00	Stem, 4", 5 oz., ice cream, #5111½	14.00	
Cup	15.00	35.00	Stem, 4½", 3½ oz., cocktail, #5111½	22.50	
Cup, demi	20.00		Stem, 5", 5 oz., saucer champagne, #5111½	18.00	
Mayonnaise, 5½" x 2½", ftd., hdld., #111	35.00		Stem, 5¼", 3 oz., wine, #5111½	32.50	
Mayonnaise, 5½" x 3½", crimped,	32.00		Stem, 5¼", 5 oz., ftd. juice, #5111½	24.00	
Mayonnaise, 5¾" x 3", w/dish hdld. tray	35.00	75.00	Stem, 5¾", 10 oz., low luncheon goblet #5111½	17.50	
Mayonnaise, w/7" tray hdld	35.00		Stem, 6", 4½ oz., claret, #5111½	45.00	
Nappy, 5½" x 2", div., hdld.	18.00		Stem, 6½", 12 oz., ftd. ice tea, #5111½	35.00	
Nappy, 6" x 1¾", hdld.	22.00	35.00	Stem, 6¾", 10 oz., tall water goblet, #5111½		24.00
Pitcher	275.00	750.00	Stem, 6¾", 14 oz., ftd. ice tea, #5111½	35.00	
Plate, 6"	12.00	25.00	Stem, cordial	17.50	
Plate, 6", hdld. lemon	14.00	30.00	Sugar, 3", 10 oz.	15.00	35.00
Plate, 6", sq.	14.00	30.00	Sugar lid	12.50	55.00
Plate, 7"	17.50	35.00	Tumbler	17.50	40.00
Plate, 7½"	18.00	35.00	Tray, 8" x 2", hdld. celery	17.50	
Plate, 7½", sq.	19.00	38.00	Urn, 4½" x 4½"	27.50	
Plate, 8½"	20.00	25.00	Urn, 10½" x 4½"	125.00	350.00
Plate, 9", sq.	35.00	75.00			

*Colored foot

TROJAN, Fostoria Glass Company, 1929 – 1944

Colors: "Rose" pink, "Topaz" yellow; some green seen

Both pink and yellow Trojan are selling very well at present. For a while, there were several sets of yellow being marketed; but these sets have been dispersed and new collectors are now having difficulty finding serving pieces.

Stemware is available except for cordials and clarets. Clarets are almost nonexistent in any Fostoria pattern. If you need them, you had better buy them whenever you find them!

Price increases for soup and cereal bowls have exceeded those for most other Trojan pieces. Stock up on them quickly before they soar even higher.

The yellow vase in the bottom photo is #4105 while the pink one is #2417.

	Rose	Topaz
Ash tray, #2350, lg.	50.00	40.00
Ash tray, #2350, sm.	30.00	25.00
Bottle, salad dressing, #2983	500.00	325.00
Bowl, baker, #2375, 9"		65.00
Bowl, bonbon, #2375		15.00
Bowl, bouillon, #2375, ftd.		18.00
Bowl, cream soup, #2375, ftd.	27.50	22.00
Bowl, finger, #869/2283, w/6¼" liner	45.00	40.00
Bowl, lemon, #2375	18.00	16.00
Bowl, #2394, 3 ftd., 4½", mint.	25.00	22.00
Bowl, #2375, fruit, 5"	20.00	18.00
Bowl, #2354, 3 ftd., 6"	30.00	35.00
Bowl, cereal, #2375, 6½"	45.00	35.00
Bowl, soup, #2375, 7"	95.00	85.00
Bowl, lg. dessert, #2375, 2-handled	85.00	75.00
Bowl, #2395, 10"	110.00	75.00
Bowl, #2395, scroll, 10"	75.00	65.00
Bowl, combination #2415, w/candleholder handles,	195.00	165.00
Bowl, #2375, centerpiece, flared optic, 12"	50.00	45.00
Bowl, #2394, centerpiece, ftd., 12"	50.00	45.00
Bowl, #2375, centerpiece, mushroom, 12"	55.00	50.00
Candlestick, #2394, 2"	22.00	20.00
Candlestick, #2375, flared, 3"	25.00	22.00
Candlestick, #2395½, scroll, 5"	65.00	60.00
Candy, w/cover, #2394, ¼ lb.	275.00	250.00
Candy, w/cover, #2394, ½ lb.	200.00	165.00
Celery, #2375, 11½"	40.00	30.00
Cheese & cracker, set, #2375, #2368	75.00	65.00
Comport, #5299 or #2400, 6"	35.00	30.00
Comport, #2375, 7"	50.00	45.00
Creamer, #2375, ftd.	22.50	20.00
Creamer, tea, #2375½	60.00	50.00
Cup, after dinner, #2375	50.00	40.00
Cup, #2375½, ftd.	20.00	18.00
Decanter, #2439, 9"	950.00	795.00
Goblet, claret, #5099, 4 oz., 6"	130.00	85.00
Goblet, cocktail, #5099, 3 oz., 5¼"	32.00	30.00
Goblet, cordial, #5099, ¾ oz., 4"	95.00	70.00
Goblet, water, #5299, 10 oz., 8¼"	37.50	27.50
Goblet, wine, #5099, 3 oz., 5½"	55.00	45.00
Grapefruit, #5282½	55.00	45.00
Grapefruit liner, #945½	50.00	40.00
Ice bucket, #2375	75.00	65.00
Ice dish, #2451, #2455	45.00	35.00

	Rose	Topaz
Ice dish liner (tomato, crab, fruit) #2451	20.00	10.00
Mayonnaise ladle	30.00	30.00
Mayonnaise, w/liner, #2375	60.00	50.00
Oil, ftd., #2375	325.00	235.00
Oyster, cocktail, #5099, ftd.	30.00	27.50
Parfait, #5099	70.00	50.00
Pitcher, #5000	375.00	285.00
Plate, #2375, canape	30.00	20.00
Plate, #2375, bread/butter, 6"	6.00	5.00
Plate, #2375, salad, 7½"	9.00	8.00
Plate, 2375, cream soup or mayo liner, 7½",	9.00	8.00
Plate, #2375, luncheon, 8¾"	17.50	15.00
Plate, #2375, sm., dinner, 9½"	22.50	20.00
Plate, #2375, cake, handled, 10"	35.00	32.50
Plate, #2375, grill, rare, 10¼"	90.00	80.00
Plate, #2375, dinner, 10¼"	70.00	55.00
Plate, #2375, chop, 13"	50.00	50.00
Plate, #2375, round, 14"	55.00	50.00
Platter, #2375, 12"	70.00	60.00
Platter, #2375, 15"	150.00	120.00
Relish, #2375, 8½"		20.00
Relish, #2350, 3 pt., rnd., 8¾"	45.00	40.00
Sauce boat, #2375	115.00	95.00
Sauce plate, #2375	45.00	40.00
Saucer, #2375, after dinner	10.00	10.00
Saucer, #2375	6.00	5.00
Shaker, #2375, pr., ftd.	95.00	75.00
Sherbet, #5099, high, 6"	25.00	20.00
Sherbet, #5099, low, 4¼"	20.00	16.00
Sugar, #2375½, ftd.	22.50	20.00
Sugar cover, #2375½	135.00	110.00
Sugar pail, #2378	175.00	125.00
Sugar, tea, #2375½	55.00	45.00
Sweetmeat, #2375	18.00	18.00
Tray, 11", ctr. hdld., #2375	35.00	32.50
Tray, #2429, service & lemon insert		225.00
Tumbler, #5099, ftd., 2½ oz.	55.00	40.00
Tumbler, #5099, ftd., 5 oz., 4½"	30.00	25.00
Tumbler, #5099, ftd., 9 oz., 5¼"	22.50	17.50
Tumbler, #5099, ftd., 12 oz., 6"	37.50	30.00
Vase, #2417, 8"	145.00	120.00
Vase, #4105, 8"	215.00	160.00
Vase, #2369, 9"		210.00
Whipped cream bowl, #2375	15.00	12.00
Whipped cream pail, #2378	135.00	115.00

Note: See page 93 for stem identification.

TWIST, Blank #1252, A.H. Heisey & Co.

Colors: crystal, "Flamingo" pink, "Moongleam" green, "Marigold" amber/yellow; "Sahara" yellow; some "Alexandrite" (rare)

Heisey's Twist has made some large price increases in all colors of tumblers and stemware. Since most pieces are marked, finding a bargain on a piece of Twist is quite an accomplishment!

	Crystal	Pink	Green	Sahara	Marigold Alexandrite
Baker, 9", oval	25.00	35.00	45.00	60.00	
Bonbon, individual	10.00	20.00	25.00	32.00	
Bonbon, 6", 2 hdld.	5.00	14.00	17.00	30.00	
Bottle, French dressing	50.00	90.00	110.00	135.00	
Bowl, cream soup/bouillon	15.00	25.00	32.00	50.00	
Bowl, ftd., almond/indiv. sugar	35.00	45.00	55.00	65.00	
Bowl, indiv. nut	10.00	20.00	27.50	45.00	
Bowl, 4", nappy	10.00	20.00	25.00	30.00	
Bowl, 6", 2 hdld.	7.00	15.00	18.00	20.00	
Bowl, 6", 2 hdld., jelly	10.00	20.00	28.00	30.00	
Bowl, 6", 2 hdld., mint	7.00	15.00	18.00	20.00	
Bowl, 8", low ftd.		45.00	50.00	75.00	
Bowl, 8", nappy, grnd. bottom	20.00	40.00	45.00	50.00	
Bowl, 8", nasturtium, rnd.	35.00	60.00	70.00	80.00	450.00
Bowl, 8", nasturtium, oval	35.00	60.00	70.00	80.00	
Bowl, 9", floral	25.00	35.00	40.00	65.00	
Bowl, 9", floral, rolled edge	30.00	35.00	40.00	65.00	
Bowl, 12", floral, oval, 4 ft.	30.00	40.00	50.00	65.00	525.00
Bowl, 12", floral, rnd., 4 ft.	30.00	40.00	50.00	65.00	
Candlestick, 2", 1-lite		30.00	40.00	60.00	
Cheese dish, 6", 2 hdld.	10.00	20.00	25.00	30.00	
Claret, 4 oz.	15.00	30.00	40.00	50.00	
Cocktail shaker, metal top			400.00		
Comport, 7", tall	25.00	60.00	85.00	150.00	
Creamer, hotel, oval	25.00	35.00	45.00	50.00	
Creamer, individual (unusual)	18.00	35.00	35.00	65.00	
Creamer, zigzag handles, ftd.	20.00	40.00	50.00	70.00	
Cup, zigzag handles	10.00	25.00	32.00	35.00	
Grapefruit, ftd.	15.00	25.00	35.00	60.00	
Ice tub	25.00	65.00	85.00	125.00	
Ice Bucket					400.00
Pitcher, 3 pint	60.00	150.00	170.00		
Mayonnaise	20.00	40.00	45.00	40.00	
Mayonnaise, #1252½	20.00	35.00	45.00	50.00	
Mustard, w/cover, spoon	30.00	80.00	90.00	100.00	
Oil bottle, 2½ oz., w/#78 stopper	50.00	100.00	110.00	120.00	
Oil bottle, 4 oz., w/#78 stopper	50.00	100.00	110.00	120.00	
Plate, cream soup liner	5.00	7.00	10.00	15.00	
Plate, 8", Kraft cheese	20.00	35.00	45.00		
Plate, 8", grnd. bottom	7.00	12.00	15.00	25.00	
Plate, 10" utility, 3 ft.	25.00	30.00	42.00		
Plate, 12", 2 hdld., sandwich	25.00	40.00	50.00	55.00	
Plate, 12", muffin, 2 hdld., turned sides	30.00	40.00	55.00	65.00	
Plate, 13", 3 part, relish	10.00	17.00	22.00	35.00	
Platter, 12"	15.00	40.00	60.00	75.00	
Salt & pepper, ftd.	100.00	140.00	160.00	200.00	
Saucer	3.00	5.00	7.00	10.00	
Stem, 2½ oz., wine, 2 block stem	25.00	35.00	40.00	45.00	
Stem, 3 oz., oyster cocktail, ftd.	10.00	30.00	40.00	50.00	
Stem, 3 oz., cocktail, 2 block stem	10.00	30.00	40.00	50.00	
Stem, 5 oz., saucer champagne, 2 block stem	10.00	20.00	25.00	30.00	
Stem, 5 oz., sherbet, 2 block stem	10.00	18.00	24.00	28.00	
Stem, 9 oz., luncheon (1 block in stem), also made 2 block stem 9 oz.	40.00	60.00	70.00	70.00	
Sugar, ftd.	20.00	30.00	37.50	60.00	
Sugar, hotel, oval	25.00	35.00	40.00	50.00	
Sugar, individual (unusual)	18.00	35.00	38.00	65.00	
Sugar, w/cover, zigzag handles	25.00	40.00	60.00	80.00	
Tray, 7", pickle, grnd. bottom	7.00	15.00	22.00	25.00	
Tray, 10", celery	10.00	20.00	27.00	30.00	
Tray, 13", celery	12.00	25.00	37.00	50.00	
Tumbler, 5 oz., soda, flat bottom	10.00	22.00	32.00	36.00	
Tumbler, 6 oz., ftd. soda	10.00	22.00	32.00	36.00	
Tumbler, 8 oz., flat, grnd. bottom	15.00	25.00	30.00	40.00	
Tumbler, 8 oz., soda, straight & flared	12.00	25.00	30.00	40.00	
Tumbler, 9 oz., ftd. soda	20.00	40.00	50.00	60.00	
Tumbler, 12 oz., iced tea, flat bottom	20.00	45.00	60.00	70.00	
Tumbler, 12 oz., ftd. iced tea	20.00	40.00	50.00	60.00	

VALENCIA, Cambridge Glass Company

Colors: crystal, pink

Valencia is often confused with another Cambridge pattern, Minerva. Notice in the photo of Valencia that the lines in the pattern are perpendicular to each other. On Minerva, the lines in the pattern meet on a diagonal forming diamonds instead of squares.

I never can write about this pattern without thinking how expensive the pieces pictured would be if they were only Rose Point! All of these pieces are highly coveted in Rose Point, but are only just being noticed in Valencia. Valencia items are, of course, rarer than the highly promoted Rose Point. Yet, there are thousands of collectors searching for Rose Point and only a few looking for Valencia; so, the immense discrepancy in price on identical pieces in these patterns is due to demand.

Some of the more unusual and interesting pieces pictured include the covered honey dish, six-piece relish on #3500 12" plate, and the 15" long, three-part, two-handled relish. That metal-handled piece on the left of the photo behind the squared honey dish was called a sugar basket by Cambridge. This is similar to Fostoria's sugar pail. Terminology used by different companies sometimes causes today's collectors problems.

	Crystal		Crystal
Ash tray, #3500/124, 3¼", round.	10.00	Relish, #1402/91, 8", 3 comp.	30.00
Ash tray, #3500/126, 4", round	14.00	Relish, #3500/64, 10", 3 comp.	32.00
Ash tray, #3500/128, 4½", round	18.00	Relish, #3500/65, 10", 4 comp.	35.00
Basket, #3500/55, 6", 2 hdld., ftd.	22.00	Relish, #3500/67, 12", 6 pc.	125.00
Bowl, #3500/49, 5", hdld.	18.00	Relish, #3500/112, 15", 3 pt./2 hdld.	90.00
Bowl, #3500/37, 6", cereal	22.00	Relish, #3500/13, 15", 4 pt./2 hdld.	90.00
Bowl, #1402/89, 6", 2 hdld.	18.00	Salt and pepper, #3400/18	65.00
Bowl, #1402/88, 6", 2 hdld., div.	20.00	Saucer, #3500/1	3.00
Bowl, #3500/115, 9½", 2 hdld., ftd.	38.00	Stem, #1402, cordial	70.00
Bowl, #1402/82, 10"	35.00	Stem, #1402, wine	35.00
Bowl, #1402/88, 11"	40.00	Stem, #1402, cocktail	22.00
Bowl, #1402/95, salad dressing, div.	45.00	Stem, #1402, claret	45.00
Bowl, #1402/100, finger, w/liner	35.00	Stem, #1402, oyster cocktail	20.00
Bowl, #3500, ftd., finger	30.00	Stem, #1402, low sherbet	14.00
Candy dish, w/cover, #3500/103	110.00	Stem, #1402, tall sherbet	17.00
Celery, #1402/94, 12"	32.00	Stem, #1402, goblet	25.00
Cigarette holder, #1066, ftd.	42.00	Stem, #3500, cordial	70.00
Comport, #3500/36, 6"	30.00	Stem, #3500, wine, 2½ oz.	32.00
Comport, #3500/37, 7"	45.00	Stem, #3500, cocktail, 3 oz	20.00
Creamer, #3500/14	17.00	Stem, #3500, claret, 4½ oz.	45.00
Creamer, #3500/15, individual	20.00	Stem, #3500, oyster cocktail, 4½ oz.	18.00
Cup, #3500/1	20.00	Stem, #3500, low sherbet, 7 oz.	14.00
Decanter, #3400/92, 32 oz., ball	165.00	Stem, #3500, tall sherbet, 7 oz.	16.00
Decanter, #3400/119, 12 oz., ball	125.00	Stem, #3500, goblet, long bowl	25.00
Honey dish, w/cover, #3500/139	125.00	Stem, #3500, goblet, short bowl	22.00
Ice pail, #1402/52	75.00	Sugar, #3500/14	15.00
Mayonnaise, #3500/59, 3 pc.	45.00	Sugar, #3500/15, individual	20.00
Nut, #3400/71, 3", 4 ftd.	55.00	Sugar basket, #3500/13	95.00
Perfume, #3400/97, 2 oz., perfume	110.00	Tumbler, #3400/92, 2½ oz.	25.00
Plate, #3500/167, 7½", salad	10.00	Tumbler, #3400/100, 13 oz.	25.00
Plate, #3500/5, 8½", breakfast	12.00	Tumbler, #3400/115, 14 oz.	27.00
Plate, #1402, 11½", sandwich, hdld.	25.00	Tumbler, #3500, 2½ oz., ftd.	20.00
Plate, #3500/39, 12", ftd.	35.00	Tumbler, #3500, 3 oz., ftd.	16.00
Plate, #3500/67, 12"	30.00	Tumbler, #3500, 5 oz., ftd.	15.00
Plate, #3500/38, 13", torte	35.00	Tumbler, #3500, 10 oz., ftd.	16.00
Pitcher, 80oz., Doulton #3400/141	295.00	Tumbler, #3500, 12 oz., ftd.	20.00
Relish, #3500/68, 5½", 2 comp.	20.00	Tumbler, #3500, 13 oz., ftd.	20.00
Relish, #3500/69, 6½", 3 comp.	25.00	Tumbler, #3500, 16 oz., ftd.	22.00

VERSAILLES, Fostoria Glass Company, 1928 – 1944

Colors: blue, yellow, pink, green

I have tried to list all Fostoria line numbers for each piece of Versailles. These line numbers can also be utilized for June listings. The sugar and creamer are sitting on the lemon tray in the green Versailles photo. This tray is rarely seen. There is a plain, six-sided insert that fits in the center which is missing in the photo. The 7" soup bowl shown next to this tray is the nemesis of many collectors.

Be sure to see page 93 for Fostoria stemware identification. Many people confuse stems because their heights are so similar. Shapes are more important. Clarets are the most difficult stem to find; cordials are the next most troublesome.

If you order or ship using ads, you need to know the following Fostoria facts: liners for cream soups and mayonnaise liners are the same piece; two-handled cake plates come with and without an indent in the center. The indented version also serves as a plate for one of two styles of cheese comports; bonbon, lemon dish, sweetmeat, and whipped cream bowls all come with loop or bow handles; and sugars come with a straight and ruffled edge. The ruffled top sugar is the one that takes a lid.

	Pink, Green	Blue	Yellow
Ash tray, #2350	24.00	30.00	25.00
Bottle, #2083, salad dressing, crystal glass top	395.00	695.00	395.00
Bottle, #2375, salad dressing, w/ sterling top or colored top	395.00	695.00	395.00
Bowl, #2375, baker, 9"	55.00	125.00	55.00
Bowl, #2375, bonbon	15.00	25.00	17.50
Bowl, #2375, bouillon, ftd.	20.00	35.00	20.00
Bowl, #2375, cream soup, ftd.	22.00	30.00	22.00
Bowl, #869/2283, finger, w/6" liner	40.00	60.00	40.00
Bowl, lemon	15.00	22.00	17.50
Bowl, 4½", mint, 3 ftd.	27.50	40.00	27.50
Bowl, #2375, fruit, 5"	22.00	35.00	25.00
Bowl, #2394, 3 ftd., 6"			30.00
Bowl, #2375, cereal, 6½"	30.00	55.00	30.00
Bowl, #2375, soup, 7"	60.00	100.00	60.00
Bowl, #2375, lg., dessert, 2 hdld.	30.00	95.00	50.00
Bowl, #2375, baker, 10"	50.00	95.00	50.00
Bowl, #2395, centerpiece, scroll, 10"	55.00	75.00	55.00
Bowl, #2375, centerpiece, flared top, 12"	40.00	60.00	45.00
Bowl, #2394, ftd., 12"	35.00	60.00	45.00
Bowl, #2375½, oval, centerpiece 13"	55.00	85.00	
Candlestick, #2394, 2"	20.00	27.50	20.00
Candlestick, #2395, 3"	17.50	35.00	22.00
Candlestick, #2395½, scroll, 5"	35.00	50.00	35.00
Candy, w/cover, #2331, 3 pt.	155.00	225.00	
Candy, w/cover, #2394, ¼ lb.			195.00
Candy, w/cover, #2394, ½ lb.			175.00
Celery, #2375, 11½"	40.00	95.00	45.00
Cheese & cracker, #2375 or #2368, set	75.00	110.00	75.00
Comport, #5098, 3"	25.00	40.00	25.00
Comport, #5099/2400, 6"	30.00	50.00	30.00
Comport, #2375, 7"	32.50	65.00	
Comport, #2400, 8"	65.00	110.00	
Creamer, #2375½, ftd.	17.50	22.50	15.00
Creamer, #2375½, tea	45.00	60.00	45.00
Cup, #2375, after dinner	40.00	60.00	40.00
Cup, #2375½, ftd.	17.50	21.00	19.00
Decanter, #2439, 9"	1,200.00	2,000.00	750.00
Goblet, cordial, #5098 or #5099, ¾ oz., 4"	80.00	100.00	65.00
Goblet, #5098 or #5099, claret, 4 oz., 6"	85.00	135.00	85.00
Goblet, cocktail, #5098 or #5099, 3 oz., 5¼"	25.00	37.50	28.00
Goblet, water, #5098 or #5099, 10 oz., 8¼"	27.50	40.00	30.00
Goblet, wine, #5098 or #5099, 3 oz., 5½"	40.00	75.00	45.00
Grapefruit, #5082½	50.00	75.00	45.00

	Pink, Green	Blue	Yellow
Grapefruit liner, #945½	40.00	75.00	40.00
Ice bucket, #2375	65.00	95.00	80.00
Ice dish, #2451	35.00	50.00	35.00
Ice dish liner (tomato, crab, fruit), #2451	20.00	20.00	10.00
Mayonnaise, w/liner, #2375	35.00	50.00	40.00
Mayonnaise ladle	30.00	40.00	30.00
Oil, #2375, ftd.	375.00	575.00	325.00
Oyster cocktail, #5098 or #5099	22.50	32.50	25.00
Parfait, #5098 or #5099	35.00	45.00	35.00
Pitcher, #5000	325.00	500.00	350.00
Plate, #2375, bread/butter, 6"	4.00	5.00	4.00
Plate, #2375, canape, 6"	25.00	40.00	32.00
Plate, #2375, salad, 7½"	6.00	10.00	7.00
Plate, #2375, cream soup or mayo liner, 7½"	8.00	15.00	9.00
Plate, #2375, luncheon, 8¾"	8.00	12.50	9.00
Plate, #2375, sm., dinner, 9½"	22.00	35.00	25.00
Plate, #2375, cake, 2 hdld., 10"	26.00	37.50	30.00
Plate, #2375, dinner, 10¼"	65.00	95.00	60.00
Plate, #2375, chop, 13"	50.00	75.00	45.00
Platter, #2375, 12"	75.00	100.00	75.00
Platter, #2375, 15"	110.00	165.00	110.00
Relish, #2375, 8½"	30.00		35.00
Sauce boat, #2375	80.00	145.00	80.00
Sauce boat plate, #2375	25.00	55.00	25.00
Saucer, #2375, after dinner	7.50	10.00	7.50
Saucer, #2375	4.00	6.00	5.00
Shaker, #2375, pr., ftd.	95.00	150.00	95.00
Sherbet, #5098/5099, high, 6"	20.00	27.50	22.50
Sherbet, #5098/5099, low, 4¼"	20.00	25.00	22.00
Sugar, #2375½, ftd.	15.00	20.00	15.00
Sugar cover, #2375½	140.00	195.00	125.00
Sugar pail, #2378	155.00	225.00	145.00
Sugar, #2375½, tea	42.50	55.00	42.50
Sweetmeat, #2375	14.00	20.00	15.00
Tray, #2375, ctr. hdld., 11"	30.00	45.00	35.00
Tray, service & lemon	325.00	425.00	250.00
Tumbler, flat, old-fashioned (pink only)	95.00		
Tumbler, flat, tea (pink only)	100.00		
Tumbler, #5098 or #5099 2½ oz., ftd.,	40.00	60.00	40.00
Tumbler, #5098 or #5099, 5 oz., ftd., 4½",	20.00	35.00	22.00
Tumbler, #5098 or #5099, 9 oz., ftd., 5¼"	20.00	37.50	21.50
Tumbler, #5098 or #5099 12 oz., ftd., 6",	35.00	55.00	32.00
Vase, #2417, 8"			165.00
Vase, #4100, 8"	135.00	250.00	
Vase, #2385, fan, ftd., 8½"	125.00	225.00	
Whipped cream bowl, #2375	15.00	18.00	13.00
Whipped cream pail, #2378	125.00	165.00	125.00

Note: See page 93 for stem identification.

VESPER, Fostoria Glass Company, 1926 – 1934

Colors: amber, green; some blue

A blown style of grapefruit with an etched liner is shown in Vesper in the top row. Some companies called these shrimp dishes. You filled the inside compote with shrimp or fruit and put ice in the larger container to keep it chilled. Since ice was a valuable commodity in those days, only the well-to-do had these items and that resulted in short supplies today.

Vesper comes on stem line #5093 and tumbler line #5100. I have an example of each piece in row 2 on the next page. The shapes are slightly different from those Fostoria etches found on the Fairfax blank. The #5093 stems are as follows: cordial, low sherbet, cocktail, wine, high sherbet, claret, parfait, and water goblet. The #5100 footed tumblers include: ice tea, water, juice, oyster cocktail, and bar glass. I hope this will eliminate any confusion.

Row 3 shows the flat creamer, footed bouillon with liner, footed cream soup with liner, flat cream soup with liner, and the finger bowl with liner.

Row 5 shows shallow soup, fruit, cereal, deep soup, and 8" vegetable bowls.

All other pieces should be easily identified. We tried showing these on rows this time. I hope you like the way it turned out.

Amber Vesper is not as collected as some other Fostoria colors; but as you can see here, this amber pattern has a multitude of pieces! Many are easily found; others will take some patience and searching. Etched amber Fostoria patterns may be the "sleepers" in the Elegant glass collecting field. I've seen gorgeous table settings made with amber glass.

The amber butter dish was the only one known for a while. Another one was found in Texas a few years ago; but before it could be marketed, it was broken. So for now, there is still only one existing!

In the past blue and green Vesper have been shortchanged in my books. Enjoy the new photographs on page 217! There is little blue Vesper to be found on the market at a price collectors are willing to pay! Rarely found, attractive glassware often gets priced "out of sight" as one collector put it! Green Vesper is more easily found.

	Green	Amber	Blue
Ash tray, #2350, 4"	25.00	30.00	
Bowl, #2350, bouillon, ftd.	12.00	17.50	30.00
Bowl, #2350, cream soup, flat	25.00	30.00	
Bowl, #2350, cream soup, ftd.	20.00	20.00	35.00
Bowl, #2350, fruit, 5½"	10.00	12.50	25.00
Bowl, #2350, cereal, sq. or rnd., 6½"	20.00	25.00	35.00
Bowl, #2267, low, ftd., 7"	20.00	25.00	
Bowl, #2350, soup, shallow, 7¾"	25.00	35.00	50.00
Bowl, soup, deep, 8¼"		35.00	
Bowl, 8⅞"	30.00	40.00	
Bowl, #2350, baker, oval, 9"	60.00	70.00	90.00
Bowl, #2350, rd.	40.00	50.00	
Bowl, #2350, baker, oval, 10½"	75.00	85.00	115.00
Bowl, #2375, flared bowl, 10½"	35.00	35.00	
Bowl, #2350, ped., ftd., 10½"	40.00	50.00	
Bowl, #2329, console, rolled edge, 11"	35.00	37.50	
Bowl, #2375, 3 ftd., 12½"	40.00	42.50	
Bowl, #2371, oval, 13"	40.00	45.00	
Bowl, #2329, rolled edge, 13"	40.00	45.00	
Bowl, #2329, rolled edge, 14"	45.00	50.00	
Butter dish, #2350	300.00	800.00	
Candlestick, #2324, 2"	17.50	25.00	
Candlestick, #2394, 3"	15.00	17.50	40.00
Candlestick, #2324, 4"	15.00	20.00	
Candlestick, #2394, 9"	55.00	90.00	95.00
Candy jar, w/cover, #2331, 3 pt.	110.00	110.00	225.00
Candy jar, w/cover, #2250, ftd., ½ lb.	225.00	185.00	
Celery, #2350	17.00	22.00	40.00
Cheese, #2368, ftd.	18.00	20.00	
Comport, 6"	22.50	25.00	45.00
Comport, #2327, (twisted stem), 7½"	27.50	30.00	55.00
Comport, 8"	40.00	50.00	60.00
Creamer, #2350½, ftd.	14.00	20.00	

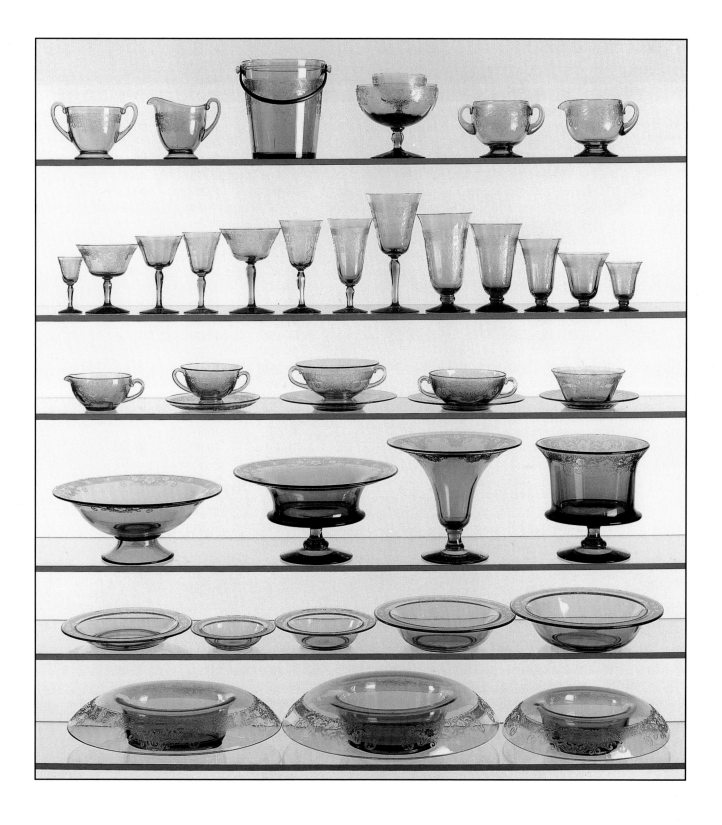

VESPER

	Green	Amber	Blue
Creamer, #2315½, fat, ftd.	18.00	22.00	35.00
Creamer, #2350½, flat		22.00	
Cup, #2350	14.00	15.00	35.00
Cup, #2350, after dinner	40.00	40.00	75.00
Cup, #2350½, ftd.	14.00	15.00	35.00
Egg cup, #2350		40.00	
Finger bowl and liner, #869/2283, 6"	27.50	30.00	45.00
Grapefruit, #5082½, blown	50.00	50.00	85.00
Grapefruit liner, #945½, blown	45.00	45.00	50.00
Grapefruit, #2315, molded	50.00	55.00	
Ice bucket, #2378	60.00	70.00	
Oyster cocktail, #5100	16.00	20.00	40.00
Pickle, #2350	22.00	25.00	40.00
Pitcher, #5100, ftd.	300.00	335.00	500.00
Plate, #2350, bread/butter, 6"	4.50	5.00	10.00
Plate, #2350, salad, 7½"	6.00	6.50	15.00
Plate, #2350, luncheon, 8½"	7.50	8.50	20.00
Plate, #2321, Maj Jongg (canape), 8¾"		50.00	
Plate, #2350, sm., dinner, 9½"	18.00	22.50	30.00
Plate, dinner, 10½"	35.00	45.00	
Plate, #2287, ctr. hand., 11"	22.50	30.00	55.00
Plate, chop, 13¾"	32.00	37.50	75.00
Plate, #2350, server, 14"	55.00	65.00	100.00
Plate, w/indent for cheese, 11"	18.00	20.00	
Platter, #2350, 10½"	35.00	40.00	
Platter, #2350, 12"	50.00	60.00	100.00
Platter, #2350, 15",	85.00	95.00	145.00
Salt & pepper, #5100, pr.	70.00	80.00	
Sauce boat, w/liner, #2350	125.00	135.00	
Saucer, #2350, after dinner	10.00	10.00	25.00
Saucer, #2350	4.00	4.50	5.00
Stem, #5093, high sherbet	16.00	17.50	32.00
Stem, #5093, water goblet	25.00	27.50	45.00
Stem, #5093, low sherbet	15.00	17.00	25.00
Stem, #5093, parfait	35.00	40.00	55.00
Stem, #5093, cordial, ¾ oz.	70.00	75.00	125.00
Stem, #5093, wine, 2¾ oz.	35.00	37.50	60.00
Stem, #5093, cocktail, 3 oz.	25.00	27.50	45.00
Sugar, #2350½, flat		20.00	
Sugar, #2315, fat ftd.	18.00	20.00	32.00
Sugar, #2350½, ftd.	14.00	16.00	
Sugar, lid	185.00	175.00	
Tumbler, #5100, ftd., 2 oz.	35.00	45.00	60.00
Tumbler, #5100, ftd., 5 oz.	15.00	20.00	40.00
Tumbler, #5100, ftd., 9 oz.	16.00	20.00	45.00
Tumbler, #5100, ftd., 12 oz.	25.00	35.00	55.00
Urn, #2324, small	65.00	80.00	
Urn, large	75.00	90.00	
Vase, #2292, 8"	85.00	95.00	150.00
Vanity set, combination cologne/ powder & stopper	225.00	250.00	350.00

Note: See stemware identification on page 93.

VICTORIAN, #1425 A.H. Heisey Co., 1933 – 1953

Colors: crystal, Sahara, Cobalt, rare in pale Zircon

At a recent Depression glass show in Dearborn, Michigan, a large set of Victorian was offered for sale. This large accumulation caught the eye of several new collectors and by the end of the show many pieces were sold with several new sets having been started. A display of any set will attract more collectors than only having a few pieces offered. Similarly, offering the pieces individually, gives several people the chance to start collecting, whereas pricing the whole set eliminates most of the market except for other dealers. Novice dealers often make that mistake. Collectors rarely buy sets of anything. They already own some pieces and are looking for additional items. The fun of the hunt is gone if everything is bought at once, and most collectors do not have the finances to buy a set all at once.

Heisey Victorian was only made in the colors listed. If you find pink, green, or amber Victorian in your travels, then you have Imperial's legacy to this pattern from 1964 and 1965. These colors are usually marked with the H in diamond trademark, but they were made from Heisey moulds after the company was no longer in business.

Imperial also made about ten pieces in crystal, but they can not be differentiated from the original Heisey... and they aren't as discriminated against by Heisey collectors as are the colored pieces!

	Crystal		Crystal
Bottle, 3 oz. oil	65.00	Plate, 21" buffet or punch bowl liner,	100.00
Bottle, 27 oz. rye	160.00	Relish, 11", 3 pt.	45.00
Bottle, French dressing	75.00	Salt & pepper	40.00
Bowl, 10½" floral	40.00	Stem, 2½ oz. wine	22.00
Bowl, finger	15.00	Stem, 3 oz. claret	20.00
Bowl, punch	250.00	Stem, 5 oz. oyster cocktail	17.00
Bowl, rose	75.00	Stem, 5 oz. saucer champagne	17.50
Bowl, triplex w/flared or cupped rim	80.00	Stem, 5 oz. sherbet	15.00
Butter dish, ¼ lb.	65.00	Stem, 9 oz. goblet (one ball)	24.00
Candlestick, 2-lite	110.00	Stem, 9 oz. high goblet (two ball)	26.00
Cigarette box, 4"	50.00	Sugar	25.00
Cigarette box, 6"	75.00	Tray, 12" celery	30.00
Cigarette holder & ash tray, ind.	25.00	Tray, condiment (s/p & mustard)	150.00
Comport, 5"	45.00	Tumbler, 2 oz. bar	35.00
Comport, 6", 3 ball stem	100.00	Tumbler, 5 oz. soda (straight or	
Compote, cheese (for center sandwich)	40.00	curved edge)	20.00
Creamer	25.00	Tumbler, 8 oz. old-fashioned	30.00
Cup, punch, 5 oz.	10.00	Tumbler, 10 oz. w/rim foot	20.00
Decanter and stopper, 32 oz.,	60.00	Tumbler, 12 oz. ftd. soda	28.00
Jug, 54 oz.	250.00	Tumbler, 12 oz. soda (straight or	
Nappy, 8"	30.00	curved edge)	24.00
Plate, 6" liner for finger	10.00	Vase, 4"	40.00
Plate, 7"	20.00	Vase, 5½"	48.00
Plate, 8"	30.00	Vase, 6" ftd.	55.00
Plate, 12" cracker	75.00	Vase, 9" ftd. w/flared rim	75.00
Plate, 13" sandwich	80.00		

VICTORIAN

WAVERLY, Blank #1519, A.H. Heisey & Co.

Colors: crystal; rare in amber

This Heisey blank is known more for the Orchid and Rose etchings appearing on it than for itself.

	Crystal
Bowl, 6", oval, lemon, w/cover	30.00
Bowl, 6½", 2 hdld., ice	50.00
Bowl, 7", 3 part, relish, oblong	25.00
Bowl, 7", salad	17.00
Bowl, 9", 4 part, relish, round	25.00
Bowl, 9", fruit	22.00
Bowl, 9", vegetable	22.00
Bowl, 10", crimped edge	25.00
Bowl, 10", gardenia	20.00
Bowl, 11", seahorse foot, floral	65.00
Bowl, 12", crimped edge	35.00
Bowl, 13", gardenia	25.00
Box, 5", chocolate, w/cover	70.00
Box, 5" tall, ftd., w/cover, seahorse hand.	85.00
Box, 6", candy, w/bow tie knob	45.00
Box, trinket, lion cover (rare)	600.00
Butter dish, w/cover, 6", square	65.00
Candleholder, 1-lite, block (rare)	100.00
Candleholder, 2-lite	40.00
Candleholder, 2-lite, "flame" center	65.00
Candleholder, 3-lite	65.00
Candle epergnette, 5"	15.00
Candle epergnette, 6", deep	20.00
Candle epergnette, 6½"	15.00
Cheese dish, 5½", ftd.	20.00
Cigarette holder	50.00
Comport, 6", low ftd.	20.00
Comport, 6½", jelly	35.00
Comport, 7", low ftd., oval	50.00
Creamer, ftd.	20.00
Creamer & sugar, individual, w/tray	47.00
Cruet, 3 oz., w/#122 stopper	60.00
Cup	14.00
Honey dish, 6½", ftd.	35.00
Mayonnaise, w/liner & ladle, 5½"	50.00
Plate, 7", salad	6.00
Plate, 8", luncheon	8.00
Plate, 10½", dinner	50.00
Plate, 11", sandwich	18.00
Plate, 13½", ftd., cake salver	60.00
Plate, 14", center handle, sandwich	65.00
Plate, 14", sandwich	35.00
Salt & pepper, pr.	50.00
Saucer	4.00
Stem, #5019, 1 oz., cordial	50.00
Stem, #5019, 3 oz., wine, blown	15.00
Stem, #5019, 3½ oz., cocktail	10.00
Stem, #5019, 5½ oz., sherbet/champagne	7.00
Stem, #5019, 10 oz., blown	15.00
Sugar, ftd.	20.00
Tray, 12", celery	18.00
Tumbler, #5019, 5 oz., ftd., juice, blown	17.00
Tumbler, #5019, 13 oz., ftd., tea, blown	20.00
Vase, 3½", violet	50.00
Vase, 7", ftd.	25.00
Vase, 7", ftd., fan shape	40.00

WILDFLOWER, Cambridge Glass Company, 1940's – 1950's

Colors: crystal, mainly; some pieces in color

Wildflower can be found on additional Cambridge blanks. I have tried to price a significant portion of the pattern, but (as with other Cambridge patterns shown in this book) there seems to be a never ending list! You can figure that, like Rose Point, almost any Cambridge blank may have been used to etch this pattern. I have given you the basics. Price yellow, green, or gold encrusted items up to 25% higher. Most collectors are searching for crystal. Possibly the most desirable piece pictured is the hat in the bottom photograph. There are collectors of glass hats searching for these as well as Wildflower collectors.

	Crystal
Basket, #3400/1182, 2 hdld., ftd., 6"	27.50
Bowl, #3400/1180, bonbon, 2 hdld., 5¼"	18.00
Bowl, bonbon, 2 hdld., ftd., 6"	17.50
Bowl, #3400/90, 2 pt., relish, 6"	17.50
Bowl, 3 pt., relish, 6½"	20.00
Bowl, #3900/123, relish, 7"	18.00
Bowl, #3900/130, bonbon, 2 hdld., 7"	20.00
Bowl, #3900/124, 2 pt., relish, 7"	22.00
Bowl, #3400/91, 3 pt., relish, 3 hdld., 8"	25.00
Bowl, #3900/125, 3 pt., celery & relish, 9"	25.00
Bowl, #477, pickle (corn), ftd., 9½"	25.00
Bowl, #3900/54, 4 ft., flared, 10"	37.50
Bowl, #3900/34, 2 hdld., 11"	45.00
Bowl, #3900/28, w/tab hand., ftd., 11½"	47.50
Bowl, #3900/126, 3 pt., celery & relish, 12"	40.00
Bowl, #3400/4, 4 ft., flared, 12"	40.00
Bowl, #3400/1240, 4 ft., oval, "ears" hand., 12"	45.00
Bowl, 5 pt., celery & relish, 12"	35.00
Butter dish, #3900/52, ¼ lb.	185.00
Butter dish, #3400/52, 5"	125.00
Candlestick, #3400/638, 3-lite, ea.	35.00
Candlestick, #3400/646, 5"	27.50
Candlestick, #3400/647, 2-lite, "fleur-de-lis," 6"	32.50
Candy box, w/cover, #3900/165	75.00
Candy box, w/cover, #3900/165, rnd.	70.00
Cocktail icer, #968, 2 pc.	65.00
Cocktail shaker, #3400/175	95.00
Comport, #3900/136, 5½"	35.00
Comport, #3121, blown, 5⅜"	42.00
Creamer, #3900/41	15.00
Creamer, #3900/40, individual	20.00
Cup, #3900/17 or #3400/54	17.50
Hat, #1704, 5"	185.00
Hat, #1703, 6"	225.00
Hurricane lamp, #1617, candlestick base,	160.00
Hurricane lamp, #1603, keyhole base & prisms	210.00
Ice bucket, w/chrome hand, #3900/671	70.00
Oil, w/stopper, #3900/100, 6 oz.	85.00
Pitcher, ball, #3400/38, 80 oz.	150.00
Pitcher, #3900/115, 76 oz.	175.00
Pitcher, Doulton, #3400/141	295.00
Plate, crescent salad	175.00

	Crystal
Plate, #3900/20, bread/butter, 6½"	7.50
Plate, #3900/130, bonbon, 2 hdld., 7"	17.50
Plate, #3400/176, 7½"	10.00
Plate, #3900/161, 2 hdld., ftd., 8"	22.50
Plate, #3900/22, salad, 8"	17.50
Plate, #3400/62, 8½"	15.00
Plate, #3900/24, dinner, 10½"	67.50
Plate, #3900/26, service, 4 ftd., 12"	35.00
Plate, #3900/35, cake, 2 hdld., 13½"	40.00
Plate, #3900/167, torte, 14"	45.00
Plate, #3900/65, torte, 14"	45.00
Salt & pepper, #3400/77, pr.	40.00
Salt & pepper, #3900/1177	37.50
Saucer, #3900/17 or #3400/54	3.50
Set: 2 pc. Mayonnaise, #3900/19 (ftd. sherbet w/ladle)	32.50
Set: 3 pc. Mayonnaise, #3900/129 (bowl, liner, ladle)	40.00
Set: 4 pc. Mayonnaise #3900/111 (div. bowl, liner, 2 ladles)	45.00
Stem, #3121, cordial, 1 oz.	57.50
Stem, #3121, cocktail, 3 oz.	22.50
Stem, #3121, wine, 3½ oz.	35.00
Stem, #3121, claret, 4½ oz.	42.00
Stem, #3121, 4½ oz., low oyster cocktail	18.00
Stem, #3121, 5 oz., low parfait	35.00
Stem, #3121, 6 oz., low sherbet	15.00
Stem, #3121, 6 oz., tall sherbet	17.50
Stem, #3121, 10 oz., water	27.50
Sugar, 3900/41	14.00
Sugar, indiv., 3900/40	20.00
Tray, creamer & sugar, 3900/37	15.00
Tumbler, #3121, 5 oz., juice	18.00
Tumbler, #3121, 10 oz., water	22.00
Tumbler, #3121, 12 oz., tea	27.00
Tumbler, #3900/115, 13 oz.	30.00
Vase, #3400/102, globe, 5"	40.00
Vase, #6004, flower, ftd., 6"	40.00
Vase, #6004, flower, ftd., 8"	60.00
Vase, #1237, keyhole ft., 9"	75.00
Vase, #1528, bud, 10"	40.00
Vase, #278, flower, ftd., 11"	60.00
Vase, #1299, ped. ft., 11"	70.00
Vase, #1238, keyhole ft., 12"	110.00
Vase, #279, ftd., flower, 13"	120.00

Note: See Pages 228 – 229 for stem identification.

YEOMAN, Blank #1184, A.H. Heisey & Co.

Colors: crystal, "Flamingo" pink, "Sahara" yellow, "Moongleam" green, "Hawthorne" orchid/pink, "Marigold" deep, amber/yellow; some cobalt

Etched patterns on Yeoman blank #1184 will bring 10% to 25% more than the prices listed below. Empress etch is the most commonly found pattern on Yeoman blanks and the most collectible. Notice some tremendous price increases on the covered lemon bowls, cologne bottles, and pitchers. The main reason this pattern is so collectible is due to the colors in which it was made!

	Crystal	Pink	Sahara	Green	Hawth.	Marigold
Ash tray, 4", hdld. (bow tie)	10.00	20.00	22.00	25.00	30.00	35.00
Bowl, 2 hdld., cream soup	12.00	20.00	25.00	30.00	35.00	40.00
Bowl, finger	5.00	11.00	17.00	20.00	27.50	30.00
Bowl, ftd., banana split	7.00	23.00	30.00	35.00	40.00	45.00
Bowl, ftd., 2 hdld., bouillon	10.00	20.00	25.00	30.00	35.00	40.00
Bowl, 4½", nappy	4.00	7.50	10.00	12.50	15.00	17.00
Bowl, 5", low, ftd., jelly	12.00	20.00	25.00	27.00	30.00	40.00
Bowl, 5", oval, lemon and cover	30.00	60.00	65.00	75.00	90.00	90.00
Bowl, 5", rnd., lemon and cover	30.00	60.00	65.00	75.00	90.00	90.00
Bowl, 5", rnd., lemon, w/cover	15.00	20.00	25.00	30.00	40.00	50.00
Bowl, 6", oval, preserve	7.00	12.00	17.00	22.00	27.00	30.00
Bowl, 6", vegetable	5.00	10.00	14.00	16.00	20.00	24.00
Bowl, 6½", hdld., bonbon	5.00	10.00	14.00	16.00	20.00	24.00
Bowl, 8", rect., pickle/olive	12.00	15.00	20.00	25.00	30.00	35.00
Bowl, 8½", berry, 2 hdld.	14.00	22.00	25.00	30.00	35.00	50.00
Bowl, 9", 2 hdld., veg., w/cover	35.00	60.00	60.00	70.00	95.00	175.00
Bowl, 9", oval, fruit	20.00	25.00	35.00	45.00	55.00	55.00
Bowl, 9", baker	20.00	25.00	35.00	45.00	55.00	55.00
Bowl, 12", low, floral	15.00	25.00	35.00	45.00	60.00	55.00
Candle Vase, single, w/short prisms & inserts	90.00			150.00		
Cigarette box, (ashtray)	25.00	60.00	65.00	70.00	80.00	100.00
Cologne bottle, w/stopper	70.00	120.00	130.00	140.00	160.00	140.00
Comport, 5", high ftd., shallow	15.00	25.00	37.00	45.00	55.00	70.00
Comport, 6", low ftd., deep	20.00	30.00	34.00	40.00	42.00	48.00
Creamer	10.00	20.00	20.00	22.00	50.00	28.00
Cruet, 2 oz., oil	20.00	60.00	60.00	65.00	55.00	65.00
Cruet, 4 oz., oil	30.00	60.00	65.00	65.00		
Cup	5.00	20.00	20.00	25.00	35.00	
Cup, after dinner	20.00	35.00	35.00	35.00	40.00	50.00
Egg cup	20.00	25.00	32.00	39.00	42.00	52.00
Grapefruit, ftd.	10.00	17.00	24.00	31.00	38.00	45.00
Gravy (or dressing) boat, w/underliner	13.00	25.00	30.00	45.00	50.00	45.00
Marmalade jar, w/cover	25.00	35.00	40.00	45.00	55.00	65.00
Parfait, 5 oz.	10.00	15.00	20.00	25.00	30.00	35.00
Pitcher, quart	70.00	80.00	90.00	110.00	145.00	160.00
Plate, 2 hdld., cheese	5.00	10.00	13.00	15.00	17.00	25.00
Plate, cream soup underliner	5.00	7.00	9.00	12.00	14.00	16.00
Plate, finger bowl underliner	3.00	5.00	7.00	9.00	11.00	13.00
Plate, 4½", coaster	3.00	5.00	10.00	12.00		
Plate, 6"	3.00	6.00	8.00	10.00	13.00	15.00
Plate, 6", bouillon underliner	3.00	6.00	8.00	10.00	13.00	15.00

YEOMAN

	Crystal	Pink	Sahara	Green	Hawth.	Marigold
Plate, 6½", grapefruit bowl	7.00	12.00	15.00	19.00	27.00	32.00
Plate, 7"	5.00	8.00	10.00	14.00	17.00	22.00
Plate, 8", oyster cocktail	9.00					
Plate, 8", soup	9.00					
Plate, 9", oyster cocktail	10.00					
Plate, 10½"	20.00	50.00		50.00	60.00	
Plate, 10½", ctr. hand., oval, div.	15.00	26.00		32.00		
Plate, 11", 4 pt., relish	20.00	27.00		32.00		
Plate, 14"	20.00					
Platter, 12", oval	10.00	17.00	19.00	26.00	33.00	
Salt, ind. tub (cobalt: $30.00)	10.00	20.00		30.00		
Salver, 10", low ftd.	15.00	30.00		42.00		
Salver, 12", low ftd.	10.00	25.00		32.00		
Saucer	3.00	5.00	7.00	7.00	10.00	10.00
Saucer, after dinner	3.00	5.00	7.00	8.00	10.00	10.00
Stem, 2¾ oz., ftd., oyster cocktail	4.00	8.00	10.00	12.00	14.00	
Stem, 3 oz., cocktail	10.00	12.00	17.00	20.00		
Stem, 3½ oz., sherbet	5.00	8.00	11.00	12.00		
Stem, 4 oz., fruit cocktail	3.00	5.00	7.00	9.00		
Stem, 4½ oz., sherbet	3.00	5.00	7.00	9.00		
Stem, 5 oz., soda	9.00	8.00	30.00	20.00		
Stem, 5 oz., sherbet	5.00	5.00	7.00	9.00		
Stem, 6 oz., champagne	6.00	16.00	18.00	22.00		
Stem, 8 oz.	5.00	12.00	18.00	20.00		
Stem, 10 oz., goblet	10.00	15.00	30.00	25.00		
Sugar, w/cover	15.00	40.00	35.00	40.00	60.00	40.00
Sugar shaker, ftd.	50.00	95.00		110.00		
Syrup, 7 oz., saucer ftd.	30.00	75.00				
Tray, 7" x 10", rect.	26.00	30.00	40.00	35.00		
Tray, 9", celery	10.00	14.00	16.00	15.00		
Tray, 11", ctr. hand., 3 pt.	15.00	35.00	40.00			
Tray, 12", oblong	16.00	19.00	24.00			
Tray, 13", 3 pt., relish	20.00	27.00	32.00			
Tray, 13", celery	20.00	27.00	32.00			
Tray, 13", hors d'oeuvre, w/cov. ctr.	32.00	42.00	52.00	75.00		
Tray insert, 3½" x 4½"	4.00	6.00	7.00	8.00		
Tumbler, 2½ oz., whiskey	3.00	8.00	10.00	12.00		
Tumbler, 4½ oz., soda	4.00	6.00	10.00	15.00		
Tumbler, 8 oz.	4.00	12.00	17.00	20.00		
Tumbler, 10 oz., cupped rim	4.00	15.00	20.00	22.50		
Tumbler, 10 oz., straight side	5.00	15.00	20.00	22.50		
Tumbler, 12 oz., tea	5.00	20.00	25.00	30.00		
Tumbler cover (unusual)	35.00					

CAMBRIDGE STEMS

1066
11 oz. Goblet

1402
Brandy Inhaler (Tall)

3025
10 oz. Goblet

3035
3 oz. Cocktail

3077
6 oz. Tall Sherbet

3104
1 oz. Cordial

3106
9 oz. Goblet Tall Bowl

3115
3½ oz. Cocktail

3120
6 oz. Tall Sherbet

3121
10 oz. Goblet

3122
9 oz. Goblet

3124
3 oz. Wine

3126
11 oz. Tall Sherbet

3130
6 oz. Tall Sherbet

3135
6 oz. Tall Sherbet

3400
11 oz. Lunch Goblet

3500
10 oz. Goblet

3600
2½ oz. Wine

3775
4½ oz. Claret

3625
4½ oz. Claret

3779
1 oz. Cordial

HEISEY'S "ALEXANDRITE" COLOR (rare)

Row 1:
Candlesticks, Trident, pr. (134)...................... 780.00
Cathedral vase (1413)............................. 800.00

Row 2:
Tumbler, 12 oz., ftd., soda,
  Creole (3381) 120.00
Tumbler 5 oz., ftd., soda, Creole (3381).......... 100.00
Tumbler, 8½ oz., ftd., soda, Creole (3381)...... 110.00
Tumbler, 2½ oz., bar, Glenford (3481) 200.00

Row 3:
Ball vase, 9" (4045).. 800.00
Ball vase, 4" (4045).. 380.00
Ball vase, 6" (4045).. 420.00

Row 4:
Plate, Colonial Star (1150) 325.00
Plate, Yeoman 40.00
Stem, 2½ oz., wine, Creole (3381) 160.00
Stem, 11 oz., water goblet, Creole (3381)....... 220.00

Row 1:

Stem, water, Plymouth (3409) 600.00
Tumbler, 2½ oz. wine Gascony (3397) 145.00
Tumbler, 11 oz. low footed goblet Gascony (3397) 340.00
Decanter, Gascony (3397) 700.00
Tumbler, 14 oz. footed soda, New Era (4044) 165.00
Stem, 10 oz. goblet, New Era (4044) 180.00

Row 2:

Plate, Cactus (1432) 250.00
Beer mug, Old Sandwich (1404) 250.00
Cream pitcher, Old Sandwich (1404)...................... 320.00
Candleholder, single, Old Sandwich (1404).......... 300.00

Row 3:

Candleholder, single, Empress (135)..................... 220.00
Floral bowl, Empress (1401)................................... 375.00

Ash tray, Empress (1401).. 300.00
Candy w/cover, Empress (1401)............................... 425.00

Row 4:

Vase, favor, Diamond Optic (4230) 170.00
Tub salt, Revere (1183) 75.00
Vase, favor, Diamond Optic (4229) 195.00
Vase, favor, (4228).. 200.00
Vase, 2", ball (4045) 460.00
Vase, ivy ball (4224)... 250.00
Ash tray, individual, Old Sandwich (1404)............. 45.00
Tumbler, Arch (1417).. 60.00

Row 5:

Vase, 6", ball (4045) 360.00
Vase, 12", ball (4045)... 2500.00
Vase, 9", ball (4045) 700.00

HEISEY'S "COBALT" COLOR (rare)

Row 1:
Stem, 10 oz., water, Spanish (3404) 140.00
Candleholder, Ipswich (1405)........................ 260.00
Plate, 8", square, Empress (1401).................... 60.00

Row 2:
Stem, 5½ oz., saucer champagne, Spanish
  (3404) 75.00
Tumbler, 12 oz., ftd., soda, Spanish (3404).... 80.00
Stem, 3½ oz., cocktail, Spanish (3404).......... 90.00
Stem, 1 oz., cordial, Spanish (3404)............... 250.00
Stem, 5½ oz., sherbet, Spanish (3404)........... 85.00

Row 3:
Candlestick, 6" (135) 220.00
Salt and pepper pr., (25) 255.00
Ash tray, Empress (1401).............................. 300.00
Candy w/cover, Empress (1401)..................... 425.00

Row 4:
Plate, 8", round, Empress (1401) 60.00
Vase, Cathedral (1413) 600.00
Candy w/cover, short, Aristocrat (1430) 800.00

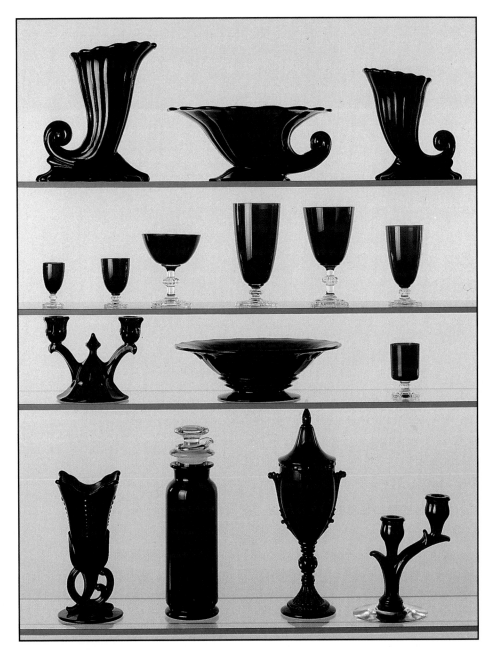

Row 1:
Vase, 9", Warwick (1428).................................. 250.00
Bowl, 11", floral, Warwick (1428).................. 350.00
Vase, 7", Warwick (1428).............................. 230.00
Row 2:
Tumbler, 1 oz., cordial, Carcassonne (3390) ... 225.00
Tumbler, 2½ oz., wine, ftd., Carcassonne
  (3390) 110.00
Stem, 6 oz., saucer champagne, Carcassonne
  (3390) 55.00
Tumbler, 12 oz., soda, ftd., Carcassonne
  (3390) 70.00
Stem, 11 oz., tall stem, Carcassonne (3390) ... 95.00

Tumbler, 8 oz., soda, Carcassonne (3390) 65.00
Row 3:
Candleholder, 2-lite, Thumbprint
  and Panel (1433).. 135.00
Bowl, 12", floral, Thumbprint and Panel
  (1433) 200.00
Cigarette holder, Carcassonne (3390) 110.00
Row 4:
Vase, 9", Tulip (1420) 425.00
Cocktail shaker, Cobel (4225) 450.00
Candy w/cover, tall, Aristocrat (1430)............1000.00
Candleholder, 2-lite, Crocus (140)................. 400.00

HEISEY'S "DAWN" COLOR (rare)

Ash tray, 6", square, Prism Square	95.00	Sugar, Cabochon (1951)	60.00
Bowl, 6¾", jelly Leaf (1565)	40.00	Tray, 12", 4 pt. variety, Octagon (500)	350.00
Butter dish, ¼ pound, Cabochon (1951)	180.00	Tumbler, 4", 10 oz., water, Coleport (1487)	30.00
Creamer, Cabochon (1951)	60.00	Tumbler, 5¼", 13 oz., iced tea, Coleport	
Sherbet, 20th Century (1415)	35.00	(1487)	40.00

Tumbler, 5 oz., ftd. soda Kohinoor (4085) .... $550.00+ ea.

Notice the top soda has a blue top and foot with a crystal stem while the bottom left one has a blue top and crystal stem and foot. The bottom right soda is all blue.

HEISEY'S TANGERINE COLOR (rare)

Row 1:
Stem, 5 oz., champagne, Duquesne
  blank (3389).. 165.00
Stem, 5 oz., parfait, Duquesne blank (3389)... 170.00
Stem, water, 9 oz., Duquesne blank (3389) 200.00
Tumbler, juice, ftd., 5 oz., Duquesne blank
  (3389) 140.00

Row 2:
Vase, favor, (4229) 700.00
Vase, favor, (4232) 700.00
Plate, 8", square, Empress (1401).................... 140.00
Tumbler, 12 oz., ftd. soda, Spanish (3404) 360.00
Stem, 10 oz., water goblet, Spanish (3404) 430.00

Row 3:
Tumbler, 3 oz., cocktail, Gascony (3397)........ 180.00
Tumbler, 14 oz., ftd. soda, Gascony (3397) 160.00
Tumbler, 12 oz., ftd. soda, Gascony (3397) 150.00
Goblet, 11 oz., low ftd. Gascony (3397)......... 240.00
Tumbler, 10 oz., ftd. tumbler, Gascony
  (3397) 140.00

Row 4:
Vase, ivy (4224) 225.00
Candleholder, Trident (134).......................... 800.00
Tumbler, 10 oz., ftd. soda, Gascony (3397) 300.00
Fruit cocktail or finger side bowl, 6 oz., Gascony
  (3397).. 225.00

Creamer, Empress blank (1401) 650.00
Cup, Empress blank (1401) 800.00
Saucer, Empress blank (1401).. 200.00
Sugar, Empress blank (1401) 650.00

TIFFIN'S TWILIGHT COLOR (rare)

There are two colors of Tiffin's Twilight; the older is represented by the last two items in the top row. This glass has the ability to look blue in artificial light and pink in natural light. It is sometimes confused with similar colors of other companies, namely Heisey's Alexandrite, Cambridge's Heatherbloom, and Fostoria's Wisteria. All the above colors are enjoying a surge in collecting popularity. Tiffin's Twilight just happens to be the "new kid on the block," so to speak.

Row 1:

Bowl, Canterbury	100.00
Ash Tray	50.00
Martini pitcher, Modern	300.00
Water goblet	35.00
Juice tumbler, #17594	30.00
Bud vase	135.00
Cordial, #17501	75.00
Cordial, Fontaine, #15033	135.00
Cordial, #15033	85.00

Row 2:

Bowl	95.00
Bowl, Modern	175.00
Cordial	50.00
Cordial	65.00
Bowl, Empress	85.00